This Rough Game

Fascism and Anti-Fascism

David Renton

SUTTON PUBLISHING

First published in 2001 by
Sutton Publishing Limited · Phoenix Mill
Thrupp · Stroud · Gloucester · GL5 2BU

British Library Cataloguing in Publication Data
A catalogue record for this book is available from the British Library

ISBN 0 7509 2515 9

Typeset in 11/14.5pt Sabon.
Typesetting and origination by
Sutton Publishing Limited.
Printed and bound in England
by J.H. Haynes & Co. Ltd, Sparkford.

Contents

Preface and Acknowledgements

This is a book about fascism and its opponents. Its themes include ways of understanding fascism (in other words, theories of fascism), and also the tactics of fascism's opponents. Much of the book is focused on events in Britain in the 1930s, '40s and '70s. Other sections look at several aspects of Hitler's fascism in Germany, and also more recent events in France, Austria, America and elsewhere. The starting point of the book is the rather unexceptional premise that the appropriate response to fascism is opposition to it. Indeed this imperative can be said to apply equally to the activist and to the historian. The introduction describes my personal and historical background, while the subsequent chapters address key moments in the history of fascism and anti-fascism in Britain, Europe and America.

I would like to thank the many people who have helped me to prepare this book. Over the past three years, I have taught courses in the history of fascism at Nottingham Trent University and Edge Hill College in Ormskirk. Several of my students knew I was preparing this book, and offered suggestions which made their way into the final text. Even without these direct comments this book has benefited from a constant connection with its audience. The best way to write, I am convinced, is to teach. The staff at the inter-library loans desk at Edge Hill were consistently helpful, and I am also grateful to the librarians at the British Library, the British Newspaper Library and the National Museum of Labour History for access to their material. As well as those friends separately mentioned in the text, I would like to thank Steve Silver of the magazine *Searchlight*, Toby Abse, Anne Alexander and Sean Kelly for reading through the entire first draft; also Christopher Feeney of Sutton Publishing for his many useful suggestions on the book's title and structure. I could not have asked for a more helpful editor.

Like any book, this was a collective project. The chapter on German exceptionalism benefited from conversations with Chris Brooke. Although he would disagree with the argument here, I am grateful to him for several important suggestions. Another writer I have debated with is Philip Coupland – the chapter on British fascism is stronger for his advice and comments. Tom Brass and Gareth Dale gave valuable advice on the chapter which examines German exceptionalism. Discussions with Bruce Howard, Mike Taylor and Matt Zepf also helped me to complete the section on Albert Einstein's politics. Several chapters were informed by David Turner's email correspondence, which suggested a number of useful leads. Rick Kuhn also read several chapters of the book in advance. Sally Davison and Helen Collins advised with the chapter on women and fascism. The chapter on Rock Against Racism was influenced by my interviews with a number of activists from this period. They include Pete Ainsley, Peter Alexander, Mike Beaken, Bev Bennett, Ian Birchall, Richard Buckwell, John Burton, John Diamond, Keith Flett, Alan Gibbons, Ruth Gregory, Caroline Harper, Martin Kellett, Caroline O'Reilly, Dick Pole, David Rosenberg, John Shemeld, Andy Strouthous, and Syd Shelton. Despite the assistance I have received, all errors are, of course, my own.

Some of these chapters use material which has appeared previously in a different form in magazines and journals including *Changing English*, *Contemporary Politics*, *Jewish Culture and History*, *Race and Class*, *Rethinking Marxism*, *Searchlight*, *Socialist History*, *Socialist Review* and the web-magazine *Voice of the Turtle.* Where there was an earlier article, this point is referenced in the footnotes. On each occasion when ideas have appeared elsewhere, they were significantly revised for the book.

Introduction: Writing about Fascism

At the outset, I would like to explain how and why I came to write this book. First, this introduction will say something about my background, and the original motives which shaped my interest in the history of fascism and anti-fascism. My hope is that in doing this, readers will understand something of the issues which run through this work. Second, the chapter will explain how this book fits into the existing literature on fascism, and especially how it relates to my previous books. I have already published a number of studies looking at the history and theory of fascism and anti-fascism, and readers may be interested to read my opinion of what distinguishes my work.

From an early age I was fascinated by history, and especially labour and social history. At school, I was fortunate to meet one founder of the History Workshop movement, Raphael Samuel, who taught at Ruskin College in Oxford. As an undergraduate student, I was supervised by another social historian, Ross McKibbin. Christopher Hill himself spoke at Oxford while I was there, and he seemed to represent a living link to the radical students of the 1930s. His work in turn pointed me towards the books of a distant relative, another left-wing historian Dona Torr, who had been Hill's mentor in the Communist Party of Great Britain. David Widgery was another inspiration. His books showed me that there was a connection between the politics of the first Anti-Nazi League (ANL) and the radical music (reggae, punk, soul) of the 1970s. I was now an active socialist, but one whose ideas remained unfinished. I was looking for work in which I could think. I wanted to become a historian, and labour history seemed to me to be the obvious field to pick.

These youthful goals were thrown off course by events which took place in my second year as a university student. In East London, Derek Beackon of the far-right British National Party (BNP) was elected as a councillor for Tower Hamlets. Suddenly, there were groups of fascists springing up all over London and southern England. Oxford, where I lived, was no exception. In the spring of my second year, neo-Nazi graffiti appeared around the local areas. That May a middle-aged Somali man, Said Guleid Ahmed, was killed in a racist firebombing. The police announced that this could not have been a racist murder, a line agreed by each of the local anti-racist organisations with the single exception of the ANL. The local press blamed the series of racist attacks in Oxford that summer on Palestinian extremists, while other anti-fascists brought out a special leaflet accusing the members of the ANL of encouraging alarmism, saying 'East Oxford is not East London'. Because the police line was accepted, the victims of this racist attack were not granted even the limited support which other families have received.

Together with a number of close friends and other political allies, I threw myself into the campaign in support of the victims of this racist attack. Why did the members of the ANL claim that this was a racist murder? One reason was that we met members of the family within days of the attack. Another factor was that a supporter of ours lived on the road and was a witness to the incident. Indeed, he was told by the local police that he would be the chief witness when the prosecution began. Our friend was told that a court case was imminent, although it never came. The Anti-Nazi League was the only group to take collections for the family, to provide security to people afraid of being attacked again, and to call a march in support of the dead man, which I helped to organise, and in which the family and many other local people took part.

Back in university, students were encouraged to complete a long dissertation, a work of original research based on our own historical interests. My intention had been to write about local strikes, or some other moment in working-class history. Given what I had seen in Oxford, I chose instead to write about the history of fascism and anti-fascism in Oxford. It was not the first, formative political experience I had lived through – but it was an important moment which challenged some, and reinforced other ideas which were already in my head. Informed by these experiences, my writing became less abstract, more relevant and much more fully formed. The dissertation I wrote about Oxford in the 1930s was later published with the help of David Horsfield at Ruskin College.[1] From these experiences, a research studentship at Sheffield University seemed the logical next step. The research would have to be on fascism or the far right, and as I had finished my own work on that topic, this next step seemed the right one to take. Another friend, Pete Alexander, was instrumental in persuading me to accept a scholarship to fund research in this field. For most of the time since, I have worked as a lecturer in the history of fascism, teaching in Nottingham, London, at Rhodes University in South Africa, and most recently at Edge Hill College in Ormskirk.

Several themes follow from this brief history. For one thing, I came to the study of fascism and anti-fascism from without. My primary interest has been in the history of labour activists and other champions of the dispossessed. Even now I still feel half-embarrassed when I take my books on public transport to work – 'What are you reading?', 'Oh, the new biography of Hitler.' You can imagine how that sounds! I do feel as though my work has so far been on a detour, even if the point of arrival is closer now. In addition, I would say that my books combine (at times, uneasily) the perspective of the historian and the activist. I continue to write for the anti-fascist magazine, *Searchlight*, while I have also been an active member of several anti-racist groups, including most recently the Merseyside Committee to Defend Asylum Seekers. Other writers will claim to stand above the mêlée – even if I believed that such a neutral position was possible, I would not place myself there.

I have always believed that the most appropriate way to write about fascism is to write against it. Although the far-right parties still remain on the fringes of European political life, they do play a role in present-day politics. There is no prospect of any far-right party seizing real state power in any country in Europe, now or at any time in the next ten years. Yet despite their seeming isolation, fascist and other far-right parties are still able to do damage. At many times over the past ten years, the existence even of an isolated far right has been enough to encourage mainstream parties to adopt racism. The tightening of immigration laws in France and Germany through the 1990s, was justified by the need to prevent the growth of the extreme right. That centre-party politicians have had this excuse is bad enough – just think of the consequences. Meanwhile, the electoral success of Jörg Haider's Freedom Party, which won 27.6 per cent of the vote in the 1999 Austrian elections, is another reason to guard against complacency. The same is true of the recent wave of hostility towards asylum seekers in Britain. Although this was a campaign started by the traditional parties, it is an issue from which the influence of the far right has grown.

Having described my background, what about the approach in my writing? The best way to understand my work is by comparing it to the rival theories which exist within the study of fascism. Over a particular period, either since the publication of Ernst Nolte's *Three Faces of Fascism*,[2] or certainly since the success of the Front National in the French Euro-elections of 1984, I would argue that there has been a trend towards writing about fascism in a new and distinct way. Undoubtedly the champions of the so-called 'new consensus' in fascism studies would argue that they have created a new academic field. Fascism studies has only recently separated itself from its parents, but it exists, and is different. The new subject exists as a distinct literature because it already has its own fixed rules. These laws state that fascism studies should be written in just one of a limited number of styles: as apologetic biographies of aged or dead fascists; or in the form of meticulous footnotes to the history of policing, as complacent narratives of the 'age of fascism' which is now over; or in the form of exotica or other pornography of violence. For those of us who work in the field such a list is depressingly familiar – the vast majority of these studies fit into these camps. Many readers interested in fascism studies will be able to join up the dots, connecting these brief descriptions to the writers they have read and known.

My main criticism of fascism studies has been with the method of those historians who develop this approach, which method seems to me to be derived from the philosophical tradition of idealism. By 'idealism', I do not suggest that the authors are naive – although some are. Instead, my point is that they overemphasise the ideas of fascism. It is useful to understand this fascism studies approach as a partial response to postmodernism; certainly its preoccupation with the language of fascist intellectuals mirrors the so-called 'linguistic turn', which has left its mark on all social theory. The champions of fascism studies are more positive about the new method. Roger Griffin describes the 'new consensus' as a value-free approach, transcending the emotive historiography of the post war years. Stanley Payne argues that fascism 'was an historical phenomenon primarily limited to Europe during the era of the two world wars'.[3]

The era of fascism is over, so we can approach these questions in a new and dispassionate way.

THE IMPACT OF FASCISM STUDIES

To give a sense of the impact of the fascism studies approach, two books will be discussed which are profoundly shaped by its method. The first is George Watson's *The Lost Literature of Socialism*, the second is Mark Neocleous's *Fascism*. The two authors start from different positions and discuss fascism in different ways, but there are also important similarities in their approach. The content of their argument is not determined by their own beliefs, but by their method; in both books the approach towards fascism is shaped by the idealism of fascism studies. Both authors define fascism primarily in terms of the ideas and language of fascist intellectuals. These ideas are taken as being significant, even determinant in terms of understanding fascism. The problem comes when the ideas and actions of fascism were at odds, as they very often were. At this stage fascism studies has much less to say.

George Watson is a Fellow in English at St John's College, Cambridge, and an editor of the *New Cambridge Bibliography of English Literature*. His book, *The Lost Literature of Socialism*, maintains that socialism was a conservative and even nostalgic reaction to the radicalism of capitalism.[4] Apparently, there have been socialist monarchs; Watson names Napoleon III as his example. Meanwhile, according to Watson, 'the whole of National Socialism' was based on Karl Marx. Watson's approach is that of a literary critic; texts are examined for their common links, words are blasted out of time. It does not matter if what an author wrote contradicts Watson's argument. Beneath any text, Watson finds evidence of something else. In addition, George Watson is quite happy to disagree with every historian who has studied Karl Marx, or Robert Owen or George Bernard Shaw. As postmodernism has taught us, all texts are open to any possible reading, and Watson's analysis is no more contradictory (or so he would claim) than most.

To back up his claim that fascism was invented by left-wing socialists, Watson quotes selectively from Hitler's friends and correspondents. Herman Rauschning is quoted as having heard Adolf Hitler say 'I have learned a great deal from Marxism', but no mention is made of Hitler's 1924 trial speech at which he promised to be 'the destroyer of Marxism'. George Watson also avoids *Mein Kampf*, a text dripping with anti-socialism and anti-communism from beginning to end. Having published extracts from his book in the *Independent on Sunday*, Watson was criticised by a number of readers for his cavalier approach to the interpretation of the records of the past. One reader condemned Watson as a revisionist, his 'diatribe . . . shows an astonishing consistency of distortion, bogus analogy and half-baked truths that defy any kind of historical professionalism'. This letter-writer, Neil MacMaster, concluded that George Watson's 'revisionist thesis is well-worn, and has been peddled for years by neo-Nazi hacks in Germany and elsewhere'. In his defence, Watson made no attempt to deny that his work was skewed, or that its effect could give succour to such supporters of the contemporary right. Instead of justifying his book's argument, he claimed that his motives were innocent of revisionist intent. 'I am an active member of the Liberal Democrats', Watson wrote – as if the benign motive of his work, and not its revisionist consequence, were the matter at stake.[5]

The problems with the idealistic approach towards understanding fascism can also be seen in Mark Neocleous's very different book, *Fascism*. In contrast to Watson, this book is an analysis of fascism written by a clear anti-fascist. Neocleous describes fascism from an external and hostile position, 'Fascism appropriates socialist language, slogans and, occasionally, arguments, but by incorporating them into a broader ideological framework with nationalist, elitist and conservative intentions it dissolves socialism's key premises into a politics of reaction and . . . reveals itself as a counter-revolutionary phenomenon in defence of capitalism.'[6] Yet for all its quality, Neocleous's argument is undermined by a method which again treats fascism simply as a set of ideas. Neocleous describes fascist language, the importance of the idea of war to fascism, the importance of the idea of nation. His book describes again and again what fascists thought, their public pronouncements, and what they said. But what did they do? How can you evaluate fascism's belief that it is utopian except by demonstrating how false this claim has been in history?

The idealistic method of fascism studies leaves its mark. In Neocleous's *Fascism*, there is no mention of Antonio Gramsci, nor of Daniel Guérin, Leon Trotsky, August Thalheimer and Victor Serge, nor of any of the dozens of socialists and other activists who spent years fighting fascism tooth and nail. There is one further important omission. Nowhere in *Fascism*, does Neocleous engage in any detail with the events of the Holocaust.[7] This is a symptom of the greater weakness. As this chapter has argued, the fascism studies approach describes fascism as a set of ideas. Because it does not look at their consequences, these ideas become disembodied. Mark Neocleous describes the ideology of murder at length, without adequately discussing the murders themselves. As a result, the book reads as the work of a prisoner, desperate to escape the hold of a philosophical idealism, but trapped, and unable to free himself from his chains.

There are reasons for focusing on these two books in particular. Although the writers start from very different ideological positions, both accounts are distorted by their adoption of a historical method which emphasises the importance of ideas and language over historical context and social meaning. In Watson's case, the effect is to produce an unduly positive account of fascism. With Neocleous, the complaint is that his critique of fascism does not go far enough. Neither author possesses any revisionist intent. George Watson is a liberal, while Mark Neocleous is an active socialist, and a correspondent for the left journal, *Radical Philosophy*. My criticism of these writers is that the effect of choosing the fascism studies method is to produce a theory which explains less about fascism than the authors want. The consequences of adopting the method are at odds with the authors' intentions. This is why I have argued against fascism studies, and in favour of a historical analysis in which the ideas and actions of fascism are linked.

IF NOT FASCISM STUDIES, THEN WHAT?

Against fascism studies, I have argued that fascism should be analysed from an external and critical (that is an anti-fascist) position. It seems to me that the only way to generate a consistently anti-fascist approach towards the history of fascism is by relating the ideas of fascism to its actions. What is needed, therefore, is a historical and materialist theory of fascism which relates fascism to the historical forces at the moments of its birth. My first full-length book, *Fascism:*

Theory and Practice, was a theoretical critique of the fascism studies method, which attempted to give substance to this approach. A second book was based on my doctoral research. *Fascism, Anti-fascism and the 1940s*, was a more historical account of the rise and fall of one specific postwar fascist party, Sir Oswald Mosley's Union Movement, which achieved the height of its influence in Britain in the decade immediately following the Second World War.[8]

The purpose of each of my books on fascism, and indeed of this book, has been to express the outlook of fascism's opponents, and especially the views of the left-wing anti-fascists of the 1930s and 1940s. Rather than looking first at the ideas and propaganda of fascism, I have looked first for its deeds and actions, and then used the deeds to explain the meaning of the words. In all movements there is a continuity between the people charged with expressing the goals and aspirations, and those people charged with putting them into effect. My approach has followed the interwar anti-fascists when they used Karl Marx's dictum, 'it is not the consciousness of men that determines their existence, but their social existence that determines their consciousness'.[9] In general terms, I have argued for an anti-fascist approach towards the history of fascism and anti-fascism alike.

Fascism: Theory and Practice gives a one-line definition of fascism, as 'a specific form of reactionary mass movement'. This simple definition implies at least four claims:

1. that fascism has been a specific form of politics, with a family resemblance to other similar movements, but also important points of difference;
2. that fascism has possessed a reactionary ideology;
3. that fascism has set out to be a mass movement, with real popular support;
4. that a contradiction has existed between the fascist ideology and the fascist movement.[10]

The key point is the fourth which explains how fascism worked, and how it changed and developed over time. The alliance between the goals and movement of fascism was inherently unstable. If fascism was a movement shaped by both mass support and reactionary goals, then there was a conflict at the heart of the movement. The mass fascist party could only be built on the basis of popular hopes, which fascism always planned to crush. Adolf Hitler and Benito Mussolini promised to bring the old capitalist order to its knees, but were then invited to power by the politicians they had attacked. This contradiction also explains why fascism could grow so fast at times of crisis, but has been generally unable to dominate politics at moments of social peace.

CONTENTS

Having said something about my own background, the common anti-fascist method which I bring to the study of fascism, and the historical literature which I reject, this introduction will end with a summary of the chapters ahead. Those which follow are all primarily historical, in other words they address different aspects of the history of fascism and anti-fascism, in the light of the comments I have made here. In order to come to a coherent sense of the past, not just describing events but also analysing and interpreting them, the structure of this book is thematic. Episodes are chosen for their lasting significance, and chapters are structured around important debates between historians.

The first section addresses key debates within the history of fascism. The first chapter in this section, aimed at readers new to the topic, offers a brief chronological history of fascism in Britain, America and Europe, from its beginning to the present day. The second chapter criticises the historians who identify a German 'Sonderweg', the claim that fascism came to power in Germany because of a peculiar flaw structured into German historical destiny. The third chapter examines women and fascism, and the question of how the movement was able to recruit women to a politics which was clearly not in their interests. Other chapters in this section examine the ideology of postwar British fascism; the ways in which historians have written the biography of Adolf Hitler; the upsurge of activity among fascist parties in Europe in the 1990s, the recent success of the far-right Austrian Freedom Party, and the way in which over the last thirty years the Holocaust has become such an important symbol in our collective memory of the past.

The second section examines moments in the history of anti-fascism. One intention is to show how anti-fascist memories of the past add extra depth to our understanding of fascism, as well as anti-fascism. The first chapter in this section addresses Weimar culture, the so-called 'Degenerate' art and music which was banned in Hitler's Germany. The second chapter examines physicist Albert Einstein's anti-fascist politics. Einstein is one of the most analysed thinkers of the twentieth century, yet few historians consider either his general politics, or their relation to the European left and anti-fascist milieu of his time. Subsequent chapters examine the battle of Cable Street in East London in 1936; the International Brigades in Spain; and also anti-fascism in Britain in the 1940s and 1970s.

One final point, the title of the book is taken from Nicholas Mosley's memoir, *Beyond the Pale*, which was written some time after Nicholas had left his father's party[11] – Oswald Mosley was then the leader of the fascist Union Movement. One of his foot-soldiers was accused of taking part in a violent attack on one of the movement's many adversaries. Mosley senior took the man into his office, and proceeded to reprimand him. Yet even while ticking off his junior, by his facial expression and his body language, Sir Oswald Mosley managed to communicate his real support for the man's actions. Such behaviour was (as he told his son) to be expected in this 'rough game'.

> There was an incident from the early days of Union Movement just after the war that stuck in my memory. My father had summoned to him one of his lieutenants who had disobeyed orders that members should not become involved in the breaking-up of opponents' meetings: my father reprimanded the man in a room next door to where Rosemary and Diana and I were having dinner. My father shouted at him for a time; the man was saying, 'Yes sir, sorry sir'; then my father said quietly, 'Well don't do it again.' And as he showed the man out into the passage some sort of wink seemed to pass between the man and my father – some touch on the arm perhaps – a recognition of comradeship or complicity beyond the demands of discipline. And it was as if we all knew that the man would of course do whatever he had done again; my father knew this; the man knew that my father knew this – it was as if the reprimand was just some ritual by which my father might effectively not quite let his left hand know what his right hand was doing. And it must have been something like this,

> I supposed, that had happened in the thirties – both with my father, and with other national socialist leaders.
>
> When I talked to my father about such incidents he would say – with his half-self-mocking half-smile-half-frown – 'It's a rough game' – or – 'One must keep the boys happy.'[12]

For Oswald Mosley, his own behaviour as leader was positive; it demonstrated his fundamental loyalty to the fascist movement. The leader could not pretend to be above the party, he must be part of it as well. For Nicholas Mosley, the action was more ambivalent. It was just one of the many signs that his father had deluded himself when he claimed that fascism was a generous and noble movement. For the later, critical reader, the message of the story is overwhelmingly negative. Sir Oswald Mosley's behaviour demonstrates that there was a regular contest between the fascist movement and the frequently employed fascist rhetoric of justice and equality. Indeed, when the two principles came into conflict, it was the demands of the movement, rather than the vision represented in fascist propaganda, which won out. Thus fascism was always the property of violent men like Adolf Hitler and Oswald Mosley – it was never anything better or more complex than that.

PART ONE

ONE

Fascism: A Brief History

FASCISM AS A MASS MOVEMENT

The origins of fascism date back to the last decades of the nineteenth century. If the mid-century was an age of liberalism, a time of democratisation and minority rights, then the 1890s were a time of reaction. All throughout Europe, the educated and the propertied felt threatened by the rise of the workers' movement. The great depression of these years also encouraged an atmosphere of paranoia and general mistrust. In France, a Jewish staff officer was jailed for espionage. No one in power believed that Captain Alfred Dreyfus was guilty. Their point instead was that the honour of the army should be defended at all costs. In Germany, Nietszche penned his syphilitic praise to the strong in conflict against the weak. In Britain, Charles Darwin's account of natural selection was transformed into a history of conflict within the human race. Social Darwinism implied that the natural condition of man was to be at war. Every country witnessed a growth in nationalism, militarism and xenophobia.[1]

The sense of crisis in Europe intensified with the First World War. This was the first 'mass' war. The factories and the machines of Western civilisation were fully employed to secure the slaughter of millions. It was also the first 'total' war. Each state compelled its population to produce for the front. Even the weak and underdeveloped Russian economy found that it could manufacture 4.5 million shells per month. This was the bloodiest war that humanity had known, with ten million people killed. As a result of the war, production fell, there was less wealth in society, and people suffered from worse health. Millions died in the postwar flu epidemic. Most important for the success of fascism, the experience of war shaped a generation. The former soldiers returned brutal and angry. They had learned to kill and were impatient for change. Many ached for a return to the discipline of the front.

Across Europe, the postwar years saw a recurrence of the same pattern. In each country, the forces most clearly opposed to the war had been the radical Socialists and Marxists on the extreme left. Consequently, they were the first groups to gain in popularity, and in several countries the initial postwar governments were alliances between Socialists and Communists. Soon, though, this moment was lost. The mid-years of the 1920s were a period of defeat for the radicals: witness the triumph of Benito Mussolini in Italy, the defeat of the General Strike in Britain. The last years of the decade saw a brief shift to stability. Then the return of financial chaos – marked by the Wall Street crash – pushed many societies back to the right. The 1930s were 'the devil's decade', a period of unemployment and military coups. Such misery extended well beyond the classic fascist regimes in Italy and Germany. Expressed as a percentage of society, the largest fascist parties in Europe were in Hungary and Romania. In Austria after the defeat of the February 1934 workers' uprising in Vienna, the only choice was between Italian- or German-style fascism.

The first fascists were Italian, taking their name from the bundles of wood that trade unions used as a symbol of workers' unity. Indeed, Mussolini, the founder of Italian fascism, stole more than this from the political left. The son of a left-wing blacksmith, the young Mussolini was a member of the Italian Socialist Party. A militant with no politics but a willingness to fight, Mussolini was rapidly promoted within the left and briefly edited the Socialist paper, *Avanti* (*Forward*). He opposed and then supported the First World War, and was expelled by his comrades for his patriotic stance. Thrown out of the socialist movement, Mussolini determined to remain in the public eye. He received backing from local businessmen, and some anarchist supporters of the war, to found an anti-Socialist newspaper, *Il Popolo d'Italia* (*The Italian People*). Mussolini campaigned for Italian entry into the conflict, and served without distinction at the front.[2]

The rise of Mussolini was a product of the political crisis in postwar Italy. Although Italy had joined the war on the side of the victors, the Italian state gained few advantages from the Versailles peace treaty. In an attempt to undo the 'humiliating victory', one adventurer, the poet and air ace Gabriele D'Annunzio launched a raid to annexe Fiume, a port on the Yugoslav coast. Back in Italy, 1919 and 1920 were the 'two red years' (*il biennio rosso*), a time of strikes and protests. The largest Italian union federation saw its membership double three times in two years. On the land, rural co-operatives attempted to expropriate the landlords. Then in September 1920, 500,000 metal workers occupied their factories. In Turin armed workers established factory councils copying the Russian Soviets. The philosopher of the council movement was Antonio Gramsci, a future leader of the Italian Communist Party. He wondered why the workers were unable to seize state power, and predicted gloomily that such an opportunity would not come again.

The first public meeting of Mussolini's *fascio di combattimento* (assault squads) was held in Milan on 23 March 1919. The 100 men present included former leftists, current supporters of D'Annunzio and *arditi* (special troops). At the end of the year, Mussolini's supporters were still a marginal force. In the 1919 elections, no fascists were chosen for parliament, not even in Milan. When fascism started to grow, it did so by presenting itself to the leaders of the *Confindustria* business federation and the *Banca Commerciale* as a non-political army of professional strike-breakers. As the movement grew, local militants emerged, men such as Italo Balbo, who had no aspirations beyond a life of violence. Fascism was a movement and a milieu before it was a party.

Meanwhile, none of the postwar Italian governments was able to resolve the crisis in society. In May 1921 the liberal parliamentarian Giolotti attempted to create a majority in parliament by forming an alliance with Italy's right-wing parties. These included the nationalists and the fascists. From this extraordinary pact, thirty-five fascist deputies were elected. Six months later, a National Fascist Party (the PNF) was formed. Mussolini's forces appeared to be growing – his presence in the newspapers was out of all proportion to his popular support. Yet in parliament, the nationalist-liberal coalition was unable to sustain a majority. Even in coalition, the right was no larger than the Catholic or the Socialist bloc. As the crisis deepened, fascist armies marched across Italy, attacking Marxists and trade unionists in one city after another. Finally, in October 1922 Mussolini threatened to stage a coup. Business was friendly, and King Victor Emmanuel refused to send his troops to defend the republic. With the king's support, Mussolini was invited into power. The widely publicised fascist 'March on Rome' happened only after the PNF's successful coup.

This fascist regime was a product of manoeuvre, chance, and the mistakes of Mussolini's opponents. Even after it took power, the king remained head of state. In the cabinet, Mussolini's supporters controlled one-third of the seats. There were also divisions within the PNF, between those who wanted an alliance with the nationalist right, and other fascists who remembered their earlier promises to rule in opposition to both Labour and Capital. Mussolini's purge of anti-fascists in the civil service failed. No new fascist system emerged. Then, during the 1924 elections, Mussolini's supporters unleashed a wave of terror against their opponents. This violence was denounced by the moderate socialists, and Giovanni Amendola and Giacomo Matteotti were killed. Suddenly the regime was on the defensive. Conservatives and the *Confindustria* attacked the government. Trade unions called a general strike, while anti-fascists boycotted the sham parliament. In December 1924, Mussolini's involvement in the Matteotti murder was proved. But Mussolini's enemies relied on the king to push the fascists out, and he would not take this step.

Having survived the Matteotti crisis, Mussolini now felt for the first time that his position was secure. The remaining years of the decade witnessed the creation of a one-party state. Local government was closed down, and elected councils and mayors were replaced by fascist *ras*. Education came under government supervision, press censorship was tightened. The fascists created a new security police. Even a new fascist calendar was launched. In 1926, parliament was replaced, and elections ended. This 'second wave' of Italian fascism continued at least until 1929 and the Lateran Treaty with Pope Pius XI. In this overwhelmingly Catholic country, to obtain the support of the Pope was to achieve security. A subsequent plebiscite gave the regime 99 per cent approval.

Germany witnessed the same succession of revolt and counter-revolution. Yet here the effects of revolution were, if anything, more dramatic. The naval mutinies which began in Kiel at the end of October spread from the seas to the cities of northern Germany. Berlin fell on 9 November, and the Kaiser abdicated. The war ended because ordinary Germans refused to fight. One of the revolutionary sailors was Richard Stumpf. His diaries record a mixture of nationalism and working-class internationalism: 'As a good German and as a Catholic, I hope that we might emerge from this war with a total victory . . . From the opposite point of view everything is different. Then I am not a German but a proletarian, and as such, I hope for a great, but not an annihilating defeat. Why should I feel this way? Past experience tells me that the lower classes stand to benefit from a defeat while the rich stand to lose.'[3] Such an unstable mixture of ideas was common at the time.

Following the revolution in Berlin, the German state was initially governed by an alliance of pro-war (SPD – German Socialist Party) and anti-war (USPD – Independent Socialist Party) socialists. A new republic was proclaimed, taking the name Weimar after the town where its constitution was signed. This was the moment for the Social Democrats to remake German society. Only within the forces of German socialism was there hesitation. Finding enemies only on their left – and anxious to avoid the requirement of the Versailles Treaty that the German army should never again exceed 100,000 men – the SPD established an unofficial army of former officers, extreme nationalists and right-wing students, who had been too young to serve in the war. This 'Free Army' (*Freikorps*) popularised the swastika symbol and introduced political murder into Weimar society. Many of Hitler's key lieutenants, including Ernst Röhm the future leader of the Nazi stormtroopers, first achieved prominence in this milieu.

The moment of revolutionary victory was short-lived. In southern Germany, Kurt Eisner's march on Munich led to the creation of a Bavarian Soviet. For six months, the state was ruled by a Soviet republic. Yet the actual support for the regime was limited. Both the Socialist SPD and the Communist KPD (German Communist Party) held back from full support. Finally the Soviet republic was defeated in May 1919. Meanwhile, in January 1919 the police chief of Berlin was sacked. A left-wing socialist, many radicals saw his dismissal as a provocation. Spartacists led by Rosa Luxemburg and Karl Liebknecht responded with insurrection. Their revolt was put down by soldiers from the *Freikorps*. The German state openly celebrated Luxemburg's murder. In Britain *The Times* was shocked by the open support for the defendants manifest at their trial: 'The accused were not brought to the dock in the normal way, but were introduced from the judge's room. They arrived laughing and radiant, their breasts decorated with orders. They gave the impression of going to a wedding rather than to the dock to be tried for murder.' Communists blamed the SPD for the murder of Luxemburg and Liebknecht. Mutual suspicion cut the German left in two.

Yet the defeat of the first revolutionary wave did not end the revolution. In 1920, Gustav Kapp attempted a *Freikorps* putsch. This was met by a united and victorious general strike in Berlin. German workers defeated Kapp in a week. The momentum shifted back to the left, and through 1920–3, the possibility of a German revolution remained open.

The decisive year was 1923. Having written German responsibility for the First World War into the peace treaty of Versailles, France and Britain demanded compensation. As the economy began to collapse, French troops entered the Ruhr. This army of occupation was met with passive resistance. The year 1923 became one of inflation. At its start, 192 German marks could be exchanged for one dollar. By November, the ratio was 4,200,000,000,000 to one. Summer 1923 witnessed strikes by miners, printers, metal workers and steel workers. The KPD grew rapidly, and a second October revolution was predicted, to match the October revolution in Russia. Hopes were pinned on a Socialist–Communist coalition in Saxony. But when troops were sent in, no general strike was called. In the absence of the left, the German right took the initiative instead.

The National Socialist Workers Party emerged at the end of a series of attempts by members of the German ruling class to bind workers to the German war effort. One of its founders, Anton Drexler, had been for several years a lone working-class champion of the war.[4] When Hitler joined the party, the DAP (German Workers' Party, later NSDAP or National Socialist German Workers' Party) had recruited a few dozen members in Munich, at most. Over the next five years, the party began to grow by accumulating the fragments of the far right. By November 1923, Hitler felt confident enough to emulate Mussolini, and attempt his own march on Berlin. Yet Hitler's 'Beer Hall putsch' was an embarrassing fiasco. Rather than backing Hitler, such local worthies as state commissioner von Kahr, and Generals von Lossow and Ludendorff, manoeuvred to place themselves first at the head of the movement, and then, when it appeared doomed, elsewhere in safety. The conspirators were arrested, and Hitler jailed for treason; he served just nine months.

The years from 1923 to 1929 saw a temporary respite for the republic. This was the short heyday of interwar German democracy, when centre parties (the Liberals, SPD and the Catholic *Zentrum*) controlled between them 75 per cent of the vote. These were also the high years of Weimar culture. The German film industry became the most advanced in the world. Weimar was blessed with an abundance of talented writers, architects, playwrights, poets and artists, including Bertolt Brecht, Walter Gropius, Johnny Heartfield, Fritz Lang, Thomas and Heinrich Mann, Carl von Ossietzky, Erwin Piscator, Eric Remarque and Kurt Weill.[5] Led by Chancellor Stresemann, the Weimar economy enjoyed a brief but important moment of wealth and stability, before the crisis returned at the end of the 1920s.

The Wall Street crash of October 1929 brought an end to this moment of hope. Within twelve months, unemployment had risen from 1.3 to 3 million. By September 1932, it stood at 5.1 million. The economic crisis tore apart the Weimar coalition. The SPD refused to cut unemployment benefit – but the Liberals and the centre demanded that the burden fall on workers. In September 1930, Hitler's NSDAP achieved its first breakthrough in elections, winning 18.3 per cent of the vote. By April 1931, Hitler's personal share of the vote had risen to 37 per cent. The Nazi Party was transformed from a minority sect into the largest electoral machine in Germany. Now that over 50 per cent of the vote was in the possession of parties that were opposed to Weimar democracy – the NSDAP and the Communists – the parliament lost all pretence of authority. Within President Hindenburg's circle, debates raged as to who should become military dictator. The aristocrats von Schleicher and von Papen were both appointed Chancellor, but neither of them could claim majority support. Eventually, on 30 January 1933, Hitler became Chancellor.

How did the Nazis achieve state power? Some historians have explained Hitler's rise in terms of the organisational machine built by Hitler in the years following his release from Landsberg prison in 1925. Linked to this was the use of political violence. Adolf Hitler's ascendancy within the NSDAP was based on his control of the stormtroopers, the SA. It was this ascendancy which saw off rival party factions, and then enabled the Nazis to attack the bastions of the powerful German left. Other writers have explained Hitler's victory in terms of the novelty of Nazi propaganda; the NSDAP's use of film and posters to blast the party's message into people's minds. In Hitler's account, the contest was his fight, his personal battle – a theme expressed in the title of his book, *Mein Kampf* (*My Struggle*).

Why did Adolf Hitler's opponents fail to stop the NSDAP? In the last free elections, the Nazis won just 33 per cent of the vote. Democrats could draw on the example of Italy to warn of the dangers of fascism. The workers' movement possessed the memory of 1920, when strikes in Berlin alone were enough to prevent Kapp's attempted coup. The socialist parties possessed three or four members for every one National Socialist. Yet in 1933, the SPD and the KPD were paralysed. The socialists were too timid to resist, while the nature of German Communism had been changed by events in Russia. Dependent on Stalin's orders, the KPD determined to turn its fire against the SPD. Its leaders made too much use of the slogan, 'After Hitler us'. The largest workers' movement in the world fell without any class resistance – there was no action, no mass strike.

The centre and the right believed that they had less to fear than the left. In any case, the right was in no fit state to resist fascism. As the Nazis grew, the middle-class parties lost support. The army refused to back Weimar, finding security in the figure of President Hindenburg. The ruling class – with its backing from the Prussian military and rural caste – looked for a dictator. It saw no reason to oppose Hitler. Business and the army were not naturally fascist, but at the height of the crisis they saw an overlap of interests with the Nazis. For respectable Germany, no alternative was on offer.

FASCISM IN POWER

Now that fascism was established and secure in Italy, Benito Mussolini was faced with the task of distinguishing his regime from the other societies of Europe. The main claim to novelty lay in the field of economics. Here, Mussolini claimed that fascism represented a 'third way', opposed to both capitalism and communism. Certainly, on the surface fascism felt different. In place of economic policies came regular battles for increased production, the 'battle for the lira' and the 'battle for grain'. Mussolini was filmed working at the harvest, huge projects were promised, which would require the building of new towns and the draining of wasteland. Yet the actual performance of the economy could not conceal the reality, that Italy was a poor country with stagnant finances. The government introduced higher taxes and price controls. Huge cartels were formed in steel and naval construction. As much as 20 per cent of the Italian economy was purchased by just one arm of the state, the Institute for National Recovery. Strikes and trade unions were banned; the balance of power shifted in favour of business. Between 1927 and 1932 nominal wages fell by 50 per cent – a catastrophic decline only partly offset by falling prices.

Elsewhere, the fascists still maintained the independence of their corporate state. The economy was divided into twenty-two corporations, roughly one for each industry. Within this unit, workers and employers were supposed to meet as equals. Among Mussolini's clients within the fascist international, the corporate state was taken as the highest form of industrial self-management. Alexander Raven Thomson in Britain was just one author who celebrated corporatism as Mussolini's great achievement. He described the principle as 'a syndicalist system upon which has been superimposed a powerful central government'.[6] Despite such optimistic definitions, the problem with the corporate state was that real workers' involvement was minimal. Bosses can be blamed for fearing scrutiny, fascism can be blamed for creating a culture of cynicism towards all public authority, but for whatever reason the corporations were a meaningless sham. In the words of Gaetano Salvemini, 'The mountain travailed and gave birth to a mouse.'

Before taking power, Italian fascism promised its people grand principles, such as life, revolution and justice. In power, it offered lesser, material rewards: cars, sport, radio, cinema and motorcycles. Yet each of these promises was reduced until nothing was left. Exiled in southern Italy, Carlo Levi was astonished by the extraordinary lack of support for the regime. He explained its survival in terms of the cynicism shown towards any alternatives.[7] Meanwhile, the growing success of German fascism radicalised the regime to the right. While Mussolini established jails for trade unionists, and led successful colonial wars, it took the example of Hitler to bring Italy into the full fascist cycle of racism, anti-Semitism, and mass repression. The one popular institution was the fascist leisure organisation. This, however, was not enough to hold Italy together. After 1939, morale was low and production went into decline. Only the threat of German retaliation kept ordinary Italians in the war.

Following the Nazi seizure of power in Germany, Hitler was faced with Mussolini's old task, of turning minority government into full fascist rule. Just three of eleven seats in Hitler's first cabinet were held by National Socialists. The process of coordination (*Gleichschaltung*) – recasting the state in the image of fascism – began with a crackdown on political parties. Following the burning of the Reichstag, the Communist Party was banned. The high votes for the NSDAP and their allies in the March elections enabled the cabinet to pass an Enabling Act, postponing Weimar's democratic constitution in favour of rule by presidential decree. The Socialist Party was banned with the trade unions in May, the Liberal, Centre and Conservative Parties following over the next eight weeks. By then the cabinet had been disbanded, and Hitler's stormtroopers incorporated into the police structures. Jews, women and anti-fascists were purged from the professions.

Yet for all these changes, the NSDAP was still compelled to move more slowly than it would have liked. As the Nazis were a minority party unsure of public support, so Hitler had to create a governing coalition, an alliance with the representatives of Weimar and pre-Weimar, pre-democratic Germany. As early as July 1933, Hitler was saying that 'the ideas of the program do not demand that we act like fools and overturn everything, but that we realise our concepts wisely and carefully'. On 30 June 1934, Hitler moved against the SA. This was the institution which embodied any remaining Nazi claims to radicalism. Its leaders were killed, and several other old scores were settled. President Hindenburg told Hitler that he had 'saved the German nation' – in truth he had pacified respectable, Conservative Germany. Business, the churches and the army remained allied to Hitler – this alliance was more important to Hitler than the fate of his own supporters.

Different groups of people had different experiences of life under the Nazis. Between 1932 and 1938 gross national product doubled, while unemployment fell from a peak of 5.6 million to a low of 400,000. Coal production doubled, iron production quadrupled. Nominal wages also increased, but no faster than inflation. It has been estimated that in 1927 the average German family ate 55.2 kg of bread per year, drank 427.8 l of milk and 76.5 l of beer. Ten years later, the figures had actually fallen, to 50.8 kg of bread, 367.2 l of milk and 31.6 l of beer. Many workers benefited from falling unemployment. Yet the destruction of the unions and socialist parties encouraged German business to attempt an assault on the conditions of the German worker. Unlike in Italy, wages increased in line with inflation. Yet the length of the working week rose sharply – in some industries by as much as ten hours per week. As Ian Kershaw writes, 'Inequalities and the persistent feelings of exploitation appear to have changed little in the period of the Dictatorship.'[8]

The story was also bleak when it came to women and young people. In 1934, Hitler told NSDAP women, 'The slogan "Emancipation of women" was invented by Jewish intellectuals and its content was formed by the same spirit. In the really good times of German life the German woman had no need to emancipate herself.' Under the Nazis, the birth-rate rose sharply, before tailing off in the late 1930s. The state was committed to an ideology that wanted to push women out of work and into the home. Yet labour shortages meant that women were needed in work, and the family campaign suffered. As for youth, a generation of young Germans took full part in the regime's youth movements. The Hitler Youth and linked schemes were as popular as their counterparts in Italy. For young girls in particular, the fascist schemes offered a partial liberation from the tyranny of the home. Yet as the Hitler Youth became compulsory, so the popularity of the various organisations declined. The cult of the physical body combined with a glorification of motherhood, and a strange fear of sex. Young people were not impressed. By the time of the Second World War, many young Germans had organised themselves in movements against the state. Middle-class youth took to dancing, jazz, and other decadent pastimes. The working-class Edelweiss Pirates led attacks on the Hitler Youth. The more that the National Socialist ideology imposed itself on people's lives, the less popular it became.

So far, this chapter has focused on Italy and Germany, but the slump and crisis were global. Even countries ruled by non-fascists were influenced by the spirit of the times. The origins of the Russian tyranny were different – yet Stalinism was as murderous as fascism. There were also fascist or near-fascist regimes established in Austria, Croatia, Spain and elsewhere. Sometimes, fascist parties originated within religious bodies (Romania) or the state (Spain). At other times, they managed to persecute the 'wrong sort' of fascist. In Spain, although Franco's movement was in some ways unlike

Hitler's, it depended for its success on Italian and German military aid. In this context, Franco's opponents rightly termed themselves anti-fascist.[9]

There were few areas of state policy to which Hitler paid as much attention as he did to foreign policy. From the Nazi arrival in power in 1933, German society was recast in preparation for war. In the first stages of this process, Hitler presented himself as the champion of small nations, eager to undo the victor's peace signed at Versailles in 1919. German troops reoccupied the Rhineland, then entered German-speaking Austria. At each stage, huge majorities subsequently ratified the action in plebiscites. In winter 1938, Germany turned its attention to the Czech Sudetenland. In return for granting him control over this region, the rulers of France and Britain convinced Hitler to stay his hand, and thus delay the conflict. But the entire purpose of fascism was war. Appeasement could only delay the inevitable. Following the German invasion of Poland in September 1939, Britain and France had no choice but to fight.

The Second World War began with a series of victories for Hitler and his allies. The first was achieved against Poland in 1939. The most impressive victory was the German success against France, which was conquered in just six weeks of spring 1940. This extraordinary success stood in marked contrast to the slow warfare of the Western Front in 1914–18. Yet not everything went Hitler's way. Neither French military defeat, nor the German aerial bombardment of London, was enough to convince England to sue for peace. Seeing that his main enemy was weakened, if not yet destroyed, Adolf Hitler turned his attention east. He now determined to attack Russia, launching Operation Barbarossa in June 1941.

One of the consequences of Hitler's conquest of Poland was that his government captured the majority of Europe's Jews. Many of the remainder fell into German hands as a result of the Russian campaign. Now the Nazis were able to fulfil their long-promised goal, and begin the 'Final Solution' of the Jewish question. We can never know how many Jews, gypsies and Slavs were murdered. It is of the nature of genocide that it becomes difficult to quantify, although the most detailed figures put the numbers of Jews killed at between 5,700,000 and 7,200,000.[10] Together with the other victims of war and genocide, these killings stand as testament to the sheer brutality of fascism.

Historians have long debated whether Hitler had always intended to kill the Jews of Europe. There is no doubt that the regime was consistently racist. *Mein Kampf* drips with anti-Semitic poison. Hitler's speeches promised to deal with the Jews, although he was often deliberately vague as to what this decision would actually mean. As late as 1938, the Nazis were still discussing whether to transport Germany's Jews to Madagascar. Clearly such an operation would have required the mass use of violence. It might also have required the killing of many thousands of Jews – as the regime had already killed many thousands of disabled Germans – but the plan remained vague, and was not yet a scheme for genocide.

The trend of recent argument has been to see the Holocaust as a product of local choice. Hitler was too lazy to issue orders. Instead he expected his subordinates to work out his wishes for themselves. The ad hoc structure of the Nazi state encouraged a cumulative radicalisation of policy. Local officials competed with each other to achieve the greatest number of deaths. The point is not that Hitler was afraid of the Holocaust, nor in any way opposed to it; the rules of the game were all established at the top of the Nazi chain of command. Hitler's extraordinary racial paranoia was crucial in creating the atmosphere of racism and poison, in which genocide could become a possible option. Yet it does appear that much of the initiative was taken by relatively low-ranked Nazi officials. Such an impression also fits with recent research into the role of 'ordinary Germans' in the Holocaust. Although the murders were horrific, it appears that the vast majority remained loyal to the state. Tiny numbers refused to take part in the killings.

Following the defeat of the German armies at the battle of Stalingrad in January 1943, the German and Italian war machines went into reverse. By mid-1943, a majority in each country could see that the most likely outcome of the war would be defeat. Yet the fascist states remained surprisingly resilient. The explanation may lie in the quality of fascist propaganda. The purpose of the propaganda departments was not merely to secure approval or active consent for fascism, but also to divide or demoralise potential opposition. Coercion also played its part. At least 100,000 ordinary Germans were killed for their political opposition to the regime. Informal networks of terror, including block wardens and paid spies, kept the population at bay. But consent and coercion were linked. Certainly in Germany, it was in the depths of war that fascist propaganda secured its greatest success – persuading a tired and hostile population that the threat of invading enemies was greater than the danger posed by their own desperate regimes. There was resistance to German fascism, ranging from millions of acts of lower-level dissent, through to the actions of the Stauffenberg plotters, who came close to killing Hitler in 1944. But such opposition was not coordinated, and remained the work of a minority.

In Italy, the war ended with a wave of collective resistance. Mussolini was first toppled in 1943 – only to be temporarily rescued by German paratroopers. As the Allied forces moved north through Italy, they received the tacit and open support of ordinary Italians. Some 20,000 workers struck in Turin in March 1943; 60,000 in Milan two years later. Naples was liberated by Communists and other civilians, fighting with the guns left by fleeing fascist troops. Eventually Mussolini was captured and killed – not by the British, but by Italian partisans. In Germany, Hitler's supporters fought to the end. Even children, old men and reservists were ordered to fight. The regime finally succumbed on 7 May 1945, with the last Axis power, Japan, giving way three months later.

NEO-FASCISM?

Fascism imposed on the world two great catastrophes. The first, apparent at the time, was the Second World War. Some 50 million people were killed, as a direct result of the aggressive militarism which was inherent in fascism and national socialism. The second catastrophe was the Holocaust. If anything this crime was the greater – the systematic and cold-blooded murder of millions of civilians, merely because they belonged to the wrong 'race'. Yet the extent of the Holocaust was not immediately apparent to most people living in Europe and America. Their rulers were ashamed of the atrocity propaganda of the First World War, and would not announce deaths which they could not prove. Many politicians and journalists also mistrusted their own people – they feared that in describing the terrible tragedy Hitler had unleashed against the Jews of Europe, they would somehow give sustenance to the myth that this had been a 'Jewish' war. Yet the Holocaust has now fixed itself in the public mind, even more so, it seems, in the last thirty years.[11] The effect of these two catastrophes should have been to push the far right permanently into the margins of public life. Yet history has not worked out that way.

Ironically, one of the first countries to witness a rebirth of the far right was Britain, a country in which fascism had enjoyed relatively little success before 1939.[12] The key figure was Sir Oswald Mosley, whose Union Movement profited from a moment of anti-Semitism during the winter of 1947/8. By the autumn of 1947, British fascists were holding around a dozen weekly public meetings, with up to 3,000 people present at the largest rallies. Much of the style of postwar fascism derives from this moment. Mosley insisted on the need for European alliances with other fascist parties. Indeed, he proclaimed that fascism could only come about at a pan-European level. The Union Movement also directed its racism against black or Third World immigrants to Britain – in contrast to the imperialist racism of Mussolini, or the anti-Semitism of Hitler and the NSDAP. Finally, the Union Movement claimed to stand for ideas and cultural values – in variance to the militarism of the classical fascist movements. This shift proved unpopular with Mosley's supporters, who left his party like rats fleeing a sinking ship.

Mosley's movement went into decline by 1948, but its existence raises an important question – how useful is it to see the postwar movements as fascist? One approach is to describe them as 'neo-fascist'. The implied argument is that fascism has altered. Old enemies – such as the trade unions – have declined in significance, while racism has come more to the fore. Surely it is correct to say that any tradition must reflect the changed circumstances of the people who have supported it. Thus the 'Marxism' of the German SPD meant one thing when it was an outlawed revolutionary party in 1890, and something quite different after 1918. But does the analogy work – has 'neo-fascism' actually been different from fascism? The postwar leaders of European fascism clearly attempted to modify the style of their movement. In Mosley's case, *The Alternative* was published to act as a bible for a new fascist generation. Although the presentation is different, there is less evidence that the movements have changed in substance. Almost all of the postwar fascist movements share a curious ambiguity towards the past. While every party has attempted to win a new periphery of supporters, most have been led by interwar fascists, and most have gone out of their way to signal their loyalty to the past. Ultimately, this question can only be resolved if these parties gain control of the state under conditions of crisis similar to those which enabled Mussolini and Hitler to hold power. Surely it is better to oppose fascism now – rather than to wait and see how destructive the children of fascism will become.

As well as Britain, several other countries witnessed the birth of postwar fascist movements eager to take power. The Italian Social Movement (Movimento Sociale Italiano) was initially little more than a fan club for Mussolini's disappointed followers. Its very initials, MSI, were a pun in Italian, 'Mussolini-Yes'. One of the ironies of the Cold War was that official anti-fascism quickly gave way to anti-communism. Nowhere was this more evident than in Italy and West Germany, where former fascists were first tolerated, and then encouraged, as a useful counterweight against the left. The MSI received some backing from the US National Security Council,[13] but few votes. The party remained stuck at around 5 per cent in the polls, until it achieved an unprecedented breakthrough in 1983. Socialist Party premier Bettino Craxi consulted the MSI before forming a left–right coalition in 1983. Craxi had several allies on the right – he would also acted as the chief patron of Silvio Berlusconi, the media boss who invited the MSI into government in the 1990s.

The timing of Craxi's initiative was no accident. Throughout Europe, the 1980s and 1990s were a good time for fascism. A gap appeared in the market. The crumbling of Cold War alliances combined with a disabling nostalgia on the left for the declining Soviet Union. A downturn in the global economy led to mass unemployment for the first time in Europe since the war. Meanwhile, the disintegration of the Russian state ushered in a new era of radical nationalism. For the fascist parties, the turning-point arrived in 1984, when Jean-Marie Le Pen's Front National (FN) achieved 11 per cent of the vote in French Euro-elections. By 1985, the FN's claimed membership had rocketed to 60,000. From Le Pen's success, other movements were able to increase their support, including Jörg Haider's Freedom Party in Austria, Vladimir Zhirinovsky's Liberal Democrats in Russia, and the Flemish Bloc (VB) in Belgium. In 1994, at the crest of this wave, the MSI led by Gianfranco Fini, Northern Leagues and Berlusconi's

Forza Italia joined forces and triumphed in Italy's general election. Gianfranco Fini's party claimed five seats and the MSI became the first fascist party to join a European government since 1945.

The parties mentioned above were primarily electoral machines. While they grew, almost every country in Europe also witnessed the parallel rise of skinhead, racist gangs. In the early 1990s, these movements appeared to represent a growing threat. Britain, Germany and whole swathes of eastern Europe witnessed an epidemic of racist attacks. The position of the gypsies in Romania, the Czech Republic or Slovakia has become weaker than the position of Jews in pre-1933 Austria or Germany. Even today the terrible condition of asylum seekers is a shame on liberal Europe. But rather than comparing the present day to the 1930s, a more accurate analogy is perhaps with the Europe of pre-1914. An atmosphere of pervasive xenophobia exists, which could yet poison the entire continent.

How about fascism outside Europe? Two of the distinctive features of interwar fascism were its ideology (which was anti-democratic, racist, and so on) and its movement (usually a mass movement originating outside the state). Over the past fifty years, there have been many nationalist movements in the Third World, several led by men who expressed admiration for the fascist governments of the 1930s. Yet there are important markers which have distinguished these parties from the European fascists. The armed rulers of South America have typically been closer to the older formation of 'Bonapartism', a military dictatorship relying on an equilibrium between the ruling class and the dispossessed. In consequence, such movements as Peronism in Argentina enjoyed a connection to the workers' movement, which was inconceivable with Mussolini or Hitler. As for the Islamic fundamentalists of the Middle East, who are often described by their opponents as fascists, the dynamics and function of the movement are different. Like fascism these movements are based on a coalition between the urban poor, and the urban and rural petty bourgeoisie. Unlike fascism, Islamism has emerged in poor countries ravaged by the forces of global military competition. The ideology has so far possessed a levelling, anti-imperialist edge which was absent from the goals of the European right. Again, it is the contrasts between these movements and fascism, which stand out.

One country which has given birth to a recognisable fascist milieu is the United States. Historically, American fascism has had to compete with a diversity of far-right traditions. Racism and ultra-nationalism drew on pre-fascist forces, including notably the Ku Klux Klan. Yet since 1945, many American fascists have been fixated – like their counterparts in Europe – by the mystique of Adolf Hitler's national socialism. With the success of the Institute of Historical Research, America has become the global home of Holocaust revisionism, the noxious claim that the Holocaust did not happen. Indeed some of the most recent trends in European fascism have been borrowed from American experience, including the use of the Internet to spread publicity; the use of bombs to create racial terror; and the strategy of 'leaderless resistance' which emulates the cell-tactics of national liberation movements. London nail bomber David Copeland was no reader, but one book he named in his confession was *The Turner Diaries*, written by US Nazi William Pierce.[14] Pierce is the guru of leaderless resistance.

Although the activities of such people demand continued vigilance, it would be wrong to end by exaggerating the threat posed by fascism or neo-fascism today. Since 1984, the most important party of European fascism has been the French FN. Yet Le Pen's party came under sustained challenge in the 1990s, before finally splitting into two rival factions. Political life in every country in Europe has become more dynamic, more fragmented and more diverse over the past ten years. When Jörg Haider's Freedom Party took power in Austria, it was immediately met by resistance from a powerful anti-fascist movement, the largest democratic movement in Austrian history. Austria's anti-fascists were inspired by anti-capitalist protests at Seattle in 1999. They reflected the vitality of that movement in their numbers, their youth and the style of their propaganda.[15] Nothing in history is fixed. The best way to approach the contemporary fascist movements is with hostility, but also with a confidence that an alternative, radically democratic political culture can be built.

TWO

One of the Causes of Fascism? German Exceptionalism Revisited

Almost everyone, it seems, likes to think in terms of the nation. Exotica sells, newspapers fill with stories of how strangely life is lived elsewhere. According to myth, France is a nation of romantics, America a country of Bible-Belt Christians, and Italians run away from a fight. Listen to international sport, and you will find the clichés reflected even in the words of intelligent commentators who should know better. Africans like to play flowing football, they say; even victorious Brazilians cannot defend. In the cinema, national stereotypes form a common basis on which to develop an individual character. So in *Star Wars, Episode One*, while the 'Japanese' build robots, the 'African' character is a loveable but cowardly rogue. Elsewhere in American films, it is the rich Englishman who is the one to avoid. Even in discussion of economics, the same myths stand out. The Japanese are industrious, the Chinese are profligate, the Americans are successful, the Russians are beset by Mafia gangs and always on the way out. Certainly in Britain, the most widespread and pervasive national myths seem to involve rivalry with the Germans. Teach a course on British fascism to English students and you will encounter one frequent explanation for the parallel rise of Adolf Hitler and defeat of Oswald Mosley: 'We don't do things like fascism here.' The British were born democrats, or so the popular myth goes, the Germans were inherently susceptible to the wiles of an autocrat.

Leaving aside such popular notions of national difference, this chapter examines one important academic explanation for the triumph of fascism – namely that the peculiar and interrupted course of German history made Adolf Hitler's victory more likely. The previous chapter began by mentioning the origins of fascism before 1914. If the theory of German exceptionalism is correct then the different paths of national development were in fact established many centuries before even Mussolini and Hitler were born.

Although Italy and Germany are said to have shared a similar pattern of development, it is the German path which has received most comment. According to such historians as Ralf Dahrendorf, Gregory Luebbert and Hans-Ulrich Wehler, Germany's late industrialisation explains her failure to establish democracy before 1914.[1] The weakness of democracy then played a role in enabling Hitler's fascists to destabilise the Weimar system. In this theory the exception or 'special route' (*Sonderweg*) which makes German history different was late industrialisation.[2] Such late development left nineteenth century Germany in the hands of an agricultural and military ruling class, the Prussian Junkers, who shaped the reactionary political and social climate which aided the growth of fascism following the fall of the Kaiser in 1918. This account of German history is expressed succinctly in a quotation from the Hungarian Marxist Georg Lukács: 'The tragedy of the German people lies in the fact that it entered into the modern bourgeois line of development too late.'[3]

One key figure in the emergence of the Sonderweg theory was the American sociologist Barrington Moore Jr. In his book, *Social Origins of Dictatorship and Democracy*, the German Sonderweg became a general theory of historical development and under-development. Moore described three general paths to modernity: an Anglo-French–American route, which culminated in liberal democracy; a German–Japanese one, which led to fascism; and the Russian–Chinese path which led to Communism. In Germany and Japan Moore described a 'reactionary' route to capitalism. What he meant by this was that the popular and revolutionary forces of the nineteenth century suffered defeats which conditioned later developments. 'Agrarian conditions and the specific types of capitalist transformation that took place in the countryside contributed very heavily to these defeats and the feebleness behind any impulse towards Western democratic reforms.'[4] This theory corresponds to clear aspects of historical reality, and it is certainly significant that the only two agreed fascist countries both industrialised late. In Germany, the right had little need to organise in political parties before the First World War, as the barely democratic Reichstag possessed relatively few powers of its own. Meanwhile in Italy, a restricted franchise was in place for far longer, and democracy was reduced to clientism and patronage. Neither democracy was strong enough to resist the rise of the fascist parties after 1918. In both countries, possibly because of their late conversion to democratic forms, the political ruling classes ended up by inviting fascism into power.

In the field of peasant studies, Barrington Moore's work has been complemented by Terry Byres's recent and important book, *Capitalism from Above and Capitalism from Below*. Byres considers the different Asian paths to capitalist agrarian transition (including above all India) in the light of historical models based on early modern European and American developments.[5] Terry Byres distinguishes between processes of transition 'from below', where peasants overcame serfdom through struggle against the landlord class, and transition 'from above', where the peasantry was subordinated to a successful landlord class which went on to engage directly in capitalist farming. Following the arguments of pioneers in the field, including Karl Marx, Frederick Engels, Karl Kautsky and Vladimir Lenin, Byres suggests that where capitalism grew from below, as in Britain and the northern United States, it was both economically and politically liberal. By contrast, where capitalism was imposed from above, as in Prussia, it was generally reactionary. Like Barrington Moore, Byres was less concerned to discuss the specific case of German history than to set forward a general or normative explanation of why different countries have taken different routes to modernity. As well as Terry Byres, other recent authors have also adopted the Sonderweg method. In his last book, *Envisioning Power*, the anthropologist Eric Wolf expressed sympathy with this approach.[6]

The Sonderweg thesis is a composite theory which borrows heavily from different fields of knowledge. From American sociology comes the emphasis on different routes to modern industrial development. The argument also relies on a certain reading of nineteenth-century Germany history, one which was especially popular among German historians in the 1970s. From Marxism comes the notion of a pure bourgeois revolution, to which other revolutions can be compared in the search for peculiarities. Sonderweg theory is thus one area in which different scholars have been able to contribute insights across the theoretical dividing lines. Yet as David Blackbourn and Geoff Eley pointed out some twenty years ago, this marriage of different theories does not always work. 'This rather disjointed eclecticism needs to be discussed. At the least it makes for obscurity. At the most it brings contradiction and logical inconsistency.'[7] There is a tendency for writers to confuse questions of economics and questions of state power, arguing for example that if the German bourgeoisie failed in the sphere of politics then it must by definition have failed in economic terms as well. Some versions of the Sonderweg theory describe a 'conjuncture' of economic and political factors; others insist that economics were decisive. Typically, the relationship of cause and consequence is unclear.

As well as borrowing from different fields, the Sonderweg thesis also lends itself to arguments outside its ranks. A recent article in the *Journal of Peasant Studies* suggested that Turkish peasant movements of the 1930s were built around a conservative and anti-socialist ideology. Comparing the Nazi *Erbhof* (Reich Entailed Farm) law of 1933 to the 'Farmer Homestead' reforms in Turkey, M.A. Karaömerlioglu maintained that in both cases land reform was carried out at the expense of people living in the cities. One point which follows is that fascism was a rural movement. This argument is reinforced by the claim that fascism grew in backward societies, and by the notion that rural underdevelopment enable the rural fascist parties to seize power.[8]

The purpose of this chapter is to offer a critique of this notion of German and, by extension Italian, exceptionalism. It is appropriate at this stage to outline the case that I will put forward. First, I will make some general criticisms of this method of looking at the past, which I will describe as a form of historical determinism. Second, I will attempt a brief critique of the agrarian history implied in the Sonderweg theory. Rather than describing Germany as especially backward, I would argue that it reached capitalist modernity in a relatively early and even unproblematic way. Third, I want to look briefly at the role of peasant ideology in Nazi thought. My argument will be that this strand of conservative ruralism was relatively weak in fascist propaganda, and that the main trend was instead reactionary modernism. The notion that the Nazis sincerely hoped to recreate a mythical Nordic or Aryan past is a mistake. Instead the Nazi future was electrified, industrial and urban. My overall point is not that there was no national exceptionalism, but rather that those who would make it determinate, seeing fascism as an inevitable response to retarded agricultural development, are giving one factor too much weight in their explanation.

EXCEPTIONALISM: A FLAWED HISTORICAL METHOD?

One of the pillars of Sonderweg theory is the claim that within broad patterns of historical development, different nations can be said to have taken very different routes towards modernity. Thus the German Sonderweg is in the same camp as the theories which exist of English, French and American exceptionalism. It is interesting that many of these countries' claimed exceptional character rests on what is described as a failed bourgeois revolution. For England, there is the argument of Perry Anderson and Tom Nairn, that the British bourgeoisie was supine, lacked consciousness and failed to achieve its revolution. According to Anderson, the English revolution was 'the first, the most mediated, and the least pure bourgeois revolution of any major European country', and its consequences were felt in the 'permanent partial interpretation' of the bourgeoisie and the aristocracy, on the terms of the latter.[9] Instead of becoming a normal capitalist society, England was dominated by its feudal aristocracy, which controlled the state and came to govern the most dynamic economy in the world.

It is not only Britain which has been described as having taken an exceptional path to capitalist development. When it comes to the French Revolution of 1789, a generation of revisionist historians have recently emphasised the agrarian and landowning character of the eighteenth-century capitalist class. Georges Comninel is perhaps the most original of these historians, for the reason that he defends his model of French exceptionalism from within the Marxist camp. As he argues: 'Since both the nobility and the bourgeoisie had marked internal differentiation, and no impermeable boundary existed between them, and the two statuses had a good deal in common in terms of their forms of wealth, professions and general ideology, it therefore would be more accurate to recognise a single "elite" in the ancien régime.' If there was a single elite, then there can have been no rising class. No gap between the aristocracy and other privileged classes means no bourgeoisie, no bourgeoisie means no bourgeois revolution; not in Germany as we have seen, and neither in Britain nor in France.[10]

Beyond the French Revolution, similar claims have also been made for a number of other countries as well. In Rodney Hilton's collection, *The Transition from Feudalism to Capitalism*, based on an important debate which took place in the journal *Science and Society* in the 1960s, the Japanese historian Kohachiro Takahashi locates Japan as an example of bourgeois revolution from above, in the same mould as Germany.[11] Another Marxist, Antonio Gramsci, argued in the 1930s that Italy had been built on the basis of an incomplete national revolution. In his account, the incomplete nature of the *Risorgimento* helped to explain Mussolini's rise to power.[12] There is also a healthy literature of American exceptionalism, going back to the pioneer work of Werner Sombart. The purpose of these works is to explain why America lacked a significant workers' party, in the style of the German SPD, or the French or Italian Communist Parties.[13] Meanwhile, as I have mentioned, Barrington Moore would also give Russia as a case of failed modernisation.

Even this brief summary of these theories of national exceptionalism should point to some of the problems in this genre. Eric Wolf defends a general emphasis on national peculiarities: 'I remain partial to the concept of the Sonderweg, which stresses the historical peculiarities of development in the Germanies, because I think that local, regional and national divergences matter everywhere. The trajectory of the Germanies did not duplicate what happened in England or France, Russia or Poland, and there is much to get from trying to define what made the Germans historically "peculiar"'.[14] Yet Eric Wolf's approach in this case must be flawed. The explanatory power of the Sonderweg thesis lies not in a general model of national diversity but rather in the contrast between a perceived general pattern and the exceptionalism of a particular case. If everyone is exceptional then no one is different. The notion of a specifically French exceptionalism is diminished when Britain is shown to have experienced a failed bourgeois revolution. And once historians have denied the revolution of 1789, what space is left for the (missing) German revolution?

More than this, the very method of exceptionalism seems to be very deterministic in its approach. The historians of American exceptionalism attempt to prove that organised labour never had a chance. At the end of the German Sonderweg is Hitler's victory in 1933. To explain this event historians find a moment, perhaps the manorial reaction of early modern Germany, or the rise of the Junkers many years later, and describe the rise of fascism as an inexorable process which from then on could hardly have been reversed. In Ralf Dahrendorf's account, the children of the failed imperial middle class of the nineteenth century become the Nazi voters of 1933. In the 1870s and 1880s, 'the traditional leading stratum managed to turn the rise of the entrepreneurial middle-class to its own use and thus rob it of the revolutionary potential of its social position and mentality'.[15] Failed revolutionaries became reactionaries, and an illiberal result is described as inevitable. Yet most historians of fascism would describe the victory of Nazism as a contingent process. Before the election of September 1930, the rise of the NSDAP was hardly assured; Hitler's party was backed up by less than 3 per cent of the vote. Even after Hitler's accession to the Chancellorship in January 1933, the Nazi Party controlled only a minority of seats in the cabinet. Hitler's victory depended not only on economic and social circumstances, but also on the mistakes of his opponents – and they were legion.

A number of historians have attempted to construct alternative theories of national development which avoid some of the problems that I have observed in the exceptionalist approach to history. In the English language, the best known of these critics is Edward Thompson. His article, 'The Peculiarities of the English', defended the substance of the classical Marxist theory of bourgeois revolution. Where he distanced himself from Perry Anderson's approach was in describing this change as a long and drawn-out process. 'I am objecting to a model which concentrates attention upon one dramatic episode – *the* Revolution – to which all that goes before and after must be related; and which insists upon an ideal type of this Revolution against which all others must be judged.' Faced with the evidence of different routes to modernity, Thompson simply shrugged his shoulders: 'It happened in one way in France, and another way here.'[16] His argument was that the general process of development to industrial capitalism was only a combination of separate national routes. Differences were neither surprising nor determinate.

Although I would accept much of Thompson's critique of Anderson's theory, there are still gaps in his approach. Edward Thompson's interest was in the British case, consequently he neglected to outline an alternative model of the general process of transition. One writer who has recently attempted to fill this gap is Alex Callinicos, in a review essay on 'Bourgeois Revolutions and

Historical Materialism'. His alternative is to define bourgeois revolutions 'not as revolutions consciously made by capitalists, but as revolutions which promote capitalism'. By focusing on the consequences of revolution, rather than the sociological question of who carried it out, Callinicos defends a pattern in which capitalism came into being as a result of revolutionary change. Taking the case of German unification, Callinicos argues that this was a bourgeois revolution, being 'an episode of convulsive political transformation, compressed in time and concentrated in target'. Callinicos draws on David Blackbourn and Geoff Eley's important book, *The Peculiarities of German History*. Their work also rejected the argument that the post-1871 German state did not reflect capitalist interests. In their words: 'The *Kaiserreich* was not an irredeemably backward and archaic state indelibly dominated by "pre-industrial", "traditional" or "aristocratic" values and interests, but was powerfully constituted between 1862 and 1879 by (amongst other things) the need to accommodate bourgeois capitalist forces.'[17] According to Alex Callinicos, after 1871 Germany was one of the most modern and developed capitalist societies in Europe, and therefore the notion that it was a backward or somehow semi-feudal state is a myth.[18]

It seems to me that this approach is in line with Karl Marx's understanding of the transformation process. Yet there is still one change which I would suggest. When Alex Callinicos describes revolutions as processes which should be defined by their consequence and not by the social class that led them, the effect is to play down the significance of the literature which has addressed the very question of which classes took part in the classic bourgeois revolutions. A very large number of historians, including Christopher Hill and Brian Manning, George Rudé and Alfred Soboul, have described different bourgeois revolutions as a process in which the existing ruling class was challenged by a 'middling sort', itself in uneasy alliance with some peasants and urban artisans.[19] The class dynamics of 1640s England bear a strong family resemblance to those of 1770s America and 1789–93 France. The problem with describing the later transitions as revolutions is that the insurrectionary moment is lacking. To describe the German unification of 1866–71 as a revolution would devalue the word.

For this reason, it might be more useful to say that the first bourgeois revolutions (Holland, Britain, America and France) were necessary to break through the feudal system. By the time of the later agrarian transitions (Japan, Italy and Germany), capitalism was already growing as an international system. A different pattern of transition became possible, without the feudal orders having to suffer a revolutionary defeat. Lest anyone think that this approach would reintroduce the Sonderweg into history, one point should be clear. In this account, the effect of the bourgeois revolutions was to make certain systemic options possible, their implications primarily international rather than national. Like E.P. Thompson, I do not believe that the moment of revolution (present or missing) went on to determine the future of each country's history.

Whether this description of the general process works or not, I hope that I have shown that the notion of a pure bourgeois revolution is flawed. No historian of 1649 or 1789 would offer the simple model of an English or French bourgeois revolution which Dahrendorf, Luebbert and other historians use as a contrast to justify the German Sonderweg approach. If the French bourgeoisie failed to lead 1789 to its end, then why should we expect heroism from the German bourgeoisie? If the German ruling class was an armed and rural elite, then how far was it different from the English aristocracy? The Sonderweg theory is based on the need to explain a perceived contrast, when on closer observation there is none.

DID GERMANY INDUSTRIALISE LATE?

Having criticised the notion of the failed bourgeois revolution which is one of the pillars of the Sonderweg approach, I want to move on to address the question of whether German society did actually industrialise late. The transition to industrialised capitalism did occur after the transition in Britain, but this is not necessarily the most useful comparison. The failure to arrive first of all does not make someone late. It might be more useful to look at the earliest nations to industrialise. In global terms Britain, the first arrival, might make the more interesting exceptional case. As early as 1850, parts of the German economy were among the most advanced in Europe. Following German unification during the Franco-Prussian war, industry grew at an enormous rate. Huge cartels were formed, bringing together industrial and financial capital. By 1900, Germany was one of the world's three most significant capitalist superpowers, with highly developed techniques of production in coal, iron and steel. This was hardly underdevelopment. Indeed, if such late industrialisation doomed Germany to forfeit the liberal road to capitalism, then what fate was left open to the 100-plus states which were formed after 1871 and whose economies only industrialised after 1900?

Post-unification Germany was not a feudal society. J.A. Perkins has produced a persuasive history of the German agricultural worker between 1815 and 1914. At the risk of simplification, his model describes a succession of five overlapping stages. (1) Before the Napoleonic wars, most peasants performed labour services on Junker farms, but feudal dues began to die out following the 1807 Prussian Edict. (2) In their place grew up a new system of *Instleute*. Cottagers, mostly unmarried men, boarded as farm servants often prior to military service. These cottagers were obliged to provide two additional workers, or *Hofgänger*, which would sometimes include the cottagers' wives. (3) From the 1860s, cottagers were replaced by *Deputatisten*, or confined labourers. Soon this became the dominant form. These tied workers obtained less income from the cultivation of land, and more from the employers' payments of commodities in kind. However, this system was found to minimise employer productivity. (4) In the place of confined labour, more agricultural workers came to demand money wages, a process contested by landowners who feared that workers would flee the land. Yet as wages were higher in the cities, landowners were unable to resist the tide of urbanisation. This *Landflucht*, or flight from the land, transformed the German countryside. (5) By the 1890s, many of the old German free labourers had been replaced in Prussia by Polish immigrant workers, paid in cash but at low seasonal rates. The direction of this process is striking. By the 1870s and 1880s, the old obligations were gone, and what held the German countryside together was not custom but the sale of commodities on the market.[20]

The argument of the Sonderweg theorists is not so much that nineteenth-century German society was still feudal, but rather that its agrarian transition was somehow different from that of English or French contemporaries. Among the pioneers of peasant studies there have been several theorists who have described a special German path of agrarian development. Karl Marx famously suggested that farming would tend to develop at the same rate as big industry: 'large industry and large agriculture on an industrial scale work together'. It followed that small-scale agriculture would die out, and that the peasantry was doomed. By contrast, Karl Kautsky's *The Agrarian Question* maintained that small-scale agriculture revealed a greater endurance than Marx had suggested. What explanation did he give? One answer was that peasants were paid less and worked harder than agricultural proletarians; Karl Kautsky understood this process in terms of 'The greater diligence and greater care of the producer who, unlike the hired labourer, works for himself, and the low level of requirements of the small independent farmer which is even lower than that of the agricultural labourer.'[21] Such factors as the natural limit to the performance of land, and the employment of children at reduced rates of pay enabled peasant farmers to maintain a temporary advantage over large-scale rural capitalists.

Observing the contrast between Marx's approach and Kautsky's, Vladimir Lenin observed that Karl Marx's account was based on English evidence and Karl Kautsky's on German sources. It followed that there were 'two paths' of capitalist agrarian development: the English (or the American) route in which the feudal peasantry was broken up over time by internal differentiation to form rival classes, including a rural proletariat as well as a capitalist farming class; and the Prussian path in which the feudal aristocracy defeated hopes for popular change and became itself the capitalist landowning class. Lenin suggested that this contrast was present in Marx's economic manuscripts. One example he gave was the following extract from Marx's *Theories of Surplus Value*, quoted by Lenin in *The Agrarian Programme of Social Democracy*, a pamphlet from 1907: 'The German finds economic relations determined by the traditional common land relations, the position of economic centres, and particular conglomerations of the population. The Englishman finds that the historical conditions of agriculture have been progressively created by capital since the fifteenth century.'[22] This distinction is the one which Terry Byres has used to such effect.

This 'two path' model has both strengths and weaknesses. I would accept that in the early modern era, western and eastern Europe did take broadly different paths. Most historians agree that the aristocracy achieved a reintroduction of feudal practices in early modern eastern Europe. Yet by the nineteenth century, this contrast is less revealing. The percentage of the population engaged in agricultural work across different European countries in 1890 does not reveal two different paths of development on either side of the Rhine. Instead the figures reveal a contrast between an urbanised inner core (which was made up of Britain alone), a semi-urbanised middle group of central European states (France, Belgium and Germany), and a rural periphery (the countries of western, southern and eastern Europe).

In terms of industrialisation and modernisation, the evidence seems to be that late nineteenth-century German agriculture was relatively near the front of the European pack. At a time of a serious depression in agricultural prices, contemporary sources describe a ferment of change in agricultural technique. New practices included the replacement of animals by steam and even electrical energy, the use of steam ploughs on small plots owned by the former handworkers of upper Saxony, and the growth of steam threshing machines until they covered 61 per cent of all large farms across Germany by 1895. These years also witnessed the development of

Table 1: Urbanisation by country and region, 1890[23]

Country/Region	Urbanisation (%)	
Europe	29.0	
North and West	43.4	Scandinavia, UK, Holland, Belgium
Central	26.8	Germany, France, Switzerland
Mediterranean	22.2	Italy, Spain, Portugal
Eastern	18.0	Austria/Bohemia, Poland
England/ Wales	61.9	
Belgium	34.5	
France	25.9	
Germany	28.2	
Austria/Bohemia	18.1	
Italy	21.2	
Poland	14.6	

changing methods of agricultural supervision based on the new practices of scientific management in the factories, and also the use of the latest techniques of land reclamation in the eastern Elbe.[24] As well as this, German farming reveals many examples of peasant farmers taking Lenin's 'English route' and becoming modern capitalist farmers, or at least small landowners, in their own right. Between 1882 and 1895 the number of landowners actually increased, with the number of small farms rising by over 200,000.

Ironically, one major source for the similarity between English and German farming is Karl Kautsky's *The Agrarian Question*. I have mentioned that Kautsky observed the continuing vitality of the small farmer, and yet the purpose of his book was to argue that Marx was broadly correct, and that the small peasantry was doomed. Less definite than Karl Marx, and more aware of countervailing tendencies on the land, Kautsky still gave plenty of evidence to suggest that German peasant farming was on the way out. Working with figures derived from the 1895 German census, Kautsky listed the growth of non-farming incomes among peasants and the growth of rural proletarians. Between 1882 and 1895, the number of agricultural labourers had fallen, while farm numbers and average size grew. This combination suggested to Kautsky that centralisation was taking place.[25]

When Kautsky explained the success of large-scale production, he listed savings on animals, implements, houses – all economies of scale. He described the impossibility of maintaining a healthy family on the low wages that small peasants allowed themselves. Another factor was that specialisation of livestock could only be achieved on large farms. The crucial advantage was perhaps in the sphere of trade. Only large farmers could build up the supplies of materials and instruments of labour which would enable the latest technology to be used. From 1879 to 1897, the number of steam-driven farming machines had increased five-fold, and as Kautsky claimed, 'The more capitalistic agriculture becomes, the more it develops the qualitative difference between the techniques of small production and that of large-scale production.' Capitalist science worked in favour of the monopolist.[26]

Kautsky explained the predominance of large-scale farming in terms of economic factors; he did not argue that coercion was significant. Karl Kautsky's model fits with the suggestion here that nineteenth-century Germany witnessed a concentration of agricultural capital, and one achieved not from above, as Lenin and others maintained, but very much from below. For J.A. Perkins, the most important process taking place in the rural areas through the last decades of the nineteenth century was the flight from the land. Fuelled by cash payments, which were demanded by agricultural workers who found themselves in a strong bargaining position in relation to their landlords, the *Landflucht* gave a speed and a focus to the transition towards full capitalist relations on the land. Lenin described the English path in terms of the emergence of a capitalist division of labour, a process achieved slowly and through internal differentiation. But this model could equally be used to explain the changes taking place in nineteenth-century Germany as well.

Sonderweg theory links the ascendancy of the Junker class on the land to their hegemony within the German state. This ascendancy is said to explain the turn to agricultural protectionism which occurs earlier in Germany and is more protracted than elsewhere. Chancellor Bismarck introduced tariffs in 1879, and these were extended in 1902. By 1914, there was a strong anti-Socialist coalition in the German Reichstag, made up of parties taking their support from industry, agriculture, and the Catholic Church. Yet Niek Koning suggests that this alliance of rye and iron was not dictated on the terms of the Prussian Junkers. One point he makes is that several leading Junkers, including Johann von Thünen, were politically liberal or even leftist in the 1830s. The factors which drove this class towards protection were first the trauma of 1848, and then the sharp fall in agricultural prices after 1873. Agricultural investment fell from 576 million marks in 1860–4, to 282 million marks in 1877–81.[27] The passing of grain tariffs cannot be used as evidence to prove that Germany was run by Junkers. The 1879 tariff was opposed by Junker-dominated bodies, including the provincial parliaments of East and West Prussia. As for the 1902 tariff, this was introduced on the suggestion of industry, in the form of the Central Union of German Manufacturers. Following Barrington Moore, Koning observes the rise of an 'agrarian fundamentalist' ideology in early twentieth-century Germany. Yet unlike the Sonderweg theorists, he explains this ideology in terms of the 'decline of landed power'.[28]

One valuable phrase which Blackbourn and Eley use only sporadically is the notion of 'combined and uneven development'.

This is a formula borrowed from Leon Trotsky's *History of the Russian Revolution*, and in particular from his argument that Tsarist Russia was simultaneously an underdeveloped society and also one in which there were examples of the most modern techniques of production. In the 1930s, Trotsky pointed out that backward societies copy the most advanced economic techniques from their more developed rivals, and thus development can be a very rapid process. In the context of the Sonderweg debate, this formula offers an important set of insights. One point is that we should not understand modernisation as an either/or event, but rather as a process in which the same societies can offer contradictory patterns of development. To focus historical attention only on the difference between early and late modernisation is to obscure perhaps more revealing issues, including questions of the evenness of development and the pace of modernisation.

There is one final argument that I want to put in this section. When it comes to providing an explanation for fascism, it seems to me that Italy and Germany contained examples of both 'backwardness' and 'development'. In both countries, there were rural areas where development was unknown. Meanwhile, in both countries, there was the most advanced industry. The best way to understand the history of these societies in the interwar period is as a process in which external influences, politics, human decisions and often luck had an important role to play. Certainly there was backwardness in both Italy and Germany, but it is hard to see it as decisive. Italy was relatively underdeveloped, and a large share of the population lived in the south, which was barely industrialised. Yet the north contained some of the most modern areas in Europe, including the 'industrial triangle' of Genoa, Milan and Turin. Both societies could have gone in different directions, towards workers' control, towards bourgeois democracy or towards fascism.[29] Even after the rise of fascism had begun, politics remained contested and the outcomes were still open to challenge.

WAS NAZISM A REACTIONARY IDEOLOGY?

Having addressed the question of whether Germany did modernise late, I will now progress to the issue of fascist ideology. As already mentioned, a recent article in the *Journal of Peasant Studies* made the claim that fascism was a backward-looking and rural ideology. M.A. Karaömerlioglu quotes Nazi propaganda, in which the peasants are described as 'the cornerstone of the German state', 'the strongest custodians and bearers of the physical and spiritual inheritance of our people', and 'most faithful sons'.[30] If this argument was substantially correct, then it would support the Sonderweg thesis, with its account of Italy and Germany as peculiarly underdeveloped societies. If these were such backward societies, then it should follow that they would be especially susceptible to a rural and backward-looking ideology, such as fascism. Sonderweg theory describes a reactionary form of Prussian agriculture, which gave succour to reactionary politics. In this scheme, Hitler would be the clearest reactionary of all.

It is possible to list further examples of fascist speeches or programmes with a strong reactionary element. One example could be the article 'Fascism and the countryside', written by Benito Mussolini five months before the fascist march on Rome. Mussolini began by stressing the traditional distance between the countryside and the towns. 'During the Risorgimento', the period of national uprising leading to the 1848 revolution, 'the rural population were either left out of the account or hostile. The unification of Italy is the work of the intellectual bourgeoisie and of certain artisan sectors of the cities.' Now, Mussolini claimed, things had changed. Peasants had taken part in the battles of the war, notably during the Italian victory at Caporetto. Mussolini's party had gone on to recruit a generation of peasant fascists. 'The new petty bourgeoisie of rural producers, concentrated in the *Fasci*, is destined to become, as in France, a force of stability and social patriotism.' Mussolini's conclusion was that fascism was the only truly peasant movement. 'Fascism is transforming this rural passivity . . . into active participation in the reality and sanctity of the nation. Patriotism is no longer a feeling monopolised (or exploited) by the city, but becomes the heritage of the countryside as well.'[31] Yet although there were many instances in which both fascist states would declare their loyalty to the peasantry, there are as many speeches in which fascism declared its support for the workers, German and Italian business, small capital, the churches, women, and so on. Several writers including Roger Griffin, have maintained that fascism was a catch-all ideology.[32] If historians are to reply that fascism received greater support from specific classes, then a few speeches are not enough. More attention should be paid to the fascist–peasant relationship.

The most important Nazi spokesman for the rural politics of Junkerism was Walther Darré. His politics were nostalgic and reactionary, and were expressed in his slogan, 'a Holy Trinity of peasant, soil and blood'. The fascist believed in the breeding of a new 'nobility', to be based on the aristocracy of German history. Walter Darré's politics are summed up in *A New Nobility from Blood and Soil*, a book he wrote in 1930: 'Every available means should be used to achieve the goal that the creative blood in the body of our people, the blood of human beings of the Nordic Race, should be preserved and increased, because on this depends the preservation and development of our Germanness.'[33]

There were themes in fascist ideology which pointed towards a reactionary peasantism. Yet I would argue that these were secondary to the fascist goal. Contrary to the notion that fascism did especially well among peasants, in fact – as Conan Fischer has established – the German National Socialist Party recruited far better in the cities than on the land. Indeed, the party's well-known turn towards the countryside in the late 1920s was a response to urban failure; it was not motivated by any belief in the moral superiority of the land over the town.[34] After the formation of fascist states in Italy and Germany, agriculture was placed consistently behind industry in terms of the priorities of the regime. In Italy, farm labourers suffered wage cuts, while their unions were closed down. In Germany, the Reich Entailed Farm Law was supposed to protect the German farmer by granting secure land tenure to him. Yet the law became in reality a prison for the small agricultural producer. Because the law dictated that peasants could not lose their land, they could not raise loans on it to finance improvements. Resentment and stagnation expressed themselves in declining yields; production of wheat, barley and fodder grains declined by around 15 per cent between 1933 and 1935.[35] So although Walther Darré was given ministerial positions under the Nazis, his schemes were increasingly marginalised. Some of his ideas were seen as impractical, while others contradicted the central Nazi push towards industrial expansion for the purpose of war.[36] In short, fascism was an urban movement and not a rural one.

If fascism was not rural was it reactionary? One historian who has given a convincing account of the dynamics of the fascist dystopia is Jeffrey Herf. He describes a process whereby 'the irrationalist and romantic traditions of German nationalism were reconciled to modern technology in a cultural system one can call reactionary modernism'. These politics were manifested in a fascist glorification of the engineer. Carl Weike, the editor of the monthly journal of the national engineers' association, both during the Weimar period and under the Nazis, argued for a 'philosophy of technology' based on capitalism and 'primal will'. Other writers, including Heinrich Hardensett, portrayed a national mission of civilisation, which would be achieved by engineers and Nazis together. After 1933, the regime supported engineering businesses. Adolf Hitler personally sponsored and helped to plan the Volkswagen, or 'people's car'. The regime built monuments to the 'unknown engineer'. Fascism was an urban movement with a strong modernising element.[37]

I have argued that fascism was not reactionary in the context of economic modernisation. Fascism was not a rural force, nor did it believe in recreating a mythical idyllic past. Hitler's Wagnerian fantasies should be taken with a large pinch of salt. No fascist general ever sent his Aryan warriors into battle armed with their historic weapons, the sword and the spear. What then is the content to Herf's categorisation of fascism as a reactionary modernist movement? The fascist parties did believe in turning the clock back, but in a limited sense only. The main point that the Italian and German fascists borrowed from the reactionary politicians of nineteenth-century conservatism was a belief that capitalism had created class division. Fascism was reactionary in so far as it had a defining ambition to abolish all forms of class struggle. From this insight other things followed: fascists attempted to remove women from the workforce, they attempted to destroy modernist culture, and they launched a murderous attack on the Jews. Yet fascism did not look back to the 'classless' unity of lord and peasant in medieval feudalism. The classless future that fascism spoke of was a future where class divisions continued to exist but their expression was denied, and where the majority of the population lived in obedience to a capitalist state.

CONCLUSION: WHO'S EXCEPTIONAL NOW?

At the end of this chapter, I hope that a coherent alternative interpretation of German history has emerged. First, I have argued that the Sonderweg rests on a spurious notion of an ideal bourgeois revolution. Such a pure revolution has never taken place, and the contrasts between the real and the ideal tell us less than they are held to explain. Second, I have made the case that the causes of the rise of fascism should not be sought primarily in the long sweep of German history. My argument is that fascism was not inevitable in 1600 or 1900, or indeed in 1930. Hitler's victory was far more the product of mistakes on the part of his opponents, than it was the consequence of any high road to 1933. Third, I have argued that it is wrong to see fascism, and especially German fascism, as a reactionary movement based on peasant hostility to industrial capitalism. Instead, I have categorised fascism as a form of reactionary modernism, which sought to promote the interests of military development, and promoted heavy industry as a result. If fascism failed to modernise Germany, then this was because the desire for increased production was joined to a belief in the moral justice of racial war. At all events, those historians who have blamed the victory of Nazism on German rural underdevelopment have misplaced the responsibility. It is in the political conflicts and the class relationships of the cities that the explanation for 1933 should be sought.

THREE

Women and Fascism

This book has criticised fascism studies – a way of looking at the history of fascism which focuses on the ideas of the far right, to the exclusion of its practice. The pressure to come up with new approaches to the subject is intense. Yet the impact of new theories is not always positive. The love of controversy has given a spur towards new approaches, some of which assert the originality of their argument without providing the material which would be needed to defend their case. This chapter will criticise one strand of fascism studies, namely the recent study of the relationship between gender and fascism. The authors I have in mind are mostly writing in Britain, and several chose British fascism for the object of their historical study.[1] This chapter will first discuss and assess the work of these recent authors, and then offer an alternative theoretical model of how the relationship could be understood. That counter-theory will be based on the work of a generation of anti-fascist activists from the 1970s; historians who were part of a large anti-racist milieu, and whose theories offered more vivid insights than the approach of these more recent authors.

The literature which I criticise is one that challenges the older argument that fascism and women's interests were incompatible. I do not suggest that merely writing about women and fascism should be problematic. The study only becomes controversial when the authors have accepted fascist claims that their movement represented women's interests. One good example of the problematic literature is Martin Durham's recent book *Women and Fascism*.[2] Durham's study addresses the nature of women's support for fascism. As its author points out, millions of women voted for the fascist parties or supported the fascist regimes. Indeed women often represented Mussolini or Hitler's greatest admirers. For evidence, we only need to see the pictures of the huge fascist rallies – with teenage girls screaming with an energy that puts contemporary teen-band groupies to shame.

What is Durham's distinctive argument? The first general claim is that for too long historians have written gender out of the picture. 'Fascism has much to say about women, and discussions of the extreme right are woefully incomplete or they do not make this crystal clear.'[3] The second claim is that the traditional historical assumption that fascism was anti-female is too simple: 'It is hard now (although, unfortunately not impossible) to envisage an account of the extreme right that does not take the importance of gender seriously. Instead the great danger may now be that studies will recognise the importance of the relationship between the extreme right and women but in such a way as to obscure its complexity.'[4] The traditional approach is regarded as over-simplistic; historians 'can no longer believe that fascism is to be seen by definition as a masculine movement pursuing a misogynist agenda'.[5] The purpose of *Women and Fascism* is summed up by a sentence from its introduction: 'Conventional accounts see fascism as, by definition, an anti-feminist movement devoted to the removal of domestic servitude and the unceasing production of children . . . In important ways, this study is intended to subvert that supposition.'[6]

Martin Durham establishes that fascism was a feminist issue, but he has more difficulty in making the case that fascism was itself a feminist movement. His difficulties might be likened to those of a comparable historian of Islamic fundamentalism. It is agreed that many Islamist parties have received their strongest support from women, but how far does that make these organisations objectively *women's* parties? The most persuasive test would lie in the practice of the ideology, in the extent to which women were involved in the actual running of the organisation, in the ideas which were promulgated, and in the nature of the laws which were introduced when the movement achieved state power.[7]

Tested in these ways, Durham's own research makes it clear that fascism was an anti-feminist ideology. In Italy, Benito Mussolini campaigned to return women into the family, insisting that Italian birth rates were too low. Contraception was banned and feminism stigmatised. Within Adolf Hitler's party, women made up just 6 to 8 per cent of the membership. The British Union of Fascists (BUF) may have been more sympathetic to women than its sister parties, and a minority of its writers did accept that women might have a right to work. Yet even in this, Martin Durham's home case, the party as a whole was eugenicist, fixated with increased birth rates, and opposed to women's independence. Indeed, the third chapter of *Women and Fascism* demonstrates that the few recognisable feminists within fascism (including Mary Richardson and Mrs Carrington) left the BUF precisely because it would not meet their demands.[8]

All these examples are taken from Durham's book, although it would be possible to add further evidence of fascism's hostility to women's independence which has been discovered by other historians over the past twenty years. The obvious starting point is Weimar Germany. According to Anne Alexander, this was a relatively liberal and female-friendly society, a positive example of women's relative equality: 'Liberation meant more than the chance to vote. Weimar Germany witnessed a cultural flowering which seemed to promise both sexual and artistic fulfilment . . . More than 150,000 Germans subscribed to the journals of sex reformers such as Magnus Hirschfeld and Helene Stöcker, the leading figure in the radical *Bund für Mutterschutz*. Music hall songs celebrated women's sexual and political confidence: "Chuck all the men out of the Reichstag" was one popular chorus.'[9] The contrast with what was to follow could not have been more striking. In power, the NSDAP attempted to ban women from professional employment. The measures introduced fitted with Nazi ideology, while also increasing opportunities for men seeking work. The state introduced marriage loans, dependent both on the political loyalty of the family and the woman's consent to give up paid employment.[10] Nazi racism had a particular impact on women. It was mothers who would breed the new race of fit Germans, free from racial and political taint. The implementation of eugenic policy meant an unprecedented increase in the state supervision of the birth process. Older women were surplus to requirements. Younger women could only hope that their child would not be one of the 100,000 German children killed in cold blood for their inherited disability.

Richard Evans has described how after Hitler's victory in 1933, even Nazi women's organisations felt a need to condemn the independent status of women. So Gertrud Bäumer, the leading figure in the Nazi League of German Women (BDF), supported women who resigned from political office in the early 1930s and retreated into the home, on the grounds that the rough and tumble of politics was 'foreign to women's natures'.[11] In a similar vein, Stefan Berger points to the failure of the German government to mobilise women workers, even during the Second World War: 'In January 1943 the regime finally decreed that all women between the ages of 17 and 45 had to register with the unemployment office. Yet out of 3.1 million women, only 1.2 million were regarded as fit to work.' Democratic Britain and Stalinist Russia, neither of them exactly havens for women workers, did not make the same mistake as Adolf Hitler.[12]

Meanwhile, similar notions of eugenics and natalism reinforced the unequal status of women in Mussolini's Italy. A National Agency was established to regulate maternity and infancy. Family loans and allowances were granted to the most productive women, their production being measured in childbirth.[13] A demographic campaign was established to push up the birth rate (it largely failed).[14] Women were instructed to leave employment, both in order to 'return' their jobs to men, but also to resume their natural role as the keeper of the home. With the expansion of the Italian empire into Africa, and the copying of anti-Semitism from Hitler's Nazis, anti-feminism and racism were mixed together. White women were instructed to breed. If they failed to carry out this instruction, their failure was blamed on the memory of 'Jewish' feminism.[15] One difference, though, in the Italian experience, was the residual legacy of the Catholic Church, which reinforced the misogyny of the regime, while drawing on the values of traditional Italy to justify its role.

So there is a considerable body of established scholarship, which is rejected by the new writers because its analysis of women's roles lacks 'complexity', and because any crude account of women's lives will write real people out of history. But how do you argue against the experience of the majority; what can you say when so much of women's experience was so negative? The author of *Women and Fascism* is aware of many of the points made here, and skates over the contradiction in his book between the argument and the evidence by invoking a series of yes-buts: 'Italian Fascism was not ascribed with anti-feminism from its beginnings . . . The party was not uniformly misogynist . . . A closer examination suggests a more complex picture . . . Nazism is not to be understood as the uncomplicated expression of patriarchal power . . . There is more fluidity than we might have thought in fascist notions of the feminine.'[16] The tone of the argument is uncertain.

There are other ways to write about fascism and its impact on women. In the 1970s there was a large milieu of socialist and feminist historians in Britain, organised in the History Workshop and other Socialist History networks.[17] Members of this movement did write about fascism, but in a more critical way. One reason for the greater hostility to fascism expressed in their work is that many writers were actively involved in the large anti-racist campaign that was so important in Britain at the end of the 1970s.[18] This campaign gave birth to an array of organisations, including Rock Against Racism, the Anti-Nazi League, and Women Against Racism and Fascism. The contention of this chapter is that the activist history produced by writers sympathetic to the anti-racist movement offered a more compelling explanation of the relationship between women and fascism than that offered in Durham's book. So what did these historians argue?

One important collective was the 'Women and Fascism Study Group', based at the Centre for Contemporary Cultural Studies in Birmingham. This group contributed to a Women Against Racism and Fascism (WARF) conference held in Birmingham in early 1978, and then published a pamphlet of their own the following year.[19] Their argument was that fascism should not be seen primarily as a racist movement, but rather as a party which was sexist and homophobic as well. In their words, 'Fascism does address women *as women* – or rather, as wives and mothers, breeders for race and nation – and it aims to win support on that basis. Fascism also addresses men – it sees itself as virility personified, and regards liberalism as "feminine".'[20] Members of the group saw the phrase 'breeders for race and nation' as central to their argument, and this became the title of their pamphlet. Having criticised mainstream writers for neglecting the distorted masculine politics at the heart of fascism, the Women and Fascism Study Group sought to integrate their analysis of fascism and sexism into a total argument which emphasised the racist and nationalistic character of the movement. Sections of their pamphlet addressed racism, eugenics, and also the impact of the demand for women's liberation.

A further aspect of the Women and Fascism Study Group pamphlet is worthy of mention. In order to sustain a consistently anti-sexist understanding of fascism in interwar Italy and Germany and postwar Britain, the authors drew on an earlier generation of witnesses to fascism, including Wilhelm Reich, Virginia Woolf and Winifred Holtby.[21] I will mention only one of these earlier writers here. Virginia Woolf's 1938 essay 'Three Guineas' asked how to prevent the collapse into fascism and European war. Her conclusion described the fascist invocation of a cult of muscularity:

> Another picture has imposed itself upon the foreground. It is the figure of a man; some say, others deny that he is Man himself, the quintessence of virility, the perfect type of which all the others are imperfect adumbrations. He is a man certainly, His eyes are glazed; his eyes glare. His body, which is braced in an unnatural position, is tightly cased in a uniform. Upon the breast of that uniform are sewn medals and other mystical symbols. His hand is upon a sword. He is called in German and Italian Führer or Duce; in our language Tyrant or Dictator. And behind him lie ruined houses and dead bodies men, women and children.

The importance of this symbol to Woolf was that it raised clearly the connection between 'the public and the private worlds'. A public dictatorship must also be a private dictatorship, a society in which women would be dependent and at home. Yet if fascism made a claim to understand the universal status of humanity, so did anti-fascism. 'The human figure even in a photograph suggests other and more complex emotions. It suggests that we cannot disassociate ourselves from that figure but are ourselves that figure.' This discussion provided Woolf's conclusion, that the need was to challenge the fascist image of universal man: 'we can prevent war not by repeating your worlds and following your methods but by finding new worlds and creating new methods'. It was a message endorsed by the authors of *Breeders for Race and Nation*.[22]

Another group which attempted to study the gender dynamics of fascism was the Liverpool socialist group, Big Flame, in a pamphlet, *Sexuality and Fascism*. This was typical of the literature of the 1970s, in that it began by stressing the sexist character of fascism: 'Discussion of the ideology of National Socialism has often underestimated, or ignored, the vast importance of their anti-feminist ideas.' What made fascism sexist? First, fascism's anti-liberalism demanded an assault on women's organisation. Second, fascism's racism required control of the birth process, which justified a draconian supervision of the private sphere. Third, fascism's alliance with conservatism reinvigorated the traditional Christian dominance over women's lives.[23] The authors of this pamphlet were motivated by the rise of fascism in 1970s Britain: the threat of the National Front (NF).[24] Big Flame observed that the NF did recruit some women to its organisation. Yet this fact was connected to the contemporary crisis in the family, the rise in divorce and abortion, the emergence of alternative lifestyles and gay sexuality. One of the Front's appeals to women was that it claimed to defend the family. This call may have represented a defence of the subordination of women, but this was not the first time in history that people have supported a demand which was opposed to their own economic or political interests.[25]

Still in 1970s Britain, the socialist writer Jane Hardy wrote an important article for the magazine *Women's Voice* on 'Women and Fascism'. Her piece argued for anti-fascism from an explicitly socialist-feminist perspective. First of all, she described how Hitler's Germany had forced women back into the home. Next she gave examples of how fascist speakers, Hitler and Goebbels, had defended their vision of women's role in society. Then Hardy showed that these right-wing ideas had come back to haunt in more recent times: 'What is so sickening is that it is not so very different from what we hear every day; women should give up their jobs, the 1967 Abortion Act should be tightened or restricted or abolished; *Gay News* is threatening our moral fibre. These are not attacks by fascists, but it is a thin line that divides conservative ideas from those of the extreme right.'[26] *Women's Voice* operated around this time as the main publishing vehicle for another women's anti-fascist organisation, Women Against the Nazis. For the editors of this magazine, the question of women's relationship to fascism was a consistent theme. In February 1978, *Women's Voice* ran an interview with Miriam Karlin. She was a prominent member of the ANL, responsible for recruiting several fellow actresses, including Mia Farrow, Janet Suzman, Peggy Ashcroft, Glenda Jackson and Dorothy Tutin. Karlin felt that too many men were thinking about their careers: 'Women are far more prepared to stand up and be counted on their gut reaction to something.'[27]

Another organisation worth mentioning was Rock Against Sexism, again part of this general, anti-racist and anti-sexist milieu. In an article for the magazine *Temporary Hoarding* on Wilhelm Reich, a radical psychologist and anti-fascist from Weimar Germany, Lucy Toothpaste, the founder of Rock Against Sexism, attempted to demonstrate that fascism (and indeed all political authoritarianism) represented an onslaught against sex, not just in the 1930s, but forty years later as well: 'In case all that lot seems a bit far-fetched to you, we couldn't resist giving you some living proof of the connection between authoritarianism in the home and in the state. "Love and discipline went together. My father sometimes took his pit belt off and leathered me. I shed tears, but I knew he was right and I was wrong." That's what James Anderton said in an interview in the *Observer* in February. It was a belief that right and wrong were as distinct as black and white that reinforced his one and only ambition "to be a policeman and if possible the biggest policeman of all".'[28] Sadly by 1979 James Anderton's goal had been achieved, as Lucy Toothpaste went on to record, 'Well, he grew up to be a policeman alright, the chief constable of Greater Manchester to be exact, the second most powerful cop in the country.'

The interest in Wilhelm Reich was common among the writers in this milieu, but why did he exert such influence? Half of the answer lies outside the question of the relationship between fascism and gender. A Dialectics of Liberation Conference was held in 1968 at the London School of Economics. The speakers present at this conference included R.D. Laing, David Cooper, Lucien Goldmann and Paul Sweezy. The glue binding together this disparate range of economists, psychologists and cultural studies writers was (as one participant, David Widgery, observed) 'neither Sartre nor Fanon, but the Marxist Reich of the inter-war years'.[29] Taking place at such pivotal time and location for the counter-culture, this conference had a symbolic appeal and remained a point of reference for the British left for at least the next ten years. The other reason for Wilhelm Reich's appeal has more to do with the subject under discussion. Reich's theories appealed to anti-fascist writers in the late 1970s because of his interest in questions of gender, sexuality and the fascist mass movement. So Wilhelm Reich was a key reference point for the authors of *Breeders for Race and Nation*. For them, the significance of Reich lay in his interest in the mass psychology of fascism: 'Reich was one of the few in the '30s to pose the question of why fascism appeals to the mass of men and women. Why did so many join the Nazi movement? What anxieties and fears was fascism addressing? These questions are still central to a feminist and socialist analysis of right wing and fascist movements.'[30]

In order to explain the appeal of fascism, Wilhelm Reich's *The Mass Psychology of Fascism*, combined insights from Marxist economics and Freudian psychology. For Reich, the crisis of the 1930s was a crisis of sexuality. Capitalism was in decline, and disrupting the traditional structures of family and sexual life. As a consequence, sexual desires were repressed, among both men and women. Yet fascism appeared to celebrate the sexual unfreedom of women in particular. Political reaction consciously exploited 'the sexual effect of a uniform, the erotically provocative effect of the rhythmically executed goose-stepping'. The classic example of this process was the swastika. Reich believed that this symbol had been chosen deliberately for its historic, sexual connotations.[31] Not only did fascism exploit sexuality, but it did so in a way understood by its audience: 'The exhibitionistic nature of militaristic procedures have been more practically comprehended by a sales girl or an average secretary than by our most erudite politicians.' The rise of fascism, the adversary of sexual freedom, represented a failure of human creativity. It was an extended sado-masochistic response to 'the suppressed man of our authoritarian machine civilisation and its mechanistic-mythical conception of life.'[32]

In the 1970s, a number of writers attempted to develop and extend the insights of Reich's work. Beyond those already mentioned, Reich was also cited by David Widgery, one of the founders of Rock Against Racism (RAR), the anti-racist organisation which acted as the inspiration for the later Anti-Nazi League. This, for example, is his description of the Carol Grimes concert at which RAR was effectively launched:

> It was a success, not just packed out and a great atmosphere but highly political in quite a new way. There was one East End racist in the audience who happened to like Carol Grimes. There he was enjoying himself but there was a big banner up there saying 'Black and White Unite' and stickers and leaflets asking 'What are we going to do about the NF?' He was up to the neck in left-wing ideas

> but having a good time. Wilhelm Reich, the avant-garde German psychiatrist who diagnosed as a fatal weakness in the German Left's opposition to Hitler its refusal to take seriously the cultural and sexual tensions of fascism's appeal, would have loved it.[33]

Here Reich was used as a symbol of resistance to fascism, rather than as a detailed critic of how fascism's sexual mysticism worked.

One author who mined Reich's work most deeply was the Italian leftist Maria-Antonietta Macciocchi, whose 'Female Sexuality in Fascist Ideology' was translated by Jane Caplan for the first issue of the socialist-feminist journal, *Feminist Review*.[34] Macciocchi went out of her way to criticise those anti-fascist writers who romanticised the relationship between women and fascism, exaggerating the extent of resistance, and thus writing women out of history. She described this process as the 'new female metaphysics which risks making the women's movement digress into a childish creed: Women the Supreme Being, Women the Absolute Good'. From Reich, Macciocchi borrowed an emphasis on sex, and the manipulation of an ideology of sex, as one foundation of the regime. In her words, 'The characteristic of fascist and nazi genius is their challenge to women on their own ground: they make women both the reproducers of life and the guardians of death, without the two terms being contradictory.' Perhaps one difference which separated Maria-Antonietta Macciocchi from Wilhelm Reich was her greater emphasis on images of death: 'The body of fascist discourse is rigorously chaste, pure, virginal. Its central aim is the death of sexuality: women are always called to the cemetery to honour the war dead, to come bearing crowns and they are exhorted to offer their sons to the fatherland.' So fascism was about the denial of sexual pleasure – procreation combined with 'a violent rejection of all sex'. Did that mean that fascism appealed to a general condition, in which women would always oppose the implications of 'femininity' (feminism)? Macciocchi was less confident about the past, more so about the present: 'We are in the presence of the opening up of a *new continent* of history,' she argued. 'If all the feminist movements, if all the revolutionaries could understand this, one day we can do away forever with fascism.'[35]

These Reichian insights have not been restricted to feminists and activists of the left. Since the 1970s, several working historians have attempted to integrate them into more conventional histories of fascism. One such is George Mosse, whose account of fascist sexuality in Hitler's Germany makes much of the relative invisibility of women's bodies in fascist art, compared to the abundance of men's bodies, especially in fascist sculpture. As Mosse documents, even female fascists observed the contradiction implied in the Nazi Party's rhetorical support for procreation when this was combined with an ideological hostility to sex. One female Nazi affected by this conflict was Lydia Gottschewski, the organiser of the League of German Girls (BDM). Although Gottschewski was an extreme anti-feminist, she observed that the Nazi denial of bodily love could only reduce the status of women.[36] Similar perspectives inform Klaus Theweleit's two-volume *Male Fantasies*, a compelling reading of the books and letters produced first by members of the *Freikorps*, and then by male Nazis. His interest, like Reich's, is in the overlap between fascism as a form of class rule and fascism as a form of gender domination. In his words, 'along with capitalist relations of production, a specific male–female (patriarchal) relation might belong at the centre of our examination of fascism, as a producer of life-destroying realities'.[37]

This analysis of fascism has also spread beyond the confines of academic history. The Canadian author Margaret Attwood's novel *The Handmaid's Tale* represents an attempt to translate this understanding of fascism into the sphere of literature.[38] In her book, a contemporary clerico-fascism conquers North America, leaving Japanese tourists in their knee-length skirts to photograph the surviving and fully veiled women, divided into a complex hierarchy of wives, cooks, and biological mothers. Older women disappear, to work in conditions of extreme manual labour in the republic's colonies. The novel's heroine Offred is a handmaid, which means that she is trained to produce the children of her commander. Outside the bedroom, her day is spent wandering veiled head-to-toe, bored and desperate for amusement. Women are also denied the freedom to read and write. Of course, *The Handmaid's Tale* is not a historically accurate account of what fascism was like; indeed, its targets include American fundamentalist Christianity, as well as fascism. The truths of literature are different. Instead the book points in an exaggerated way to one real aspect of historic fascism – namely its intense restriction of the lives of women.

From the literature which has been described here, four key points emerge. First, in power fascism represented an attack on women. Considerable attempts were made to remove them from the public sphere of work and politics, and to place women instead in the private sphere of home life. Second, such misogyny was connected to other themes within the full set of fascist ideology. For example, fascism's concern with race was part of a general concern with the creation of the *Volksgemeinschaft*, or national community. Both in Germany and Italy, fascist parties attempted to supervise the birth process, increasing the number of births and decreasing women's control over their own bodies. Third, as Wilhelm Reich pointed out, fascism was a sexualised movement. A large part of its appeal (to both men and women) relied on a visual imagery, which glorified the human body, while remaining resolutely hostile to the representation of sex.[39] Fourth, fascism's hostile attitude towards women's rights was not merely a matter of past history. Fascist parties in postwar Europe have been equally hostile towards the goals of women's liberation.

In all fairness, Martin Durham could argue that these potential criticisms are tangential to his central argument, which is that at times women did join the fascist parties. If fascism was so hostile to women, then how could any woman ever join such a party? To answer this point, however, requires going beyond the recent literature. In so far as its authors have a consistent theory to explain women's occasional support for fascism, it is simply to repeat (with some distance) the claims of fascists themselves, that there was something objectively pro-female about fascism. Hence the quote cited earlier: 'fascism was not uniformly misogynist'. The alternative explanation is to indicate that (in general terms) people are capable of defending a movement which is hostile to their interests.

The best known (but not the only) theory of 'false consciousness' is the Marxist theory of ideology.[40] This maintains that at certain times people are quite capable of supporting a party or a trend which is not to their benefit. In the work of Marx himself, the classic example of such an observation was his analysis of the role of Christianity: 'Religion is the sigh of the oppressed creature, just as it is the spirit of spiritless conditions. It is the *opium* of the people.'[41] This claim is a dual observation: religion is believed by ordinary people and engages with the alienation that millions feel in their lives; but this belief is partial, and needs to be renewed if it is to be sustained. A parallel claim could be made to explain the position of that minority of women who supported the fascist parties. Although fascism was not in their interests, fascism raised enough important questions for at least some women to find its answers appealing. Fascism could not be a women's movement – but it could do enough to recruit some women. In contrast to the recent work criticised here, such an argument would be neither controversial nor new.

For the anti-fascists of the 1970s, it was not enough merely to announce that fascism was an anti-feminist ideology (in this sense of the term). Instead, this generation of writers progressed from a general theory of ideology to a much more specific and historical theory of fascism, rooted in Wilhelm Reich's work on sexuality. As such, an explanation was offered for the success of fascism, namely that this movement had a sexualised appeal to women which coexisted with the anti-feminist imperative to drive women into the home. The total impression of fascism which emerges then is of a contradictory movement, which offered young women the chance to worship their leaders, while simultaneously denying them the chance to lead fulfilling lives both inside and outside the domestic sphere. This stress on the contradictory character of fascism can coexist with an emphasis on the ultimately sexist nature of the movement. To borrow from one of the most common fascist images, under Mussolini and Hitler, women could play a role in the crowd, but they were not allowed to appear on the platform.[42] One of the motives of fascism was always to deny women a role as real agents in shaping their own lives.

The argument of this chapter should be clear. To explain the paradox of female support for Hitler and Mussolini, arguments are required which the recent literature does not supply. Here, the anti-fascist literature of the 1930s and 1970s becomes especially valuable. These writers attempt to explain fascism's gendered appeal to women, without in any way suggesting that fascism was in women's interests. Their theories offer a more compelling insight into the contradictory relationships of the past.

FOUR

Understanding Adolf Hitler

A previous chapter addressed the question of whether fascism was the product of a distorted national history. In this chapter the nature of enquiry shifts from the broad question to a narrower one – how significant were the leaders in shaping the character of fascism? For many years historians have debated the question of determinism and free will. These debates have become especially sharp when historians have discussed the lives of 'great men', acknowledged historical figures whose lives have shaped the destiny of millions. In the mid-twentieth century, textbook history often seemed to consist simply of a list of kings and queens, a top-heavy approach which was rightly satirised in Sellar and Yeatman's light-hearted guide to British history, *1066 and All That*.[1] But the alternative style which addresses longer-term factors can reduce the space for human agency.[2] E.H. Carr was just one writer to have commented on the issue. His conclusion reunites both points of view: 'What seems to me essential is to recognise in the great men an outstanding individual who is at once a product and an agent of the historical process, at once the representative and the creator of social forces which change the shape of the world and the thoughts of men.'[3]

On the left the debate has been at least as charged as it was in purely academic circles. Karl Marx is often quoted for his dictum that 'Men make their own history, but they do not make it just as they please; they do not make it under circumstances chosen by themselves, but under circumstances directly encountered, given and transmitted from the past. The tradition of all the dead generations weighs like a nightmare upon the brain of the living.'[4] It would be easy, therefore, but mistaken, to read the opening passages of his 'Eighteenth Brumaire' as a defence of historical determinism. More than one Marxist has followed this cul-de-sac, placing all emphasis on 'history' as if history was a real person, with fixed rules, and a real ability to determine the outcome of events.

One of the first Russian Marxists, Georgi Plekhanov, is often criticised for precisely such mechanical thinking. His pamphlet, *The Role of the Individual in History*, argued that economic structures were more important in explaining history than individuals, and also that individual personalities were themselves the product of historical necessity. In fairness to Plekhanov, his intentions were more dialectical than most critics allow. Rather than abolishing the space for human freedom, Plekhanov hoped to map out a more persuasive account of the relationship between determinism and will.[5] Another Russian Marxist, Leon Trotsky, offered his own synthesis. According to him, personality was not just shaped by historical factors; personality was itself a factor. Trotsky's metaphor was of a link in a chain. Attempting to explain the role of his collaborator Lenin in the Russian Revolution, Trotsky argued that without Lenin, 'there would have been no October Revolution, the leadership of the Bolshevik Party would have prevented it from occurring'.[6]

Although this discussion is important, it is perhaps one-sided. For all the participants were most interested to explain the behaviour of those with whom they identified. It is easy to debate the freedom of manoeuvre of figures that you admire. But what happens when the personality is which one you find repugnant? This chapter will consider these questions of freedom and determinism, for the figure of Adolf Hitler. It is only when all obstacles of empathy and identification have been removed that a convincing analysis of the importance of individuals in history can be made.

ADOLF HITLER

The events of Adolf Hitler's life are well known. Born to a lower-middle-class family in Vienna in 1889, Hitler attempted to establish himself as an artist, but failed, and spent several years drifting around Vienna without much success. The outbreak of war in 1914 finally transformed Hitler's life. Contemporary photographs show his eyes brimming with new-found purpose. Serving with distinction as a messenger in the German trenches, Hitler was decorated and promoted to the rank of corporal. At the end of the war, Hitler was employed by the German chief of staff. In this role, he was sent to attend the meetings of one small right-wing sect, the German Workers' Party (DAP, later NSDAP). Hitler joined the group, and as he records in *Mein Kampf*, quickly took a leading role in the movement. One important incident was the attempted Beer Hall putsch of 1923, when Hitler and his followers attempted to seize Munich with the intention of marching on Berlin. For this crime, Hitler was jailed. Yet rather than ending his career, this failure only brought new success. The publicity which followed his trial made Adolf Hitler a household name. Having been released from prison early, Hitler first reunited the NSDAP, and then set about rebuilding its organisation. The 1929 Wall Street crash sent the German economy into crisis, and following the 1930 elections Hitler's party became the second largest in Germany.

In the fifteen years between the end of the First World War and his arrival in power, Hitler's life was dominated by his political career. Nothing else mattered to him. He seems to have lost contact with his family, and had few friends outside his political life. Even his love-affairs were short and emotionally brief. In 1933, partly thanks to the machinations of a clique of conservative politicians, Adolf Hitler was invited to take on the role of Chancellor of the Germany. Successes continued, including his tactical dismantling of his own private army, the SA, during the 'Night of the Long Knives' (1934). This was followed eighteen months later by the entry of the German army into the demilitarised Rhineland area. Finally, Hitler's luck turned against him in 1939, when the invasion of Poland prompted the French and British governments to act and led to an all-out world war. In this contest, and especially following the German invasion of Russia in 1941, Hitler was able to achieve his long-standing ambition to 'solve' the racial question, murdering many millions of gypsies, Slavs and Jews. Yet the war ended with German defeat and Hitler's suicide.

The story of Hitler's life is familiar, yet the question of how to interpret that life is more difficult. The first problem is how far to see Hitler as able to control events at will? He named his own autobiography *Mein Kampf* (*My Struggle*), believing that his rise was the product of a strong self-belief, as if anyone could become dictator simply by the strength of their desire. Such an emphasis on will returned during the war. Hitler explained every German victory in terms of his own strength of character – and every defeat in terms of the weakness of his leading generals. Yet historical events are not created simply by the ambition of these so-called great men.

Individuals can play an important role in the chain of historical events, but in any large society no one is wholly free to decide their own destiny. So Hitler's explanation can be disregarded, as we search for a more compelling theory.

The second question is how to avoid glamorising Hitler's life. No historian has described Hitler as a positive figure, but in writing about him it is hard to avoid following the chronology that he set out in his own book. The danger is in making Hitler appear special, central to events, even seductive. As the sole leader of the German state Hitler had extraordinary power over his subjects. Few other figures in history have held such dominance over millions. If the devil always has the best lines, then how can the historian restore Hitler to that level of mediocrity from which he only briefly emerged?

The solution of these dilemmas can be traced through the history of the several biographies of Adolf Hitler. It is interesting to observe that although several thousand histories include Hitler in their title, there are no more than three biographies of the man available in English which are generally recognised as being of the appropriate historical standard. The first is Alan Bullock's *Hitler: A Study in Tyranny* (1952), the second Joachim Fest's *Hitler* (1973), the third is Ian Kershaw's biography, of which the first volume has appeared as *Hitler: 1889–1936: Hubris* (1998), and the second as *Hitler: 1936–1945: Nemesis* (2000).[7] The lack of historical biographies contrasts with the abundance of writing devoted to the study of the other leading figures of the mid-twentieth century, including Stalin, Churchill and Roosevelt. One reason for the lack of further studies could be the sheer quality of Bullock's initial biography. The other explanation would lie in the immense difficulty of constructing an adequate account of his life. No historian wants to be remembered as the writer who glamorised Hitler's life.

The first significant biography was Alan Bullock's *Hitler*. Written in the immediate aftermath of the Second World War, this book represented a reflection of the values for which it was fought. The tone of Bullock's book was judgemental, its method reflected the common-sense values of the time. The fact that Adolf Hitler went to war demonstrates that war was a continuous Nazi goal. Again, the fact that Hitler was a virulent anti-Semite proves that the Holocaust must have been planned, and that Hitler must have planned it. This is how Alan Bullock explained the writing of his book:

> I first began this study with two questions in mind. The first, suggested by much that was said at the Nuremberg Trials, was to discover how great a part Hitler played in the history of the Third Reich and whether Göring and the other defendants were exaggerating when they claimed that under the Nazi regime the will of one man, and one man alone, was decisive. This led to the second and larger question: if the picture of Hitler given at Nuremberg was substantially accurate, what were the gifts which Hitler possessed which enabled him first to secure and then to maintain such power?[8]

Despite the tone of sceptical enquiry, Bullock's answer to his first question was determined before his research began. Nazi Germany was (as Alan Bullock had already decided) a personal dictatorship of the most distinct kind. Enormous emphasis was placed on the single figure of Adolf Hitler, while relatively little attention was given to Hitler's lieutenants. Still less interest was taken in the important question of why ordinary Germans agreed to follow where Hitler led. The strength of this early approach lay its plausibility, its coherence, and in the clear moral judgement that fascism was wrong. The weakness of Bullock's book lay in its indifference to factors outside Hitler's control.

Towards the end of the 1960s, a new generation of historians began to emerge in Germany. As one participant, Hans-Ulrich Wehler, records, this generation emerged 'against the general background of the so-called rebellion of students and junior staff in West Germany, and this intellectual climate favoured the presentation of sharply formulated hypotheses'.[9] Their evidence suggested that in his relations to his underlings, Adolf Hitler was weak-willed, indecisive and arbitrary. In contrast with Bullock, Karl-Dietrich Bracher and Hans Mommsen preferred to describe Hitler as a 'weak dictator'.[10] The ruler who emerged from their work seemed more concerned to play off rival figures against each other, rather than to ensure that consistent policies arose. This generation of historians were quickly labelled 'structuralists' or 'functionalists', to distinguish them from the older guard of 'intentionalists' who had focused more clearly on the question of Hitler's intentions. Some structuralists were broadly Marxist, in that they explained the events of Hitler's life with reference to economic factors. Among this group one key figure was

Tim Mason, whose work is discussed below. Others were more influenced by the theories of the sociologist Max Weber, and placed greater emphasis on the structures of the German state. This group included Martin Broszat, whose *Hitler State* said little about Hitler but uncovered a great deal about the workings of Nazi government.[11] A third group attempted a synthesis of Marx and Weber. One example of this last group would be Hans-Ulrich Wehler, who popularised the 'Sonderweg' arguments which have already been discussed in this book.

Although the functionalists were committed to a very sociological approach, which placed considerable emphasis on state formation and structure, the best of their accounts retained the historian's interest in the relationship between structure and agency. In 1970, Martin Broszat published an important article which examined the role of social motivation, and the link between the Führer and his people. As with Plekhanov before him, Broszat was determined to uncover the processes which created the leader. The picture that emerged was of a man imprisoned by history, a leader dependent on his crowd:

> Hitler's sudden rise from intellectual and social mediocrity and anonymity to the stage of politics underlines that his leadership could only unfold in the fluid state of a certain crisis atmosphere and collective psychological state. The unusual passion with which Hitler succumbed to the general pathology, and the absoluteness with which he concentrated on giving it expression and translating it into action, enabled him to become 'Führer'. Against a background of general exaltation he was able to experience his own neuroses as a general truth and to use the collective neurosis as the sounding board for his own fanaticism.

This passage is reminiscent of the old saying, 'I am their leader, therefore I must follow them'. Hitler's genius is explained in terms of a dual pathology, his and the German neuroses, and the general conditions of crisis which enabled such a leader to emerge. Broszat concludes, 'Hitler's leadership was thus from the outset the pivotal point of a paradoxical situation: on the one hand, merely the exponent of a broad nationalistic psychosis, on the other hand the integrative figure of the "movement" which, without such integration, could not make its political breakthrough.'[12]

The second major biography of Hitler was Joachim Fest's *Hitler*. Although lucid and well supported by primary evidence, it was not clear that Fest's work surpassed Alan Bullock's earlier biography. In particular, Fest seems to have failed to have incorporated the insights of the new generation of structuralist historians, who were then at the height of their influence. Joachim Fest's *Hitler* emphasised the early events of Hitler's life, which were used to justify several pages of implausible and semi-psychological insights. Fest's biography also devoted a great deal of space to an arid consideration of whether Hitler should be granted the status of 'negative greatness' – Hitler's distinctiveness was found in his ability 'to ignore the weight of conditions and interests'.[13] The book famously earned the wrath of Karl-Dietrich Bracher for its failure to incorporate social and economic questions.[14] So while the fashion was for sociological or structuralist explanations of the workings of the Hitler state, Fest and Bullock's works were both criticised for their intentionalist style.

One structuralist historian, Tim Mason, did attempt in the 1980s and early 1990s to escape from the convention of intentionalist biography. Mason's books were clearly Marxist in tone, including his collection of essays, *Nazism, Fascism and the Working Class* (1995), and his better-known *Social Policy in the Third Reich* (1993), which examined the condition of German workers from 1933 to 1939.[15] This latter book maintained that 'From its inception to its demise, the regime of the Third Reich acted as though the working class was something special, with its own particular experiences and interests: experiences and interests which might one day serve as the basis for collective action that could imperil the system.'[16] A committed and polemical but also tortured writer, Tim Mason confessed that he was unable to come to terms with the sheer horror of the Nazi Holocaust. In his words, 'I have always remained emotionally, and thus intellectually, paralysed in front of what the Nazis did and what their victims suffered.'[17] Several of his obituarists speculated as to the connection between Mason's inability to comprehend the Nazi genocide and his own untimely death.[18]

At around the mid-1980s, the argument between the intentionalists and the structuralists ground to a halt. Among historians of Nazi Germany, a consensus emerged that intentionalists and functionalists were only discussing two different sides of one single reality. According to this broad consensus, the issues of the debate had been resolved. Without the figure of Adolf Hitler, and indeed the Nazi dominance of the German state, most historians now agreed, the Holocaust could never have emerged. Conversely, for the Holocaust to take place, it had to be communicated. And the actual decision seems to have taken a twisted route, with different sections of the Nazi state competing in an unplanned and chaotic way to implement what each section believed was the true expression of the Führer's will.

In the new climate of agreement, several syntheses have been attempted to establish this theoretical synthesis in a work of pure history. Of these, the most important recent study is Ian Kershaw's *Hitler*. Having been identified for many years as a functionalist, Ian Kershaw was now moving into biography, the traditional preserve of intentionalism. Pulled by contradictory pressures, Kershaw was alive to the dilemmas mentioned at the beginning of this chapter, including the question of how to relate Hitler's intentions to the impact of events outside his control. The introduction to the book outlines how Hitler's biography should be written. The best biography, Kershaw argues, must bring together the emphasis on personality and character, traditionally associated with biography, with the insights of social history. Kershaw's *Hubris* then offers its own theoretical explanation of how Hitler's dictatorship operated, borrowing from Weber's sociological account of 'charismatic leadership'. The author announces 'a new approach: one which attempts to integrate the actions of the Dictator into the political structures and social forces which conditioned his acquisition and exercise of power, and its extraordinary impact.'[19]

Kershaw is also aware of the second great dilemma faced by historians: how can a biography of Hitler avoid glamorising its subject? Hitler became the dictator of the most economically advanced state in Europe, ruling over a nation of 70 million people. As a result of the Second World War and the Holocaust, he has, more than anyone else, stamped his mark on the twentieth century. *Mein Kampf* explains Hitler's success in terms of his astute leadership, his knowledge and his powerful speaking. Fortunately, Kershaw's biography recognises that Hitler had few talents except luck. Routinely underestimated by its opponents, the Nazi Party benefited from an economic crisis which it did not manufacture, and the wavering of its opponents, who could have blocked it but failed. Anyone who has had the misfortune to read *Mein Kampf* will step with joy through the early chapters of *Hitler: Hubris*, which contrast Hitler's story to the lies, half-truths, boasts and self-deceits that Hitler produced, and which other historians have lazily repeated. These chapters describe in detail how the tiny Nazi Party, with one branch in Munich in 1920, was able to grow until it exerted a hegemony over the large forces of the German far right.

To return to questions of theory, Kershaw's approach could broadly be characterised as a form of 'interactionism'; this refers to the classic sociological argument that in order to produce a sophisticated explanation of real events, the behaviour of individuals and the weight of social factors should be combined (or to use Kershaw's phrase cited above, 'integrated'). Within this family of explanations, Kershaw sees the key factor as the creation of the personal state: 'The task of the biographer has to focus not on the personality of Hitler, but squarely and directly upon *the character of his power – the power of the Führer*.'[20] How did Hitler maintain this position of power?

Before moving on to Kershaw's application of his theory, it is worth stating clearly that an interactionist approach *should* be able to offer a level of theoretical sophistication that has been previously missing from the debate. Take, for example, the important events of June 1934, the 'Night of the Long Knives', in which Hitler purged his party of its radical wing. The leadership of Hitler's storm-troopers (the SA), including such figures as Ernest Röhm, were jailed or murdered. An interactionist perspective on these events would concentrate on both Hitler's character in shaping events, and also events in shaping Hitler's character. It is possible to envisage the sort of history writing which might emerge. First would come the intentionalist half of the argument, that Hitler's character *was* important. Hitler's fussiness and indecisiveness delayed a series of events that he had considered since summer 1933. His love of high drama led him to invent and then believe an imaginary putsch by the SA, which then justified his own action. His paranoia prevented him from trusting even loyal allies. Finally, Hitler's personal feelings of inadequacy before the army and other institutions of old Germany in turn explains Hitler's willingness to promote the interests of the army at the expense of the SA.

Second would come the structuralist half of the argument, that Hitler's character *was* influenced by external factors. His willingness to deal with the army created his ambivalence as to whether the state or the Nazi Party should prosper. Indeed, the messy and bureaucratic structure of the Nazi Party left Hitler isolated, dependent on his lieutenants, and consequently paranoid. In a situation of bureaucratic rivalry, there were even plenty of leading Nazis to encourage Hitler's attack on the SA. Both Himmler and Göring wanted to see Röhm punished. The structures of Nazi rule not only left Hitler in power, but facilitated a further situation where each success left more power in his hands. Hitler had no confidants, no allies, only underlings. This left him isolated, subject to the whims and fantasies of conspirators. It fuelled his belief in high drama, and helped to create his personal style.

The advantage of an interactionist description is that it should enable both sets of insights to be fitted together. Indeed Kershaw does attempt such an interactionist history of the events of 1934. Kershaw describes the 'psychological state' which Hitler worked himself into, in order to justify his coup. Yet this irrational state is not described as anything innate to Hitler, but instead as a response both to his character and to the turn of events. Later in the same section, the biographer describes Adolf Hitler's mood as 'blackening', and again both his prior intention and the impact of external events are taken into account. In contrast to the more conventional biography of Alan Bullock, Kershaw takes studious regard of the various plots and counter-plots, both among Hitler's immediate circle and in wider society. Indeed reading his account it would be easy to conclude that the only pure Hitler loyalist was the unfortunate victim of the coup: Ernst Röhm. As elsewhere in his work, Ian Kershaw goes to considerable lengths to convey the public reception of these events. In German society, Hitler was perceived to have been the victim of a conspiracy, when he was in fact the instigator of the coup. 'There was great admiration for what was seen to be Hitler's protection of the "little man" against the outrageous abuses of power of the overmighty SA leadership. Even more so, the emphasis that Hitler had placed in his speech on the immorality and corruption of the SA leaders left a big mark on public responses.' Thus Hitler's success on 30 June 1934 owed more to his skilful publicity than to any substance in his mythical account of his own role in the events.[21]

Having identified Kershaw's theory of 'charismatic authority' as a variant of interactionism, how does the author go on to fill out this approach? Two sources in particular are cited. One is an obscure functionary, attempting to describe to his contemporaries how Nazi rule actually worked. This civil servant described himself 'working towards the Führer along lines he would wish'.[22] In other words, the Nazi dictatorship was a process of guesswork and initiative from below. Few decisions were centralised, and Adolf Hitler did not generally take a position of control. The second source emphasised is Franz Neumann's *Behemoth* (1942),[23] in which he described Hitler's dictatorship: 'Charismatic rule . . . has deep roots and becomes a powerful stimulus once the proper psychological and social conditions are set. The Leader's charismatic power is not a mere phantasm – none can doubt that millions believe it.'[24] This insight is endorsed by Kershaw, as a powerful description of how Nazi government actually worked.

The approach of Ian Kershaw's *Hitler* seems to have both strengths and weaknesses. It is appropriate to indicate the positive aspects first. One strength is in the tone. The two volumes provide a clearly non-fascist understanding of fascism. In contrast to the 'fascism studies' approach which has been criticised elsewhere in this book, Ian Kershaw's book provides an understanding of fascism which does not duplicate (but strongly condemns) the world view of fascism itself. A further strength is that if Kershaw's position becomes general among historians, then the old debate between structuralists and intentionalists will have been finally resolved. There is a space for both perspectives, especially if the insights of each can be combined. Finally, Kershaw's argument potentially resolves a third area of debate between historians – the question of whether Nazism relied on coercion or was founded on consent. If Kershaw is correct, then much more will be understood about the dynamics of ordinary Germans' consent to the regime.

Yet it should be plain there are also potential flaws in Ian Kershaw's account. One is that it is unclear from Kershaw whether he sees this interactionist method as appropriate in general, or suited only to the German case in particular. Compared to Kershaw's case of Nazi Germany, the theory of charismatic authority might actually provide a better explanation of the social dynamics of other societies, including perhaps Stalinist Russia.[25] A further potential weakness is that it is extremely difficult to write history in the way that the author indicates. Having set forward a theoretically sophisticated analysis of Hitler's rule, the emphasis is on the author to live up to the quality of his theory. Taking up this second point, although there is much to praise in Kershaw's *Hitler*, the first volume especially does seem occasionally to lose its way. The sheer burden of facts, the historian's need to tell every aspect of the story, weighs heavy from around 1930 onwards. Kershaw seems to have no explanation of why it was that Hitler's party was able to benefit so spectacularly from the recession that began with the Wall Street crash in 1929. At this stage, the biography invokes Hitler's ambition, the flaws in his psychology, and the enormous energies that the Nazi Party put into propaganda. These are then used to explain how Hitler moved in three years from being the leader of a far-right sect, to the Chancellor of all Germany. In the first volume (although far less in the second), there is a methodological retreat, and the style slips towards a more customary biography of Hitler.

The crucial moment covered in the first volume is Hitler's accession to power. The events of 1933 seem to be described in a very conventional, narrative and biographical way. The emphasis is placed on Hitler's will and his desire in bringing the Nazis into government. Yet it is also important to remember that Hitler was invited to power in January 1933, at a time when his party was in crisis, its vote slipping, and several of its leading figures were in revolt. The Nazis then had 37 per cent of the vote, and only two seats in the new cabinet. This was an unlikely beginning for dictatorship, and Hitler's final victory had more to do with the failure of his enemies than with his own skill or determination. Crucially, the German left failed to unite. The Socialists and the Communists had between them more members, more supporters, more votes, and because of their links to the working class, more weight in society than the Nazis. Yet because of Stalin's influence on the ultra-left German Communist Party, and because of the timidity of the official German Socialists, no practical unity was reached. United action was possible, and would have reversed the Nazi rise. The failure of the German left should be brought out, if only to remind us that such a capitulation should never happen again.

By contrast Kershaw's second volume, *Hitler: Nemesis*, is strongest at the most important moment of its narrative – when Hitler and his lieutenants begin the Holocaust. Here the emphasis on Hitler's charismatic authority becomes most useful, explaining how the paradoxical situation could arise in which he both determines the Holocaust, and at the same time distances himself from it. The Holocaust was the last of a series of initiatives designed to end the Jewish presence in Europe. First, Hitler considered a scheme to deport Jews to Madagascar. Then, a second proposal was made to send Jews to Siberia. As the war with Russia became more bitter, so the plan to deport millions of Jews became instead a scheme to murder millions of Jews. In the winter of 1941, Hitler agreed to SS proposals calling for the deportation of Jews from Germany. Kershaw comments, 'Hitler's agreement to the deportation of the German Jews was not tantamount to a decision for the "Final Solution". It is doubtful whether a single, comprehensive decision of such a kind was ever made. But Hitler's authorisation of the deportations opened the door widely to a whole range of new initiatives from numerous local and regional Nazi leaders who seized on the opportunity . . . to start killing Jews in their own areas.'[26]

Ian Kershaw's emphasis on local decision-making is significant. If one man should take responsibility for the killings it is, of course, Adolf Hitler. He did more than anyone else to create the general climate of murderous anti-Semitism which dominated within the leading circles of the regime. Hitler's enormous authority was used to justify the killings – the leader willed and people obeyed. He also brought the idea of a 'Final Solution of the Jewish Question' back into the heart of Nazi thinking, through a series of public speeches, beginning with one to the Reichstag in September 1939. Yet Hitler remained terrified of the Holocaust, speaking of it only in the most general, abstract terms. He would not attend the Wannsee Conference, where the most detailed plans were laid. When subordinates attempted to confirm that the process was moving at the correct speed, Hitler allowed them to show him the figures, provided that the terms used to describe the victims were stripped of all meaning. 'Even in his inner circle Hitler could never bring himself to speak with outright frankness about the killing of the Jews. Full knowledge of their murder was evidently not to be touched upon directly in his presence, even among the close band of criminal conspirators.'[27] So the implementation of the Holocaust was left to the second rank of Nazi leaders. They were expected to work towards the Führer's wishes, filling out and giving meaning to the orders that their leader was unwilling to express.

BEYOND HITLER

To suggest that the behaviour of small numbers of people can have a deep historical significance is not to glorify these individuals. No contemporary historian would claim to see the action of these supposed great men as the source of moral instruction. Such history has been out of vogue (thankfully) for fifty years and more.[28] In the case of Hitler, a historical literature has grown up which is hostile to its subject, opposed to his desires, and welcoming to those who suffered from his hate. In all these ways, the published work lives up to the need to write critically of its subject. For many years, the main debate among historians lay over the question of how far Hitler was the master of his destiny. The biographical school tended to emphasise Hitler's freedom of manoeuvre, while economists and political scientists generally described his constraints. Ian Kershaw's recent book represents a significant attempt towards a synthesis, a structuralist biography, and as such should be welcomed. His *Hitler* points towards a resolution of the argument between structure and agency. The distinction between long-term factors (economics, state structure, national history) and short-term factors (individuals, chance, personality) is, of course, a distinction made in retrospect, at the convenience of the historians. An account which makes sense of the past must integrate the insights of each approach.

FIVE

British Fascism Reconsidered

One central theme of this book has been the criticism of the way in which many historians have begun to write about fascism. For some time, historians of generic fascism have argued that the best way to explain fascism is as a set of ideas. Thus Zeev Sternhell has argued that fascism emerged first in France in the 1880s and 1890s, born in the minds of intellectuals and artists such as Edouard Drumont, Charles Peguy, Maurice Barrès and Charles Maurras.[1] These intellectuals absorbed and then synthesised socialism and nationalism and thus created a new ideology, 'a socialism without the proletariat', which duly became fascism. Sternhell stresses the right-wing elements in the thought of such thinkers of the left as Pierre Proudhon and Georges Sorel, and the left-wing elements in the thought of such right-wing figures as Drumont, Mussolini and Barrès. As a result, Sternhell maintains that there is no real meaning to the traditional distinctions between left and right. Fascism, he says, emerges on the left while claiming to be anti-left. It is commonly described as a right-wing phenomenon, but it has no more in common with conservatism than with Communism. Fascism, therefore, is 'ni droit ni gauche' – neither right nor left.[2]

Roger Griffin, another historian of generic fascism, also defines fascism according to the myths which it has generated about itself. Moreover, Griffin argues that this emphasis on the positive beliefs of fascism is now the accepted way to understand it, the 'new consensus' in the field of what he calls 'fascist studies'. The appropriate way to define liberalism is from the perspective of a liberal, therefore the appropriate way to define fascism must be from the perspective of a fascist:

> The premise to this approach . . . is to take fascist ideology at its face value, and to recognise the central role played in it by the myth of national rebirth to be brought about by finding a 'Third

> Way' between liberalism/capitalism and communism/socialism. One of the advantages of the new consensus is that it brings fascism in line with the way other major political 'isms' are approached in the human sciences by defining it as an ideology inferable from the claims made by its own protagonists.[3]

This book has argued that Roger Griffin's method is the wrong way to understand fascism. Political theorists would not recognise a history of the Holocaust written on the basis of the perpetrators' claims. Neither should we accept a theory of fascism based on the 'claims made by its own protagonists'. It is a strange theory which accepts the definition that historical figures offer to describe themselves without asking if they were right. It would make more sense to argue that fascism should be studied critically, in an antagonistic or even hostile manner.

Once historians choose to write about fascism, they must acknowledge that their theories will have an impact. At the very least, a 'neutral' way of writing about generic fascism will tend to encourage a 'neutral' approach towards writing about specific fascist movements in each country. Two recent articles in the *Journal of Contemporary History* both made the case that British fascism should be seen primarily as an ideology. Richard Thurlow examines Oswald Mosley and the attempted rebirth of British fascism after 1945. He suggests that the most convincing way to understand British fascism is as a vehicle for the expression of Mosley's thought: 'The fact that synthesis was such a core feature of Mosley's fascism mean that the development of his thought was pragmatic and flexible, fresh emphases could be developed according to new political realities, even though the central beliefs of the fascist myth remained intact.' The judgement on Oswald Mosley's success or failure is interpreted primarily in terms of the vitality of his ideas. According to Thurlow, Mosley was 'a revolutionary whose ideas failed to register in the intellectual or cultural mainstream, even if he was a pioneer of the various syntheses of fascist, racial populist and democratic traditions which came to characterise forms of neo-fascism in Europe after 1945'.[4]

In the same issue, Philip Coupland also describes British fascism in terms of its ideas. His article suggests that British fascism should be seen as a utopian movement. Drawing on the writings of fascists such as Louise Irvine and E.D. Randell, and other members of the British Union of Fascists (BUF) in the 1930s, he emphasises the 'revolutionary' character of British fascist thought, summed up by such BUF wisdom as the saying that fascism is 'revolutionary or it is nothing'. For Philip Coupland, the BUF was 'part of the wider utopian politics and culture of the 1930s'. Of course, Coupland's point is not to celebrate fascism – rather his intention is to explore the subjective character of human aspiration. As he writes: 'Perhaps by better understanding the danger of utopianism, we will be able to keep utopia on the map but humanity off the road to serfdom.'[5]

Taking Thurlow's example of fascism in the 1940s, this chapter will argue against Coupland's notion that British fascism should be seen as utopian. What then constitutes a utopia, and how can we discriminate? The most basic, shared character of all utopias is that they do not (yet) exist – utopianism is a condition of aspiration or longing for a society which is different. Yet there are many different varieties of utopia. Conventional political language distinguishes between a policy, a manifesto, a programme, and a philosophy. At each stage the imaginative content is increased – the writing is less concerned with the present and more concerned with the future. Following this point, it seems to me that any utopian future must have an imaginative content – it should use humour, surprise, or shock – or it should have enough of these elements for contemporaries to recognise it as a utopia.

There is also the issue of what future is envisaged. Some political or fictional utopias are optimistic or generous, some egalitarian or free. Others lack these characteristics, or only share them in part. Some 'utopian' visions sit at the very opposite end of the scale – the futures which they envisage are clearly unequal, destructive or unfree. Any reader of utopian literature will be able to draw a contrast between these different varieties of utopian future. Even within one political tradition, some alternative futures are more utopian than others. For example, William Morris's *News from Nowhere* reads as the product of a milieu in which everyone is arguing about how society could change. These discussions even intrude into the opening lines of the text:

> Up at the League, says a friend, there had been one night a brisk conversational discussion, as to what would happen on the

> Morrow of the Revolution, finally shading off into a vigorous statement by various friends of their views on the future of the fully developed new society . . . there were six persons present, and consequently six sections of the party were represented, four of which had strong but divergent Anarchist opinions. . . .[6]

By the time of Beatrice and Sidney Webb's *Soviet Communism*, however, socialism seemed to have lost its utopian content.[7] Now it meant state planning, higher production and better management. Although the defenders of the Soviet Union continued to believe that they represented the future, the egalitarian-utopian content of their ideal future was less. The imagination of the labour movement had been diminished in the fifty years since Morris.

The writers associated with British fascism were members of a radical political movement. They were obliged to think of the future, and they did draw up programmes for fascist government. But their movement lacked the utopian culture of, for example, William Morris's circle. When there was a fascist future – explicit in their writing, or implied in their day-to-day conduct – this utopia was based on ideas of duty and service, hierarchy and submission. To use Coupland's own language, the fascist utopia was an *ou*topia, in the sense that it did not exist, but it was not a *eu*topia; it was not recognisably a good place.[8] Indeed, if ever a political tradition deserves the title 'dystopian' then it is fascism. Fascism set out to diminish humanity – Mussolini and Hitler promised as much – and fascism was recognised by contemporaries as a dystopian movement. In the 1930s, writers as diverse as Max Horkheimer and George Orwell reread Jack London's book, *The Iron Heel*.[9] They found in this early dystopia a guide to that worse society that fascism sought to create. What is more, they were right. British fascism as a political force represented a synthesis of ideology and practice. The ideology was reactionary, the practice violent and racist.

The argument here is that it is wrong to see fascism as being only an ideology; that simply is not how fascism was experienced at the time. Instead, the best way to see fascism is as a particular form of movement, possessing a certain ideology, and in which the ideology and movement interact. What is proposed here is in effect an alternative method of analysing either British or generic fascism, which relates the ideas of fascism to its behaviour as a political movement. Such a method does lead to a longer definition of fascism, which I have attempted to elaborate at length elsewhere.[10] The introduction to this book has already suggested that fascism represents a unity of different themes:

1. A specific form of politics, with a family resemblance to other similar movements, but also important points of difference.
2. A dystopian ideology, in which the key theme is radical elitism.
3. Political practice, conditioned by the desire to create a particular form of mass movement.
4. The fascist contradiction, a situation in which the ideology and the movement work in different directions.

This chapter will flesh out this definition, expressing disagreements with Thurlow and Coupland as it goes. It will consider fascism historically – what did the British fascists do?

BRITISH FASCISM 1945–51

There is a striking contrast between the British fascism which appears in the historical writing of Richard Thurlow and Philip Coupland, and the fascism that was experienced at the time. Both authors write as if fascism was created simply to give its leaders the opportunity to express their ideas. Thurlow's account bristles with such phrases as, 'His intention was made clear from the outset', 'The key to Mosley's postwar thought', and 'BUF ideas have been seen as one of the more impressive examples of fascist thought.'[11] However, it is not true that the primary goal of each fascist was to elaborate an ideology, nor even to develop their own political creed. Rather, the first thing which each fascist attempted was to build a fascist party. In this way, the Union Movement, the child of Mosley's prewar BUF, began in each area as a book club or society, or as a series of private groups, which 'may or may not [have been] identifiable at first glance'. Then Mosley, or Alexander Raven Thomson, would visit the groups, and merge them to form a branch of the Union Movement. The movement would begin public activities. Fascists would sell their publication *Union*, and put up slogans or graffiti on walls. Members of the Union Movement would hold their own meetings, or heckle left-wing speakers. Finally, there would be a large rally. Mosley would speak, and announce that the movement was 'coming forward as a fully fledged political party', which would stand candidates in elections, and have an open existence.[12]

These parties should not be understood simply as publishing houses, nor as other neutral sources of the printed word. They did not exist to print programmes, nor simply to sell books. Instead, they were a particular form of political structure; fascist political parties, with a strong leader, an emphasis on violence, and a typical membership. Each party had its leader, the most important of whom was Oswald Mosley. Members of the Union Movement shared a religious devotion to their 'Leader'. In detention, they arranged elaborate ceremonies on his birthday, at which they saluted his portrait and sang hymns to him. At a reunion dance in 1945, 'Mosley became the centre of a surging mob of hero-worshippers, many of whom were on the edge of hysteria.'[13] Mosley fascists wrote about their leader in tones of awe, using capitals to convey their devotion. Jeffrey Hamm wrote in the *British League Review*, 'Oswald Mosley has given us The Idea, and it is for us to build the Movement that will propagate that Idea.' Raven Thomson produced a book, *Mosley, What They Say, What They Said, What He Is*, designed to demonstrate that the leader was omnipotent, omniscient, and infallible. At meetings, the congregation treated Oswald Mosley like a god-on-earth who could be watched and adored. Trevor Grundy, then a young boy, has described the adulation of Mosley's audiences:

> In his book, *Beyond The Pale*, Nicholas Mosley, Oswald's eldest son, said that he went to an East End pub with Mosley and Diana [Mosley] and experienced what it was like to walk into a room with his father and how some of Mosley's supporters touched him to gain strength or power. He was right. It was just like that. My mother used to touch him and she'd say afterwards at home: 'That will give me strength till next year.'[14]

The ultimate sacrilege came when former supporters of Mosley, such as Beckett or Chesterton, described their former idol as the 'Bleeder'.

Richard Thurlow makes the claim that 'The BUF, despite left-wing propaganda to the contrary . . . displayed an unwillingness to use offensive violence against the state and anti-fascists'.[15] Yet many

British fascists positively revelled in the violent attacks they carried out against their opponents. In January 1946, fascists damaged bookshops in Bethnal Green, Whitechapel, and Coventry, while four months later, a Jewish shop in Hampstead was attacked. Through the winter of 1946/7, fascists set fire to synagogues in Clapton, Dollis Hill, Bristol, and Willesden. The following spring, a group called the Ku Klux Klan sent hate mail to the Edgware MP, Mrs Ayrten Gould, to Sir Hartley Shawcross, D.N. Pritt, Waldon Smithers, and the Revd Saul Amias. In July 1947, Liverpool fascists set fire to a Jewish cabinet factory, and one month later, an anonymous fascist sent threatening letters to C.H. Darke, the Secretary of Hackney Trades Council.[16]

In September of the same year, members of the British League of Ex-Servicemen shouting 'Hail Mosley' attempted to smash up a Communist meeting in Ridley Road, throwing bottles and fireworks, and injuring three people. Also that month, a gang of fascists attacked three Jewish ex-servicemen in Kingsland Road, Hackney, and beat them with knuckle-dusters. In October 1947, three fascists, John Arthur Parker, Frederick William Mendham, and Arthur Jordan, were each given twenty-eight days in prison for assaulting Jews, with John Parker later telling one of his victims that he was in charge of a fascist squad in Hackney – 'I received orders to beat you up.' Two months later, Ivor Worth, a member of the British League of Ex-Servicemen and Women, was sentenced to eighteen months in jail for placing a bomb outside the London headquarters of a Zionist organisation. In March 1948, David Barrow was fined for waving a gun while he spoke at a fascist meeting, and in April, Victor Burgess, a Union Movement speaker, was bound over for twelve months after he assaulted a man selling the anti-fascist paper, *On Guard*.[17]

What was the dominant ideology of fascism? It can be agreed that there were points of fascist ideology which did mark off individual fascists from other members of society, but these were not only or typically the ideas, nationalism and socialism, let alone 'utopianism', which our theorists have fixed upon. Philip Coupland suggests that a large number of fascists were in fact socialists, including Arthur Beavan and Alexander Raven Thomson. Meanwhile, according to Thurlow, Sir Oswald Mosley was 'a Utopian visionary', who should be compared to 'other renegade socialists, such as de Man and Deat' and who 'reverted to his left-wing roots once fascism had failed.'[18] Yet Mosley's claimed socialist credentials from the 1920s are actually rather thin. They amount to a few speeches, one pamphlet, not more. The defining continuity in Mosley's career is between the social imperialist Tory of 1918 and the fascist of 1932 and beyond. The problems with locating Mosley as a figure of the left become clear when Thurlow defines socialism as being a belief in 'expanded welfare provision from a strong state'. Under this definition Mosley could be described as a socialist, but so could any British politician, from whatever political tradition, active in the 1930s and 1940s.

As a group, the fascists put forward ideas that were the very opposite of socialism. The *Patriot* condemned the Beveridge Plan, deriding the very idea of a National Health Service: 'Those responsible for the Plan abrogated [*sic*] to themselves all the attributes of a Dictatorship.' Beveridge was 'designed to fit into a master plan issuing in a totalitarian state'. Douglas Reed's paper, *London Tidings*, denounced the activities of the Labour government, for taking money from the rich – 'those who by the wise application of their capital . . . made Great Britain what she was, are being systematically despoiled'. Fascist publications spent their every moment attacking the working-class movement. The *British League Review* described the Communist Party as 'sub-human oriental ape-men', while the Liberator Council, the Banking Reform League, the New Age Association, the Social Credit Party, the Social Credit Co-ordinating Committee and the Common Law Parliament all campaigned against local authorities who borrowed money to pay for public housing. *At Random*, the paper of the 'Modern Thought Discussion Group', warned that Communists were running British industry: 'Dare we say "it cannot happen here", when our vital mining industry is dominated by the avowed Communist Horner, who has threatened us with a coal stoppage, would we quarrel with Russia'.[19] Mosley described unemployment benefit as the negation of 'British and all human progress'. The *Patriot* defined workers as 'sub men . . . anthropoid hooligans', while the Union of British Freedom paper, *Unity*, attacked transport strikers, and Major Douglas went further still. All trade unions, he suggested, were 'an alien culture', which had to be removed.[20]

If utopianism is to have any meaning, then it must refer to the desire to create a society in which there will be more freedom or more equality. That is the whole point of a *eu*topia: here is worse, while there is different and better. Fascism, however, based itself not on egalitarianism but on elitism, on the notion that certain human beings were morally superior to others, who consequently did not have the right to exist. Richard Thurlow suggests that the Union Movement's 'most important original contribution to political life was its pioneer role in highlighting immigration as an increasingly important factor in British politics during the 1950s'.[21] Such views should not be treated simply as fascist debating points, but as open expressions of racism. The Union Movement revived the BUF chant of 'the yids, the yids, we've got to get rid of the yids'. Supporters of the movement would shout 'Get out of it, you Jew bastard', or 'Go back to Belsen'. Fascist street-corner speakers spewed out a torrent of anti-semitism. In December 1946, Victor Burgess of the Union of British Freedom called for Palestinian Jews to be publicly flogged, while in April 1947, a British League of Ex-Servicemen speaker claimed Britain was being run by a 'lying rotten Jewish dictatorship'.[22] In June 1948, a fascist speaker suggested that 'Hitler did a good job against certain people', and in December, another speaker said that, 'Jews are filthy, parasitic vermin, feeding on the political body of the country. The sooner we get rid of this lot the better. Hitler closed the doors of his gas chambers too soon.'[23]

Racism and elitism were not accidental to fascism; they were structured into the heart of British fascist thinking. For Mosley after 1945, the great idea was 'Europe a Nation'. This plan was put in Mosley's book, *The Alternative*. Europe would be amalgamated into a single state protected by tariffs, and given the best parts of Africa to exploit, under apartheid conditions. Mosley's purpose was, as Mervyn Jones commented, 'to make each eager youngster envisage himself, suitably clad in khaki shorts and carrying a whip or revolver, striding magisterially across a vast plantation where countless black backs bend in rhythm'.[24] Meanwhile, the *British League Review* denounced what it described as 'the lie of racial equality', and the *Patriot* believed that whites were naturally cleverer than blacks, who could only be 'docile and useful citizens' if they were not allowed to leave Africa. The Union Movement demanded a 'Colour Bar' against 'Black parasites', while Arnold Leese's paper, *Gothic Ripples*, argued for what it described as the natural law: 'all is race'.[25]

The most commonly expressed fascist theme, and the characteristic form of fascist dystopianism, was anti-Semitism. Anyone who has had the misfortune of reading pre-1958 British fascist literature at any length, will acknowledge the overriding, even *defining* importance of anti-Jewish racism (while since then, it has of course been anti-black racism which has played this role). G.F. Green's paper, the *Independent Nationalist*, advertised the *Protocols of the Elders of Zion*, as did the *Social Creditor*, *London Tidings*, and *Union*, while the *Patriot* contented itself with the insistence that the *Protocols* were not a forgery. A.K. Chesterton also quoted them.[26] *Gothic Ripples* gave itself the masthead, 'An occasional report on the Jewish question issued for the Jew-wise'. Leese claimed there were up to 1,500,000 Jews in Britain, and that they should be interned, or deported to Madagascar. Fascist anti-Semitism was linked to the fascist response to capitalism. What was wrong with capital, according to the fascists, was its links with finance. They argued that finance was usury, and that usury was, in the Duke of Bedford's phrase, 'what the modern Jew has successfully taught the world'. If only the financiers could be liquidated in the interests of industry, then all would be well. The National Workers Movement promised that it would introduce 'national money to be put at the disposal of all worthy enterprises at the lowest economic interest rates', and the banks would be closed down. The fascist attacks on finance were predicated on absolute support for industrial capital. *London Tidings* wanted to prevent state supervision of industry: 'the government should have no thought of intervening in the national economic life except through the medium of common law'.[27] The attacks on finance may have given the impression of an attack on business, but they were expressed by a movement which would have given all power to industrial capital.

The ideal of British fascism was a society in which the many had no rights, and would be the slaves of a few. According to Philip Coupland, 'Parties would be banned, and in place of a parliament elected on a territorial basis there would be an occupational franchise . . . A person's inclusion in the BUF's organic nation required at least a minimal conformity to a standard of conduct and would be experienced as "liberty" for those who had internalised the fascist world view.' Thurlow is more sanguine, suggesting that Mosley was converted to democracy after 1945: 'The experience of internment and the defeat of nazism, led him to modify some of his ideas within a more democratic framework.'[28] In fact, there was scant real evidence of a conversion to democracy. Fascists called their dictatorship a 'Leader state', or an 'aristocracy', declaring, in Captain R. Gordon-Canning's phrase, 'To hell with democracy'. Mosley believed that biology should be used to produce a new generation of 'Leaders', and he described this principle as 'Heredity' or 'Selection'. The Duke of Bedford wanted to see the abolition of parliament, and of all political opposition. The functions of government would be hived off to corporations, whose decisions could be validated by an occasional referendum. Alexander Ratcliffe contended that 'democracy has not benefited us not one jot or tittle', while Leese insisted that his highest idea of society was 'some kind of Aristocracy', in which there was the maximum inequality, 'we always stood for recognition of the fact of inequality both of individuals and races'.[29]

Did fascism have a mass character, as I have argued? Clearly it was not simply a party of the wealthy, as indeed there have been very few parties in history that recruited only from the bourgeoisie. In local areas, the Union Movement often received its greatest support from small businessmen and the self-employed. Among those who were members of the middle class, a very large number belonged to that small group, the four per cent or so of society that can best be described as a petty bourgeoisie. Thomas Turner possessed his own ice-cream van, while Charles and Edward Booth, fascists from Birmingham, owned a family tobacco store and had 'an interest' in a cloth manufactory. Arthur Beavans ran his own shop, making furniture, general woodwork and advertising displays, and Frederick Beet had his own business repairing electrical goods. Victor Burgess, the leader of the Union of British Freedom, was a self-employed printer and publisher, as was David Barrow, also known as David Hearns, who was arrested by the police in January 1948. Leslie Burton, another Birmingham fascist, owned a small firm making metal boxes. James Smith, arrested in June 1948, was a self-employed painter, while Spencer Comley was a wholesale coal merchant. Len Wise was a company director, while Charles Foster owned his own drapery business, and Sidney Grundy was a landlord, and worked as a self-employed photographer. The examples of fascists from this class are legion. Bertram Farland owned 'a furtive little café in Coventry', while Benny Lynch ran 'Benny's Cycles' in Birmingham. William Scannell owned his own drapery business in Smethwick, and George Dunlop, the organiser of the 18B Detainees Aid Fund, worked as a self-employed glass-blower. The fascists include comfortable farmers, small-time cinema bosses, fishmongers and a wardrobe dealer. Samuel Instone was a self-employed market gardener. Alfred Norris owned five grocery shops in Wales, and Robert Saunders owned a farm in Dorset.[30]

Having found a BUF socialism, Philip Coupland then explains its success in terms of the presence of large numbers of workers or ex-Communists to be found among the fascists: 'The utopianism of [these] fascists demonstrates a more distinctively socialist and industrial aspect, reflecting the life-world of urban and working-class Blackshirts.' Judging from the period after 1945, the former Communists seem to be largely mythical. The only one that can be named is Alexander Raven Thomson, and he had joined the Communist Party for only a few weeks in Battersea, in the mid-1920s. Raven Thomson then moved to the right, being for several years a disciple of Oswald Spengler, and it was from this right-wing background that he came to the BUF.[31] Likewise, in the period after 1945, only a very small number of working-class people joined the fascist parties, and they were mostly recruited in Mosley's old hunting grounds in south Hackney and the East End. Arthur Harding followed the fascists before the war; his brother joined then but Harding himself only joined as a retired worker after 1945. He felt that fascism was something enjoyable: 'I wanted to get out of myself. There was that urge of excitement.'[32] Wyndham Rackham, arrested at a fascist meeting in February 1948, was a postal clerk, and Margaret Hutchings, arrested in March 1948, worked as a dress finisher. Mr Couch, another Oxford fascist, was a bank clerk, while Donald Temple, arrested in May 1948, was a painter. Francis Shaw, who led a physical attack on two Jewish boys in 1949, was employed as a railway maintenance worker, while Brereton Greenhous and Barry Aitken, two members of the Union Movement fined for breaking the windows of the Russian embassy in 1950, were both clerks, as was M.J. Ryan, the member of the Union Movement charged with the responsibility for building its support among organised workers.[33]

Would it be right to describe a contradiction (as I have suggested) between the reactionary ideology and the mass character of fascism?

Fascism claimed to stand for 'British workers', but attacked working-class people, their unions, and their politics. *London Tidings* accused the unions of fomenting a general strike, which would be a prelude to a 'Jewish' takeover of Britain: 'We think the "transport workers strike" was the rehearsal for the second general strike . . . The "national strike" would begin with the usual "grievances", for the delusion of the strikers and public, but would in fact be a bid to overthrow this government and substitute another; and to inflict on the land the final leg-irons of dictatorship.' In a similar vein, the Duke of Bedford argued that full employment was a danger to be avoided, while *London Tidings* gave an offensive account of ordinary workers – 'the work-shy factory hand who has little interest in life beyond "fags" and "the Pools"'. The *British League Review* attacked families squatting in empty properties, demanding that the government prosecute them – 'a government which allows its laws to be broken with impunity is opening the floodgates of anarchy'.[34]

British fascism subordinated its ordinary members' concerns into its more important campaign against the Jews. As a result, individual fascists would express their unhappiness at the way in which leading fascists refused to speak up for the interests of ordinary people. In January 1946, A.R. Hilliard, a member of the British League of Ex-Servicemen, asked why it was that the group did not campaign for ordinary servicemen, but devoted its whole energies to anti-Semitism. According to the Special Branch witness present, 'Hilliard thought they would do better if more was said about pensions for Ex-Servicemen and less about the Jews . . . [Jeffrey] Hamm replied to this by saying that if he were to drop his anti-Jewish propaganda, the communists would be more than ever entitled to say they had defeated him.'[35] After this discussion, Hilliard soon dropped out of practical activity. At other times the contradiction between the ideology and actions of fascism expressed itself in the opposite direction, as when prominent fascists were openly dismissive of the ordinary members who made up their rank and file. After a British League of Ex-Servicemen meeting in August 1947, for example, one fascist speaker told the journalist T. Pocock, 'Don't get us wrong . . . We only appeal to the "caff boys" in these street meetings. It's no good talking to them about policy.'[36]

CONCLUSION

What is needed is a new method of looking at fascism, in which the ideology is connected to practice, and in which both are taken into account and grasped together, in order to define and understand the movement as a whole. The model suggested is provisional, but I do believe that the only way to build a sufficient theory of fascism is through employing the method here. In the process of outlining a theory of fascism which connects its ideology to its practice, and treats the fascist movement as a whole, the idea that fascism was utopian has been rejected. The genuine utopians of the 1930s and 1940s were those who believed two things:

1. That society could be transformed.
2. That the result of this transformation could either be a democratic equality, or, at the very least, a greater control for the majority over their lives.

The fascists may have believed in change, but the change they believed in was radically dystopian; they wanted to achieve a more elitist, less equal and less free society. There were plenty of utopians in Britain in the 1930s and 1940s, but neither the BUF nor the Union Movement deserve to be named among them.

SIX

Is Fascism Still A Threat?

The three sections in this chapter were originally written over a three-year period from winter 1996/97 onwards, and were published as journalism, not history. They are included to give a sense of the contemporary analysis which follows from the historical arguments developed elsewhere in this book.

FRENCH FASCISM?[1]

How should political scientists and contemporary historians understand the revival of the extreme right across Europe in the 1980s and 1990s? Two recent books both study the same case, the Front National in France. The FN was the first far-right party to achieve an electoral breakthrough after 1945, and has been an inspiration to similar parties in Italy, Belgium, Austria and elsewhere. For most of the past twenty years it has been the largest, the best known, and the leading Euro-fascist party. Since 1945, if not earlier, the parties of the far right have oscillated between two styles. Either they have turned towards an electoral strategy, taking up the same grey suits as the standard conservative politicians, and hoping to present themselves as just another political party, or these parties have moved towards political violence, attacks on their opponents and open racism. Most fascists have attempted to combine these two roads. But those which have turned most decisively towards the ballot box have found their inspiration in the Front National. This is an organisation whose significance extends beyond the national borders of France.

Although the subject is in each case the same, the two books approach the FN in different ways. Peter Davies' *The National Front in France* offers a form of discourse analysis, interpreting the Front strictly in terms of its own programme and policy statements. The result is a sympathetic, 'non-polemical' analysis of the ideas of the

Table 1: The far right in Europe[2]

Far-right percentage share of vote in most recent national elections	
Austria (Freedom Party)	26.9
Italy (National Alliance, Northern Leagues)	26.0
Norway (Progress Party)	15.3
France (Front National)	14.9
Belgium (Flemish Block, National Front)	11.4
Denmark (People's Party, Progress Party)	9.8
Germany (Republicans, German People's Union)	3.0

party. By contrast, Peter Fysh and Jim Wolfreys' *The Politics of Racism in France* is a critical and historical account of the rise of Jean-Marie Le Pen. These authors are less interested in the language and policy of the FN, and focus instead on its practice as a reactionary mass movement: 'The party has taken the lead in scapegoating gays for the spread of AIDS, supported attacks on abortion clinics and assaulted opponents on seven occasions during election campaigns between 1986 and 1995, killing three of them.'[3] With this method, their book provides a more hostile account of the French far right.

The story of the Front National can briefly be told. In the 1979 Euro-elections, the Front candidates won just 0.3 per cent of the vote. As late as 1981, Le Pen was unable to gather the signatures he needed to stand for president: 'The National Front's motley band of a few hundred fascists, racists and ex-collaborators had failed even to get a presidential campaign off the ground, their leader, a verbose former paratrooper, unable to find 500 councillors or parliamentarians to sign his nomination.'[4] The end of the movement's isolation came with the European elections in 1984. Receiving favourable publicity following its successful alliance with the conservative right in the previous year's local elections at Dreux, the FN won 11 per cent of the vote, and ten of its candidates were elected as Euro MPs. The FN moved into the political mainstream. By 1985, the party had created structures throughout the French regions, with thirty or so local offices, a youth wing, work and professional groups. Party membership rose to around 30,000, and the FN was established as a significant player in French electoral politics.

Between 1984 and 1998, the party enjoyed several years of steady growth, achieving 15 per cent of the vote in successive presidential and parliamentary elections in 1995, 1997 and 1998. Indeed, by the spring of 1998, the Front's electoral success had effectively split the two mainstream Conservative Parties, the Union Pour la Démocratie Française (UDF) and the Rassemblement Pour la République (RPR), into two complicated factions, one which was prepared to work with the Front, and one which was not. Although the direction of the FN's fortunes had been a slowly ascending curve, this ascent was punctuated by two deep crises. The first came in 1990, following the desecration of a Jewish cemetery at Carpentras. Popular protests grew against the FN, which blamed the attack on a government plot. More recently, at the end of 1998, the FN's leadership was riven by a deep split. Jean-Marie Le Pen was openly challenged by his younger deputy, Bruno Mégret, who formed a rival party and took with him the bulk of the Front's party apparatus. Even members of Le Pen's family sided with Mégret.[5] As commentators have examined the Front National, at least three issues of debate have emerged. What sort of party is the FN? What conditions made it possible for the Front to achieve its first breakthrough in 1983 and 1984? Why did the movement go into crisis in 1998?

Since 1984, the Front National has been subject to exhaustive analysis. The SOFRES polling agency has conducted a series of important surveys. In 1990, for example, it attempted to build up a total picture of the ideas held by the party's rank and file. Delegates at the party's conference were asked whether or not they agreed with certain statements. Some 80 per cent of these Front activists agreed that 'the financial power is controlled by Jews', while 60 per cent wanted to see 'the repression of homosexuality'. Just 10 per cent agreed with the statement that 'the best political system is a democracy', compared to 96 per cent who agreed that 'the best political system is a hierarchy run by bosses'.[6] The interpretation of this and other surveys remains a matter of fierce debate. For example, Jean-Yves Camus and Réné Monzat have maintained that the FN is in ways like a fascist party, except that it does not share the traditional fascist emphasis on the corporate state. Guy Birenbaum argues that the Front National is a single-issue party, based around the sole theme of immigration, while Michel Soudais sees Le Pen's organisation as an extreme (but also in some confusing sense 'democratic') inegalitarian movement. Also, Richard Golsan has described what he sees as Le Pen's ideological 'connection to Europe's Nazi past'.[7] Possibly the most important argument to come from French academics is the notion that the FN articulates one form of right-wing extremism, 'national populism'. The FN is thus held to be the latest manifestation of a French authoritarian tradition going back to General Boulanger in the 1890s or Pierre Poujade in the 1950s, rather than Hitler or Mussolini.[8] One weakness of this approach is that in stressing the nebulous character of the Front's ideas, the national populism thesis can make it harder to understand which ideas matter to the FN and why.

The method in Peter Davies' *The National Front in France* corresponds broadly to the so-called 'new consensus' in what Roger Griffin has termed 'fascism studies'. For such writers as Griffin himself – and also Roger Eatwell, Zeev Sternhell and Stanley Payne – the best way to understand fascism is through constructing a careful balance sheet of its ideas. Fascism is a 'myth', 'a political ideology', or in Griffin's formulation, a 'palingenetic form of ultra-nationalism'. It is the ideas and not the practice which distinguishes fascism from other political traditions.[9] Ironically, Peter Davies seems unaware of these writers' important works, which are so close in their concerns to his own. He argues that the FN is not fascist, yet describes it in much the same way that Griffin and Eatwell describe fascism:

> The objective of this book is to comprehend and explain FN ideology and discourse – and not to understand it in any polemical fashion. Of course, the value system of the FN will be assessed in a critical manner – its inconsistencies and defects will, naturally, be highlighted – but it is essential to note that the main aim is to understand the logic and mechanics of the party's nationalism. And we should not labour under the illusion that the FN is devoid of a coherent thought system. Both Renouvin and Samson, for example, have identified a clear 'logic' within FN ideology, and it will serve us well to remember this as the book unfolds. We should not fall into the trap of dismissing the FN as 'fascists' and worse, as 'fascists with no ideas'. This is not just an insult but a gross misconception.[10]

For this reader, the force of Davies' argument is undermined by inopportune juxtapositions. Davies suggests that a critical approach must be 'polemical'; that it is impossible to write critically about the far right without offering 'insults', and indeed that the FN is not fascist, because it has 'nationalist' ideas. To take simply his last point, if nationalism is not one constituent part of fascist ideology, then what is?

Peter Davies' own language is awkward and often euphemistic. The Front is described as 'sensitive to foreign elements'. The party's slogan 'Towards the Sixth Republic' becomes a 'forward-looking campaign epithet'. Le Pen leads an 'intriguing, fascinating and controversial movement'.[11] The tone of these and many similar phrases in Davies' book is clearly one of interest and sympathy. Yet is sympathy the appropriate response that should be shown towards what is undoubtedly a violent and undemocratic movement? This weakness becomes clear when the author addresses the FN's anti-immigrant racism:

> In essence FN philosophy demands a revolution in France's thinking on nationality legislation. FN leaders are strong in their condemnation of 'superficial' measures of detail that go no way at all to solving France's problems of naturalisation and immigration . . . Immigration is viewed as a negative, threatening political phenomenon because it bestows on France people and ways of life that are not compatible with those of the French nation.[12]

These and many similar passages would be stronger if *The National Front in France* contained sharper criticism of FN ideas. Davies is too ready to accept that immigration is really a 'problem', and not critical enough when faced with the Front's language of the nation. Far too much of this book is given over to a repetition of long passages from FN manifestos, when such quotes should be submitted to a more sustained criticism.

Peter Davies makes no attempt to offer any succinct definition of what the FN is or what it stands for. More space is given over to a criticism of 'fascism' theories than to an elaboration of any rival term. The author's theory is in this way mostly negative. Having said that, Davies does emphasise the importance within the myth of the nation of the phrase 'identity', which is also the title of the Front's theoretical journal. This is potentially an important insight. Historians have tended to assume that there is something positive about identity *per se*. Yet as Davies makes clear even nationalist and racist forces have been able to formulate their own particular identities. Such an insight can be taken further. Merely because one party has claimed to represent the historic tradition of 'France' or 'liberty' or 'democracy', that does not mean that others should see them as being in any distinctive sense democratic or liberal or whatever. Yet such a critical perspective is only developed in the second book under review.

For Peter Fysh and Jim Wolfreys, the history of the Front is a part of the history of French racism, which is discussed in detail in their book. They also argue that the FN has much more in common with classical fascist parties. The FN is a cadre party, with a strong ideology: 'The Front's discourse deliberately creates a tension between the organisation and its periphery, between "hard" and "soft" support, seeking to address sympathisers where they are and take them where the Front wants to go, converting them to the Front's world view and enlarging its core.' This ideology is described as fascist. Examples are given of Le Pen's revolutionary conservative ideas, including one speech from 1996: 'When situations are blocked, it's generally the drive of human nature which forces a breakthrough into new times . . . There is a time when all that will end and that will be the revolution. The extreme left is preparing for it . . . So I believe that you too should prepare yourselves, because at a certain point the worm-eaten structures of our system are going to collapse.'[13]

Peter Davies' *The National Front in France* is a theoretical and not a historical analysis, as its author makes clear: 'The emergence, history, organisation and electorate of the FN . . . have no real place in a study of ideology and discourse, and thus, they are referred to only in passing.'[14] Consequently, it is Fysh and Wolfreys' historical account in *The Politics of Racism in France* which provides the best starting point for an explanation of why it was that the FN achieved its take-off in 1983–4. They identify three factors which were decisive at this time: the failure of the reform programme of Mitterrand's government; vacillations on the part of the mainstream right, and the successful tactics of the FN, for whom success followed success, as the first breakthrough was solidified. One thing which comes out very clearly in their history of the rise of the Front National, is that politicians of both left and right failed each time that they attempted to outbid the Front's anti-immigrant rhetoric.

A succession of politicians, including such different figures as the Gaullist Charles Pasqua and the Socialist Edith Cresson, attempted to steal the FN's clothes. Each time, to paraphrase Le Pen, the voters preferred the original to the copy.

Although Fysh and Wolfreys' book was published before internal warfare broke out within the Front at the end of 1999, the authors argue strongly that it was popular anti-fascist mobilisation which has acted as a catalyst, intensifying the tensions within the FN. Since the mass public sector strikes of 1995, radical anti-fascist organisations have grown up, notably le Manifeste (the Manifesto) and Ras le Front (Smash the Front). In May 1997, these groups called a march of 70,000 people which threatened to shut down the FN's annual conference in Strasbourg, while on 28 March 1998, around 200,000 people paraded against fascism, on different demonstrations across France. The result of these marches has been to place the FN on the defensive, and the party lost its sole parliamentary seat in Toulon by 700 votes in a rerun election in September 1997. It was the mass hostility of the protests, Fysh and Wolfreys argue, which explains the splits within the FN: 'Mobilisation against the Front provokes internal ructions, as the example of the Strasbourg congress clearly illustrates, when tensions between Le Pen and Mégret over the party's elections strategy emerged in public for the first time. These words are being written at a time of renewed hope about the prospects of blocking a fascist revival.'[15]

Fysh and Wolfreys' book is an excellent account of the history and the movement of the Front National. By examining the long history of French racism, Fysh and Wolfreys can show how the conditions were in place for Le Pen to build his movement. The ideas of Le Pen are placed in a context, their success explained. Stressing that the Front is a fascist party, the authors categorise and make sense of Le Pen's movement. Their account is both fiercely objective, and yet critical at the same time. It is not only the FN which is subjected to scrutiny, but also its opponents. Peter Fysh and Jim Wolfreys emphasise the contrast between the parliamentary anti-fascism of *SOS Racisme* in the 1980s, which was incapable of relating to the black urban poor, and the radical anti-fascism of Ras le Front and le Manifeste in the 1990s, which has offered a greater threat to Le Pen. Different perspectives for the future are discussed, and the final note is one of cautious optimism.

REFLECTIONS ON THE 1999 ELECTIONS IN AUSTRIA[16]

On 3 October 1999, the results were announced of Austria's general election. Many Austrians were shocked to discover that Jörg Haider's Freedom Party (FPÖ) had won over 1 million votes, or 27.6 per cent of the electorate, placing it within touching distance of power. *Format* magazine spoke in despair against the complacency of the country's political elites. Outside Austria, liberal newspapers responded with confusion and shock. 'Austria thrown into turmoil', said the *Guardian*. 'Austrian political landscape turned upside down', claimed *Le Monde*.[17] Taking its cue from the Austrian Socialist Party (SPÖ), the *Financial Times* asked whether the inexorable rise of Haider's Freedom Party would take Austria outside the mainstream of European politics. Yet the most significant consequences will be felt in Austria. The country's chancellor has been forced to resign, and many socialists and anti-racists wait anxiously to see if Haider's party can be stopped.

More than any other far-right party in Europe, the Freedom Party traces its lineage directly to the fascist organisations of the interwar years. Its telegenic leader, Jörg Haider, is the son of Nazi parents. His father joined the Hitler Youth as early as 1929, and helped to found the postwar fascist organisation. Prior to Haider taking over the leadership of the FPÖ in 1986, it was a curious amalgam – a nationalist party with one free market and another national-socialist wing. Since then, Haider has brought the organisation into the electoral mainstream. Yet in a pattern familiar across Europe, Haider has taken one step forward, one step back. Publicly distancing himself from the party's past one week, he has gone out of his way to claim the fascist mantle the next. New Labour in Britain has less continuity with social democracy, less loyalty to that tradition, than Haider has with fascism.

In 1985, Jörg Haider described Walter Reder, a convicted mass-murderer and war criminal, as 'a prisoner of war'. In 1990, he praised the role of the SS in wartime as 'a struggle for freedom and democracy in Europe'. Five years later, he spoke to an assembly organised by SS veterans, describing them as 'decent people . . . people of character who have the courage of their convictions'. As recently as 1998, Haider compared the treatment of the Sudeten Germans expelled from Czechoslovakia to the Nazi Holocaust against the Jews: 'I do not want to judge what was more terrible . . . one cannot treat equal happenings differently.' Such statements are routine among Haider's entourage. They exist to convert FPÖ identifiers into hard and determined racists.

Inside Austria, Haider is often presented as a demagogue and an opportunist, but rarely as a fascist. He is a one-issue anti-immigration campaigner, not a Nazi. This absence of categorisation neglects the similarities between the FPÖ and the interwar fascist parties in Italy and Germany and elsewhere. First of all, there is an ideological continuity. Members of Haider's immediate entourage, such as Andreas Mölzer, Haider's adviser for cultural affairs, engage in open anti-Semitism. Mölzer's *Zur Zeit* has revived claims that Jews are responsible for the ritual murder of gentile children. It describes Nuremberg as 'the biggest show trial in history'. Pan-German nationalism and Holocaust revisionism are a significant part of the FPÖ's appeal. Second, there is also a strategic continuity between the Freedom Party and historic fascism. Both are radical movements, emerging outside, and in hostility to, the liberal state. Unlike the 1930s, this is not an era for large private armies, but the same extra-parliamentary strategy is there.

It is distressing to learn that more Austrian workers now vote for the FPÖ than the socialist SPÖ. It seems that Haider's party combines (like the French Front National) a petit-bourgeois cadre with a proletarian vote. Yet perhaps one area in which the Freedom Party is different from Hitler's NSDAP or Mussolini's PNF, is that the Austrian party's rhetoric combines chauvinism with free-market economics. Haider's election pledges included privatisation, tax breaks for businesses and a flat rate income tax of 23 per cent. Meanwhile, the party's leading candidate in the 1999 elections was a prominent industrialist, Thomas Prinzhorn. Anti-labour, pro-business, the FPÖ's strongest votes have tended to come from regions dependent on tourism and services. If Haider's vote has now spread, then it would follow that the potential threat of his movement has grown.

Asked in opinion polls, 65 per cent of its supporters claimed to chosen the FPÖ as a protest vote. This has led some commentators to play down the significance of the result. In the face of this vote, indifference would be a mistake. The party's first breakthrough was achieved in 1986, on the back of protest votes. The voters may have changed, but the size and racism of the party's core vote has increased dramatically. Some 22 per cent of Austrians believe that 'no Jews should live in Austria', 37 per cent that 'Jews are too influential'. Haider's fascist politics are now better known and understood across Austria. In 1991, Haider eulogised 'the correct labour policy of the Third Reich'. After this speech, the centre-right Austrian People's Party dropped its local alliance for Haider, and he was forced out of his position as Governor of Carinthia. In April 1999, however, Haider was able to return to the governorship, this time secure with a majority of the local vote. For most Austrian voters, familiarity with the FPÖ has bred acceptance, respectability, and not contempt.

Why has the far right achieved this breakthrough in Austria? According to Karl Pfeifer of *Searchlight*, one long-term factor has been the relative ease with which Austria survived the traumas of 1945.[18] Although a majority of Austrians supported the *Anschluss* with Germany in 1938, 600,000 joined the Nazi Party, and huge numbers served in the Wehrmacht, still postwar Austrian politicians described their country as a victim of Hitler's march east. While ordinary Germans have been compelled to come to terms with their country's role in the Holocaust, ordinary Austrians have been separated from this guilt. Mass-circulation dailies like *Neue Kronenzeitung* have opened their pages to Holocaust revisionists. Fascism has a dangerous and horrible place in the mind of the German public, while in Austria the feeling is more equivocal.

More recently, Austria has been ruled for thirteen years by a government consisting of the centre-left SPÖ and the centre-right People's Party. Elsewhere in Europe, the 1980s were years of conservative dominance. Following the economic downturn of the 1990s, voters turned to the left. In Italy, Britain, France and Germany we now see social democratic governments. Yet in Austria, the SPÖ is part of the problem, which needs to be changed. Threatened by the rise of Haider, the social democrats have implemented tougher anti-immigration laws, sending out a clear signal that Haider is right, and foreigners are to blame. In the absence of the socialists, opposition has come from smaller groups, the Greens (well represented in the Austrian parliament), the Communists, the Young Socialists and the socialist party *Linkswende* (whose members have been sued repeatedly by the Freedom Party). This opposition deserves wider encouragement and support.

Finally, what does Haider's vote say about the prospects for the far right? Before the 1980s, such parties were an irrelevance in European politics. Yet following the French FN's success in the 1984 European elections, a window of opportunity was opened. In the early 1990s, far-right parties grew in France, Germany, Italy and eastern Europe. By the mid-1990s, this process seemed to have reversed. In every country, the far right was on the retreat. In the key case of France, Le Pen was marginalised by the success of the 1995 public sector strikes. In a moment of popular anti-racism, the Front National found its meetings disrupted and its growth checked. The organisation split in winter 1999 and has since been in decline. It is too early to say whether Haider's success will give the European far right a boost comparable to Le Pen's victory in 1984. That will depend on events in Austria and elsewhere. One success for fascism does not yet make this a tragedy for the rest of us. Yet one lesson should be learned. Opposition to the far right remains an issue of current politics, and not simply a question of past history.

THE PROJECT OF AMERICAN FASCISM

The growth of postwar fascist movements does throw up several important challenges to historians. One such is the question of continuity – how much do present-day movements of the far right owe to their predecessors; indeed how appropriate is it to describe them as fascist? When it comes to the French and Austrian cases, there have been plenty of writers who have attempted to formulate less controversial tags more amenable to all sides concerned, including 'neo-fascism', 'national populism', and so on. The controversy is still greater in the United States, where far-right politics has an indigenous and pre-fascist tradition to draw on, namely the Ku Klux Klan, a Southern anti-black militia which pre-dated the rise of Mussolini's fascist party. Today, the wellspring of American extremism is the militia movement, a self-described 'patriotic' and 'libertarian' tradition, which in its appeal to the US constitution's right to freedom of speech, appears to stand some way apart from authoritarian European fascism. One way to get a sense of the contemporary American right is by studying its literature – not the press releases, nor the election statements aimed at first-time voters, but the material which is used to confirm the politics of activists who are already within the movement. The most important such text is *The Turner Diaries*, a fictional diary written in 1978 by William Pierce, one of the leaders of America's National Alliance. Written in the form of a novel, it is in fact a textbook of organisation, aimed at activists who are already in some way attached to his movement.

Pierce claims that his book has sold around 200,000 copies in America in Europe. Although the real figure is almost certainly much lower, influence is not always a matter of numbers.[19] The notion of 'leaderless resistance' associated with *The Turner Diaries* has become part of the common-sense value-system of the US Nazi scene. In 1983, the book inspired the formation of a real underground organisation called The Order (named after one of the secret factions in Pierce's book), whose members attempted to poison the water supplies of three US cities. Their leader, Robert Matthews, died in a shoot-out with the FBI. In 1995, three soldiers who murdered a black couple in North Carolina were found to have possessed *The Turner Diaries*. The book has also been identified as one of the influences on Timothy McVeigh and Terry Nicholls, the Oklahoma bombers. Through *The Turner Diaries*, William Pierce has become one of the best-known personalities of American fascism. Pierce owns his own radio station, a racist book club with over 400 titles, and a white power music station, Resistance Records. He is also now the leader of his own fascist party, the National Alliance.[20]

Through *The Turner Diaries*, the ideas of leaderless resistance have become a key influence on those parts of contemporary European fascism which stand at the violent edge of neo-Nazi politics. If Le Pen and Haider were the leading figures associated with the strategy of Euro-fascist parliamentarism in the 1980s and 1990s, then William Pierce is today the prophet of fascist terrorism. The British group Combat 18 named one of its magazines *The Order*, while David Myatt based his National Socialist Movement around the same influences. It was this organisation which drew the attention of David Copeland, the man who bombed Brixton, Brick Lane and Soho in summer 1999.[21]

The first thing you notice about *The Turner Diaries* is how badly written the book is. Although the author claims to have been employed once as a university professor, most of the book stumbles by in language that would make an articulate thirteen-year-old blush: 'Wow! Are things tense in here!', 'It is not safe to talk here.

The walls are quite thin, and the neighbours might wonder at a late-night conference.' It would be wrong to sneer. Even badly written books can have an influence. The same criticism was made of Hitler's *Mein Kampf*, a book which Hitler's friends had to re-draft a dozen times. Perhaps the author of *The Turner Diaries* did not have enough friends to repeat the trick.

The second thing you notice about the book is the author's evident hatred of all humanity. Scene after scene of killings take place, each one more destructive than the last. Yet the monotonous race ideology of the narrator allows no shock, no horror at the unfolding deaths – 'I have become much more realistic about life recently'. Throughout the book, violence and pain are described in welcome, loving detail. This is the description of a murder committed by the 'patriots': 'Above the placard leered the horribly bloated, purplish face of a young woman, her eyes wide open and bulging, her mouth agape. Finally I could make out the thin, vertical line of rope disappearing into the branches above. Apparently the rope had slipped a bit or the branch to which it was tied had sagged, until the women's feet were resting on the pavement, giving the uncanny appearance of a corpse standing upright of its own volition.' Although the love of causing pain is evident, by contrast, any sexual action is taboo. The one sexual experience which the narrator describes in twenty-six months is his own violation with a metal pole during an act of state torture.

In one of the best-known passages of *Mein Kampf*, Hitler expressed his desire to kill Jews – 'the sacrifice of millions at the front' would not have been necessary if 'twelve or fifteen thousand of these Hebrew corrupters of the people had been held under poison gas'.[22] Such passages are rightly remembered for their murderous intent. But Hitler's book does not possess one-tenth of the murderous imagination of his disciples today. In *The Turner Diaries*, the apple-pie patriots kill dozens, then hundreds, then thousands, then millions: 'An hour earlier, in New York, the Organization used a bazooka to shoot down an airliner which had just taken off with a load of vacationing dignitaries, mostly Jews.' Near the end of the book, two nuclear attacks take place – on America – each the act of angry 'libertarians'. When the marauding 'Organization' enters Detroit, practically the entire white population is butchered (as well as blacks and Jews). No explanation for these killings is required, and none given.

Pierce's book is not simply a hymn to violence, but there are signs within it of a more worked-out ideology. The complaints of its narrator are those of the small man threatened by bureaucracy (a new passport system), angry about extortionate prices ($5 for a gallon of gasoline), under attack from the big corporations above and big labour below. The measure which encourages resistance is the impounding of privately held firearms. The 'Revolution' manifests itself in a slaughter of the races, blacks and Jews. Old lies find a new form – one character 'learned the truth about the System's "equality" hoax. She gained an understanding of the unique role of the Jews as the ferment of decomposition of races and civilisations.' The harshest words are reserved for the narrator's former allies within the far-right camp – patriots who hand in their guns. The American people themselves receive no more praise. 'If the freedom of the American people were the only thing at stake, the existence of the Organization would hardly be justified. Americans have lost their right to be free. Slavery is the just and proper state for a people who have grown as soft, self-indulgent, careless, credulous, and befuddled as we are.'

At the end of the novel, the final fascist vision is established. All enemies, racial or ideological, are murdered. A condition of extraordinary dictatorship is established for the survivors, and 16 million square miles of the earth are 'sterilized', killing all Africans, Asians and east Europeans who live there. No ideal future is developed; the goal is defined simply by the absence of 'enemies', who have all been killed.

What should a rational audience make of *The Turner Diaries*? It would be tempting to ignore this murderous rant, but mistaken. As I have already mentioned, the book is a best-seller. The anti-fascist magazine *Searchlight* describes its author as 'the world's most dangerous Nazi', and notes his more-than-friendly links with Britain's own fascist party, the British National Party.[23] If figures like McVeigh and Copeland could find in this book an answer to their deep sense of alienation from society, this fact suggests that there must be something deeply wrong with the societies that spawned them. Perhaps most depressing is the thought that *Mein Kampf* has been rewritten in a way which translates the paranoid vision of Hitler in the 1920s into a language acceptable to the twenty-first-century generation of fascists. Truly this demands vigilance.

SEVEN

The Meaning of the Holocaust, Fifty Years On

The study of German fascism seems to go in cycles, like fashion. In the mid-1980s, the most important argument was taking place in Germany. There, the 'historians' controversy' (*Historikerstreit*) raised the issue of 'normalisation'. Writers such as Ernst Nolte suggested that it was time for Germany to shed the burden of guilt for the Holocaust. Instead patriotic Germans should console themselves with the thought that totalitarianism began in Russia. It followed that a foreigner – Stalin or Lenin – should be blamed for the Holocaust, and not Adolf Hitler.[1] In the late 1990s, the dispute of the moment surrounded Daniel Goldhagen's book, *Hitler's Willing Executioners*. Goldhagen's argument stood in direct opposition to Nolte's. Rather than minimising German guilt, Daniel Goldhagen insisted that all Germans were accountable for the killings, even ordinary, civilian Germans. Each one of the people responsible for the Holocaust was German – therefore every single German was to blame.[2] Most recently historical attention seems to have moved on from Goldhagen to one of his most trenchant critics. Norman Finkelstein, author of a detailed attack on *Hitler's Willing Executioners*,[3] has now returned to print, to argue that the very discussion of the Holocaust has gone wrong. In his words, '"the Holocaust" is an ideological representation of the Nazi holocaust . . . through its deployment, one of the world's most formidable military powers, with a horrendous human rights record, has cast itself as a "victim" state, and the most successful ethnic group in the US has likewise acquired victim status'.[4]

Not surprisingly, Norman Finkelstein's book has stirred the most extraordinary controversy. Extracts from *The Holocaust Industry* were initially published in the *Guardian*, to hostile comment. Greville Janner, chair of the Holocaust Educational Trust, described the work as 'nauseous'. Colin Schindler and Shalom Lappin attacked Finkelstein's 'imbalanced and often bigoted views'.[5]

Elan Steinberg, executive director of the World Jewish Congress, claimed to find Finkelstein 'revolting', saying, 'I simply don't accept him as a researcher.'[6] Writing in the anti-fascist magazine *Searchlight*, Kate Taylor argued that Finkelstein was 'reductive and bitter in tone. He dismisses much survivor testimony as worthless and falsely declares that Jewish groups in the US are motivated by greed.' Taylor points to the positive response to the book from the far-right British National Party's journal *Spearhead*: 'The BNP has jumped on Finkelstein's ideas with glee and relish.'[7] *The Holocaust Industry* was written by an anti-Zionist Jew to protest at the commercialisation of the Holocaust. If socialists and Jews are critical of Finkelstein, and neo-Nazis are welcoming, then surely the author has got something wrong.

The Holocaust Industry is a short text, only 150 pages long, and without an index. You would hardly guess that such a slender book could draw so much ill-feeling. One of the reasons for the enormous criticism of it is the sheer range of Finkelstein's targets, which include the governments of America and Israel, Holocaust spokesman Elie Wiesel, official Jewish bodies including the World Jewish Congress, and Holocaust hoaxers including Jerzy Kosinski and Binjamin Wilkomirski. Another impersonal target is the widespread conviction that the Holocaust was somehow a unique or irrational event. There are a lot of enemies in this book and few friends, although one ally – US radical Noam Chomsky – is thanked for his help in preparing the manuscript. Indeed one way to read *The Holocaust Industry* is as a long elaboration of the Chomskyan precept that the enemy is always at home.

Another explanation for the unusual anger raised against this book is the tone of Finkelstein's polemic. At times, he suggests that the only problem out there is the Holocaust industry – as if domestic racism, anti-Semitism and Holocaust denial were matters of no concern. Take for example, Norman Finkelstein's comment on Deborah Lipstadt's *Denying the Holocaust*; 'To document widespread Holocaust denial, Lipstadt cites a handful of crank publications.'[8] The author forgets that such 'crank' parties have 10 per cent of the vote in France and Italy, and are partners in government in Austria.[9] Another questionable passage is the defence of David Irving, 'Irving: notorious as an admirer of Hitler and sympathizer with German national socialism, has nevertheless, as

Gordon Craig points out, made an "indispensable" contribution to our knowledge of World War Two.' As evidence, Finkelstein cites not Irving himself, but Craig's review of Irving's book *Hitler's War*, which appeared in the *New York Review of Books*.[10] I suspect that had the author read any of Irving's interminably dull racist prose, then his opinion would have been less friendly.

Any sustained polemic is likely to miss at least some of its targets, but with this book, Finkelstein's 'miss rate' has risen alarmingly. One of the least convincing sections is his attack on the recent processes since 1945 which have encouraged many people to declare themselves to have been Holocaust survivors:

> Another strong motive behind this misinterpretation, however, was material. The postwar German government provided compensation to Jews who had been in ghettos and camps. Many Jews fabricated their pasts to meet this eligibility requirement. 'If everyone who claims to be a survivor actually is one,' my mother used to explain, 'who did Hitler kill?'[11]

That last sentence is wretched. By invoking the fate of his parents, Norman Finkelstein is playing the same game which he rightly detests in his opponents – you cannot question me, because I *represent* the dead millions. Such lapses of judgement do the author no credit.

All the same, it would be foolish to pretend that all of Finkelstein's arrows miss the mark. His criticisms of the Holocaust museum in Washington, which ignores the killings of the gypsies to concentrate only on Hitler's Jewish victims, seem just.[12] Again, *The Holocaust Industry* is rightly critical of the Simon Wiesenthal Centre, which awarded its 1988 prize as Humanitarian of the Year to Ronald Reagan, just thirty months after Reagan claimed that the members of the Waffen SS were 'victims of the Nazis', at least as much as the Jews.[13] Finkelstein also points out the size of the figures which have been paid in compensation to victims of the Nazi slave-labour camps. This process of recovery would be praiseworthy – if the money was likely to reach the victims. But the sums are so large and survivors so few, that the compensation must be diverted. Instead, the lawyers running these cases charge $600 per hour for their support. Finkelstein cites one advocate who was paid $2,400 just to read Tom Bower's book, *Nazi Gold*![14] The largest share of the missing billions will be spent on 'Holocaust education'. Finkelstein lists the results. There are seven major Holocaust museums in the United States. Fifty American states sponsor annual days of remembrance. Over a hundred recognised Holocaust institutions exist in the USA, alone.[15] Something strange must have happened for the murder of the Jews of Europe to become the major moment of commemoration in *American* history.

This last point deserves comment. The most important section of *The Holocaust Industry* is the first third, in which Norman Finkelstein sets out to explain why the Holocaust has become such a dominant theme in contemporary history. Inevitably this is a question which matters. We expect that as an event recedes into history, so its contemporary relevance will decline. No one speaks now with sadness of the terrible killings which took place in Armenia in 1913. We assume that memory should work like two friends parting – the further off an event stands, the smaller it should appear. Yet the Holocaust steadfastly refuses to go away. Indeed, its memory has grown considerably in the last thirty years. Just in Britain, recent years have seen innumerable events whose social meaning was influenced by our memory of the Holocaust. They include the bombing of Serbia, which was justified by the claim that Slobodan Milošević was the 'new Hitler'; the libel case begun by Holocaust-denier David Irving against Deborah Lisptadt; and also the wave of bombings by far-right activist David Copeland. Over the same period of time, the British government has announced that there is to be a national day of Holocaust memorial, and the Holocaust has been placed as a subject of study on the national curriculum. If anyone can explain why the Holocaust has grown in significance over the decades since it ended, so that it can exert such an terrible fascination for people fifty years on – then they will have understood something of significance indeed.

FROM FINKELSTEIN TO NOVICK

Norman Finkelstein's explanation of the growing memory of the Holocaust is based on a reading of Peter Novick's book, *The Holocaust and Collective Memory*. In his book, Novick shows that the way we view the Holocaust is constructed. For one thing, this memory is very recent. Through the 1950s and early 1960s, the subject was taboo:

> The two historical accounts of the Holocaust available in the United States during this time were both imports from abroad, and neither attracted much attention. Gerald Reitlinger's *The Final Solution* was distributed in this country by an obscure publisher, and as far as I can tell was never reviewed in the general-circulation press. The same was true of Léon Poliakov's *Bréviaire de la haine*, it was translated into English, as *Harvest of Hate*, thanks to a subsidy by a Jewish businessman, but sold only a few hundred copies. Neither Reitlinger's nor Poliakov's book was noted by the major historical journals. Treatment of the Holocaust in high school and college history textbooks was extremely skimpy – indeed often nonexistent. Mention of the Holocaust in other than Jewish newspapers and magazines was rare and usually perfunctory.[16]

Peter Novick claims that it was only after the 1967 Arab–Israeli War that the Holocaust became a major reference point in American-Jewish life. Novick cites the case of Lucy Dawidowicz, an anti-Zionist before 1967, who now declared that Israel was 'the corporate paradigm for the ideal image of the Jew in the modern world.'[17] There were many such transformations. Novick also argues that the memory of the Holocaust has been dominated by the experience of American Jews. A relatively affluent group in the most powerful country in the world, these people are a long way from the poor Jews of 1930s Europe. Communist and non-Jewish groups have been written out of the history of the Holocaust. Instead, Jewish-American bodies have given their support as the US government has used the memory of the Holocaust to justify its own initiatives abroad. Less certain and polemical than Finkelstein's book, it is nevertheless easy enough to see how the themes of *The Holocaust and Collective Memory* encouraged Finkelstein to write.[18]

In *The Holocaust Industry*, Norman Finkelstein objects to what he portrays as the incomplete nature of Peter Novick's analysis: 'Root assumptions go unchallenged. Neither banal nor heretical, the book is pitched in the controversial extreme of the mainstream spectrum.'[19] One of Novick's claims is that the (historical) discovery of the Holocaust came about as a result of the 1967 Six Day War. Fearful of a second Holocaust, American Jews woke up to the plight of their brethren in the Middle East. Finkelstein makes short work of this claim. As he argues, the danger to Israel in 1948 was much greater than the threat in 1967. American Jews could not have feared Israel's annihilation in 1967, because such an outcome was simply impossible. Again, Finkelstein points out that few American Jews publicly defended Israel during the 1967 war – loyalty followed the crisis, and its successful outcome. In contrast to Novick, Norman Finkelstein's explanation for the increased American support for Israel is that the overwhelming Israeli victory enabled the US government to reorientate its entire strategy in the Middle East, towards a new situation where Israel would become the regional power, loyal to America, and armed to the teeth. One of Finkelstein's most controversial claims is that Israeli military success transformed Zionism from an ideology of separation into an ideology of assimilation:

> Zionism had sprung from the premise that assimilation was a pipe dream, that Jews would always be perceived as potentially disloyal aliens . . . Israel's founding exacerbated the problem, at any rate for diaspora Jewry: it gave the charge of dual loyalty institutional expression. Paradoxically, after June 1967 Israel facilitated assimilation in the United States . . . Whereas before 1967 Israel conjured up the bogy of dual loyalty, it now connoted super-loyalty . . . unlike the American GIs in Vietnam, Israeli fighters were not being humiliated by Third World fighters.[20]

Finkelstein's criticisms of what he calls the Holocaust industry are motivated by his commitment to the political tradition of Jewish anti-Zionism.[21] Some readers will complain that in his righteous anger at the use of Zionist ideas to deny freedom to other peoples, Finkelstein paints all the colours of his picture too clear. Perhaps, but Finkelstein's criticisms of American responses to the 1967 war seem just.

Where Norman Finkelstein's book goes wrong is in the one-sidedness of its author's critique. In saying this, I do not mean for an instant that Finkelstein is wrong to criticise the behaviour of the Israeli state or its supporters in America or anywhere else. Instead, my objection to *The Holocaust Industry* is that its author explains the historical fascination of the Holocaust simply in terms of the behaviour of American Jews. These are, of course, an important people, who have helped to shape the historical memory of the killings. As an American Jew himself, Finkelstein has every right to criticise their prejudices. But I suspect that the really interesting question is to ask why have so many non-Jews, in America or Britain or elsewhere, been fascinated with the Holocaust? In *The Holocaust Industry*, all explanations start with the American Israel lobby, the 'Holocaust industry', and American Jews. We should not have to remind the author that neither American Jews nor indeed the 'Holocaust industry' controls the press, the cinema, the magazines, the arts and the theatre. Indeed, I suspect that no ethnic minority composing less than 5 per cent of the population is ever capable of winning a majority to their concerns, unless the minority is able to persuade the majority that their hopes and fears are somehow the same. Ideas which are imposed on people lose their ability to persuade – memory only becomes 'fascinating' because it touches the hearts of many. The rest of this article is therefore an attempt to explore what I see as the missing core of Norman Finkelstein's argument. It is concerned above all with the non-Jewish memory of the Holocaust.

MEMORY AND IDENTITY

According to Peter Novick, Holocaust memory is 'more often than not' arbitrary. The choice is made not from 'calculation of advantages and disadvantages' but 'without much thought for . . . consequences'.[22] Finkelstein criticises this passage, suggesting that the nature of collective memory is determined by the consequences of the playing out of vested interests. This is true – or at least partly true. As I argue elsewhere in this book, collective memory is a process which is largely shaped by the nature of the events themselves. The process by which memory becomes collective memory is a process of comparison, and revision. For an account of the past to be persuasive, it must endure the criticisms implied in subsequent versions. False histories are compared to the record of previous events, and corrected or lost.[23] The direction of this process is towards a more truthful history, closer to what we know about previous generations, closer to what actually happened in the past. It is not true that historical texts are open to any possible reading. People can write whatever they like about Macbeth, but the play is not about slavery. Anyone can say what they choose about the events of the Holocaust, but they cannot change the date or location of the killings, the identities of the perpetrators or the victims. The exact numbers of the dead can never be known (in real life, the figuring out of genocides is always approximate), and the most accurate scholarly estimates will vary. But the number known to have been killed will never be less than 5 million, and never more than 7.

Which elements of the Holocaust story are the ones that draw the greatest interest? One pillar of the collective memory is clearly the *Diary of Anne Frank*. In the 1950s and 1960s, the book sold over 5 million copies in America alone. The *Diary* has been among the most successful books ever published; adapted by Broadway and Hollywood, the book kept alive a memory of the Holocaust, which would only be rediscovered fully from the late 1960s on.[24] Despite the great success of the book, a number of writers have recently criticised the use of the *Diary*, particularly in the United States. Their objection is that when the diary is represented in film or in the theatre, and indeed when it is taught in schools, attention moves away from the episodes where the impact of the Holocaust is most bitter and most clear. Anne Frank's nightmares, the Hannukah celebration, and the Gestapo hammering on the Franks' door – all these scenes are routinely excised. The result is an optimistic narrative of human triumph over adversity. The survival of the *Diary* becomes Anne Frank's victory over fascism. As in a good Hollywood film, the moral integrity of the heroine is sufficient to keep evil at bay. This new and optimistic story of Anne Frank bears little relation to the actual, terrible events of the Holocaust. Such has been the attack on the teaching of the Holocaust by means of the *Diary*, that the respected Jewish–American author, Cynthia Ozick, has wondered out loud whether it would not have been better if Anne Frank's diary had never been found.[25]

As with the argument in Finkelstein's book, it seems to me that these claims are wide of the mark. It is said that the play did not do justice to its heroine's Zionist sympathies, but the *Diary* describes Anne's sister's desire to become a midwife in Palestine as an example of that 'narrow cramped existence' on which the author was 'not at all keen'. It is said that the play ignored Anne Frank's Hannukah celebrations, but the *Diary* referred to Hannukah just once, adding that 'St. Nicholas Day was much more fun'.[26] These criticisms are wholly anachronistic – wrapping themselves up in the onslaught against the naive, feel-good universalism of the 1950s, the critics require that Anne Frank should have been more like a late 1990s US Jew, and less like the European woman she actually was.

Of course, we should be glad that Anne Frank's diary survived. The dangers of too much study of the Holocaust are less than the dangers of too little. But the important truth implied in critical readings of the *Diary* is that the memory of the Holocaust has been changed by the extraordinary reception of one text. The Holocaust itself has become a story of entrapment, and suffocation, rather than collective death. The story takes its appeal from the victims' location. They are caught even in their own homes, in their private lives, which we like to imagine as sacred.[27] The Holocaust has in this way become a story of private suffering, rather than mass murder. It is also a story which is now and will be inseparable from the life of this one young adult.[28] So why has Anne Frank taken on this iconic role? Part of the answer might simply be linked to her age. The figure of the adolescent young woman is clearly an enormously powerful symbol in both literature and history – hence the importance of Joan of Arc in France, Nongqawuse for the Xhosa in South Africa, Antigone in Ancient Greece.[29] People identify with Anne, through her suffering. The use of the book for teaching succeeds when it generates identification, the recognition of Anne Frank's hopes and fears. The usual problem of asking people to empathise with someone very different from them falls, because Anne Frank is so similar to so many young girls.

Before the late 1960s, Anne Frank's *Diary* was perhaps the only account of the Holocaust which had intruded into people's collective memory. Yet since the 1960s there have been a series of incidents which have brought the memory of the Holocaust into the minds of millions. Over the same period a number of books, films and plays have created a similar effect. Among the events that have worked to raise public consciousness, Novick's account mentions William Shirer's *The Rise and Fall of the Third Reich*; the capture and trial of Adolf Eichmann; Hannah Arendt's *Eichmann in Jerusalem*; the first controversies surrounding wartime Pope Pius XII; Israel's 1967 and

1973 wars; the American TV series *Holocaust*, and the Palestinian *intifada*. If we are to include literature among the milestones in the popular memory of the Holocaust, I would add Primo Levi's extraordinary books – for the emotional depth of the testimony contained in them, and for their wide audience, especially in continental Europe.[30] Since the 1960s artists, novelists, poets and historians have satisfied themselves that the memory of the Holocaust was inadequate when faced with the enormity of the human loss. It is only at the end of Novick's list that we approach the present-day situation, where Holocaust museums have become common across America, where Britain has an official day of memory, and where the Holocaust is remembered across Europe as the paradigm case of historic suffering.

A second great pillar of the Holocaust, in our collective memory, is the film *Schindler's List*, which first appeared in America in 1993. It is forgotten now that this film was expected to crash at the box offices; the subject was seen as too harrowing for the normal cinema audience. Even if it failed, that would be no problem – this was the director Steven Spielberg's private project. Actors were even encouraged to study and copy the physical mannerisms of the director's executive friends.[31] Yet in reality the film was an enormous success: it won seven Oscars and raised over $100 million. In 1997, it was shown on American network television, with the rare announcement that it would not be interrupted by commercial breaks. But what of the film itself; what picture of the Holocaust emerges from it? One point to stress is that this film is primarily a work of fiction. The style of the film reinforces this impression – the use of colour and pacing remind the audience that this is no documentary, but a standard feature film. Added to Anne's diary, a pattern emerges: it seems that millions of people can only learn about the Holocaust through the medium of literature. The horror is too great for a 'factual' history to convey. Albert Friedlander explains the need for a literary memory of the Holocaust: 'A whirlwind cannot be taught; it must be experienced . . . Facts, figures and explanations are necessary. But we must also touch and feel and taste the dark days and the burning nights. Our hearts must constrict in terror and grief. Our minds must expand to make room for the incredible.'[32]

Like all good fiction *Schindler's List* is mannered – the style of the director intrudes into the narrative. Often the effects are well judged; against a black and white background, the red coat of one young victim stands out clearly. Such colour symbolises our hero's growing alienation from the Nazi war machine. At other times, the style of the director intrudes against the story – as in the shower scene, which rests too long on the naked bodies of the dead. Kitschy, mawkish, this scene adds nothing to the narrative. Another theme is pure Spielberg. As in *Armistad*, where the abolition of slavery is achieved not through a revolt by slaves but as a result of courtroom drama, a benign, powerful rescuer is required, to lead the oppressed to victory. Our hero is Oskar Schindler, a well-meaning German businessman and a real historical figure who did save hundreds of Jewish lives. It is curious that Steven Spielberg's film, which exists at one level as an affirmation of his Jewish identity, should take for its hero a Nazi, an Aryan, a non-Jew.

The success of *Schindler's List* depends on a tension between hope and despair. The film follows the use of the *Diary of Anne Frank* in its balance between misery (which demands empathy or identification) and release (the victory of human choice over Nazi evil). In real, lived, history this tension was decisively resolved; the Holocaust happened, and millions of people died. Such an outcome must be communicated when history becomes cinema. When it came out, *Schindler's List* was a film, a commodity to purchase. Oprah Winfrey told her viewers that she was 'a better person' for having seen the film. People do not consume naively. If you wanted to watch an uplifting and optimistic comedy you would not go to watch this film about the Holocaust. But the film itself constantly searches for hope. A good German is shown rescuing Jews. Then at the end of the film, an Israeli flag is shown. Despite everything, it seems, the good guys do conquer. So it was in the film, but not in its reception. This was Novick's experience: '*Schindler's List* left all of those who saw it – however much or little they'd previously known of the Holocaust – overwhelmed by the horror of the events and deeply moved, often to tears. This was my own experience, and I think it is likely that for the majority of viewers, responses of horror and grief overwhelmed whatever redemptive message is carried by the movie.'[33] What I remember of watching *Schindler's List*, is the sound of hearing an entire cinema cry. The despair of the situation, the terrible misery represented in the middle scene, these overwhelm the falsely optimistic notes struck at the end of the film.

Both in Anne's *Diary* and in *Schindler's List* the most important theme is human defeat. Although this takes place off-camera, millions of people are taken away to die. Indeed, the horror is more effective when it is secret; death is most frightening when it is not directly witnessed, but experienced indirectly, through the imagination. What we guess or imagine is in this case the truth. The Holocaust was the most one-sided defeat of human aspiration. The destruction of the Jews itself rested on a series of prior defeats. They include Hitler's seizure of power, which was resisted neither by Conservatives, nor Liberals nor Socialists; the destruction of the largest trade-union movement in the world, which was not opposed by mass strikes or any form of class resistance; the murder of the disabled, which was not opposed by any number of people; and then the defeat of the Jews.[34]

Perhaps this bleakness explains our fascination with the Holocaust. What matters is not the specific situation of the deaths, but the terrible emotions which they bring out. Even for people who were not themselves at the camps, or lack the bonds of family ties to survivors, the emotion required of their encounter with the Holocaust is one of sympathy; of identification with another human who suffers. In Lawrence Langer's words, 'the Holocaust is an event without a future – that is, nothing better for mankind grew out of it'.[35] Or, to quote Friedlander again, 'There are no silver linings surrounding the unrelieved blackness of the Holocaust.'[36] There is no redemption in the story of the Holocaust, only suffering, and then . . . greater suffering. Somehow this story appeals to people who see around them only misery. In this sense, the public fascination of the Holocaust is part of a broader story, namely the spread of images associated with loss and mourning across European cultural life.[37] For a hundred years Western society has been fascinated by stories of loss. Certainly in our literary culture the notion of decline permeates the work of such diverse authors as Beckett, Joyce and Kafka, Koestler, Mann, Proust and Spengler. Following Marx, I would explain this desire for stories with a theme of loss in terms of human alienation. Because people do not find satisfaction in their working or domestic relationships, so they look for stories that can help them to make sense of the absences in their own lives. In this way, the story of the Holocaust plays to a real human need.

CONCLUSION

This chapter opened with a detailed review of Norman Finkelstein's book, *The Holocaust Industry*, but as it has progressed, the subject has shifted towards the themes of Peter Novick's earlier text, *The Holocaust and Collective Memory*, which was such an inspiration for Finkelstein's work. The conclusions of the two books could not have been more different. Norman Finkelstein's *The Holocaust Industry* argues clearly and with passion for a different memory of the Holocaust – one which is true to the event itself, but has been purged of the commercialism and state politics which marks the memory today. By contrast, Novick's *The Holocaust and Collective Memory* argues against any lessons, any closure: 'If there *are* lessons to be extracted from encountering the past, that encounter has to be with the past in all its messiness; they're not likely to come from an encounter with the past that's been shaped and shaded so that inspiring lessons will emerge.'[38]

Ultimately, it seems to me that Novick raises more profound and more interesting questions. His polemic is more vague, his target less clear. But what Novick seeks to explain is our fascination with an event which becomes closer the further we travel from it. I agree with Finkelstein that power politics has played its part in the process. I welcome his book, in that it seeks to challenge one dominant reading of the past, opening up public discussion of the Holocaust, so that the question at issue is no longer the sterile and offensive debate over 'did it happen, or not?', but rather 'what are the lessons that we should draw from the murders?' There is no reason why the conclusion of the story should be that Jews are better off in Israel. A majority of Jews today find that they can live without fear of racism, in America or Europe, but not in the Middle East. Finkelstein's book fails, not because of its intention – to rescue the memory of the past from the causes for which it has been used – but for the more mundane reason that its polemic against the Zionist memory of the Holocaust is entirely one-sided and therefore fails to persuade. But Novick's book points us towards the more important debate, why is the Holocaust so crucial *today*?

One point I do take from Finkelstein: somehow, our memory of the Holocaust has become the memory of the Jewish Holocaust. This is a reduction of the past. It is not remembered that Hitler's first enemy was the German left. Nor are museums dedicated to the disabled and other victims of the Nazi euthanasia project. Yet it was here that the mass killings began, years before the invasion of the Soviet Union and the subsequent murder of the Jews. The Roma and the Slavs are forgotten, although their killings were at least as bloody and traumatic. Somehow human beings are only allowed to take in one story at a time – that of the Jewish Holocaust is told to the exclusion of other victims.

As the memory of the Holocaust has become the memory of the Jewish Holocaust, so the memory of it has become a matter of secondary or transferred emotions. The Holocaust is about empathy now, and identification with others. But this is an empathy without assistance – charity, not solidarity. It could not be solidarity, because solidarity was not given. Several of the critical voices I have mentioned suggest that the Holocaust has been taken over by Hollywood, becoming a naive story of human victory (in the secularised Christian sense of 'love conquers all'). In contrast, I would argue that these themes are secondary to the story of the Holocaust. The Holocaust has actually become the ultimate human story of suffering and pain. In this sense, one of the reasons for its enormous fascination – at least for people who can claim no ethnic or family identity with the dead – is the fact that this was *the* story of human defeat. All of us can share the pain.

PART TWO

EIGHT

Degenerate Art and Music

In the 1920s and early '30s, Weimar Germany was at the centre of an artistic revolution. Film makers such as Fritz Lang, architects including Walter Gropius, novelists like Thomas Mann and dramatists such as Erwin Piscator and Bertolt Brecht, all contributed to the creation of new artistic forms. The new visual style which emerged attempted to break down the traditional idea that art should represent the reality of a static image. The new artists combined different forms, music with images, movement with comedy. They wanted to portray feeling and emotion, to present a society which was in flux. Many of these artists were overtly political. Erwin Piscator's *Volksbühne*, or 'people's stage', put on plays beside socialist banners, slogans and posters. His theatre distributed free tickets in factories. The idea was to link art to people's real experiences. The plays that were produced, such as Brecht's *Threepenny Opera*, portrayed a world of poverty and exploitation. They turned the audience of spectators into participants, and consciously tried to change the world. Even the 'non-political' artists set themselves the task of transforming their art. Weimar composers, including Erik Korngold and Ernst Krenek, introduced into opera the sounds of everyday life under capitalism: the noise of trains and cars, sirens and industrial machinery.

When the Nazis came to power in 1933, they sought to eradicate this entire culture. They had their own vision of art, neo-classical architecture, paintings of rural idylls, portraits of the Führer. Any art or music which did not conform to the nostalgic and reactionary taste of the Nazis was banned. Even those few genuine artists like the expressionist Emil Nolde and the author Gottfried Benn, who had been political Nazis for years, found themselves the victims of state hostility.[1] When the Nazis sought to explain what they disliked and feared about pre-1933 Weimar Germany, they commonly found their examples in the sphere of art. In the 1940 Nazi film, *Der Ewige Jude* (*The Eternal Jew*), Weimar art is portrayed as a disturbing mixture of styles. Cabaret, cartoons, atonal music, expressionist art, Negro spirituals, theatre, architecture, and a dozen different forms of 'modern art' are mixed together. The combination of these different forms of art appears neurotic, cacophonous and misshaped. Art was also one victim of the Nazi burning of books in May 1933, where the targets included the novelists Heinrich Mann, Lionel Feuchtwanger and E.M. Remarque, the author of *All Quiet on the Western Front*, also the journalists Kurt Tucholsky and Carl von Ossietsky from the satirical journal *Weltbühne*.[2] Some 35,000 musicians were killed in the Holocaust, and many survivors refused to return after 1945.

The Nazi hostility to what they called 'degenerate' art and music was expressed in two notorious exhibitions, staged in 1937 and 1938. Weimar art was shown in the worst possible light. The catalogue placed works by modernist painters such as Klee alongside drawings by schizophrenics, in order to demonstrate the 'similarities'.[3] Speaking at the opening of the House of German Art in Munich in 1937, Adolf Hitler eulogised the qualities of Wagner: 'Before the critics did justice to the genius of a Richard Wagner, he had the people on his side, whereas the people had nothing to do with this so-called "modern art"'.[4] Yet these shows proved counter-productive. The July 1937 exhibition of 700 pieces of degenerate art drew up to 2 million visitors, vastly more than its official counter-part.[5] Indeed, its success demonstrated that many more people were interested in the 'diseased' and 'degenerate' art of Weimar than in the 'healthy' art of Hitler's Germany.

One of the Nazis' chief targets was Weimar music. Cabaret was a particular victim. Scatological and debauched, cabaret songs dealt with lesbianism, homosexuality, Reichstag corruption and female emancipation. Each theatre had its own MC, or *Conferencier*, to introduce the show. Werner Fink, the anchorman at the Katakombe, 'risked his life in the interests of his jokes. He would raise his hand to the Hitler salute, and say "that's how deep we're in the shit", and if there were Nazis in the audience he would ask them politely if they would like him to proceed a little more slowly.'[6] After the *Conferencier* came the songs. One typical Weimar number called upon women to 'Chuck all the men out of the Reichstag'. Another favourite was *Munchausen*, a half-humorous, half-honest description of the world that Hitler's opponents sought to create:

I saw a film the other day
That really varied from the norm,
There were no soldiers on parade
And no one marched in uniform . . .
I saw a court of law where all
The justices were young again,
Their hearts were young, their minds were free
They judged all men equally.[7]

It was not only the content of the music that brought the displeasure of the regime. The form itself combined humour with debauchery, pleasure, politics and sex. Rulers were mocked, the mighty humbled. It was not a style which endeared itself to the rulers of Weimar Germany, and still less could cabaret have survived under Hitler. Yet if cabaret was a favourite target, it was not the only victim of Nazi censorship. In power, the fascists set themselves against opera, jazz and atonal music. Many of the best-known musicians were forced into exile after 1933; others did not survive the camps.

Yet this chapter is concerned not with the Nazi hostility but with its object, the democratic art of the earlier, Weimar period. Anyone can visualise the staple images of fascist art. Immediately you think of filmed crowd scenes, in which the leader addresses a huge, amorphous crowd; healthy Nordic mountaineers; Roman statues; sports festivals; semi-pornographic paintings of healthy young women; uniforms, flags, guns; sculptures of near-naked Aryan men. Whether in the cinema of Riefenstahl, or in the paintings of Adolf Ziegler, these are the images which stand out. But are there equivalent and distinctive images for Weimar art, and if so, what do these images tell us about the character and the dynamics of the society in which these artists lived?

WEIMAR: SOCIETY IN FLUX

Seeking to explain the victory of Benito Mussolini in Italy in 1922, the famous Italian Marxist Antonio Gramsci described what he saw as the key explanations of fascist victory. His *Prison Notebooks* sought to explain how ‘a part of the social group’ could establish its domination over ‘the entire group’, society as a whole. This ‘hegemony’ could only be established by consent, that is by persuading wider layers of people to support the regime. In the case of 'Caesarism' (a broad concept in Gramsci's work, but here fascism), Mussolini's victory could be explained with reference to the 'passive revolution' of 1919–21, when Italian workers had taken control of their factories but proved themselves incapable of extending their hegemony to society as a whole.[8] A large part of Gramsci's explanation for the triumph of fascism relied on the partial success of the Italian revolution. His point was that the consequence of a partial revolution was not half a revolution, but something different in itself. This insight was developed to explain events in Italy, where the intervening period (between the rise of the revolution and its defeat) was brief, and the consequence of a partial revolution was fascism. Yet Gramsci's argument is potentially still more valuable when it comes to Weimar Germany, where the intervening period lasted for anything up to fifteen years. It is no coincidence that Gramsci's jottings on the passive revolution were recorded in 1933, the fateful year of the German workers' defeat.

The Weimar republic can be seen as a compromise between the working class and the German bourgeoisie, dependent on the unconsummated rise of the working-class movement in 1918–23. It follows that Weimar was a conditional society, incapable of long life. The symbol of this unsustainable equilibrium was the terrible inflation of 1923, when the value of the mark collapsed until billions were needed to purchase one British pound. All life, all property, lost value. Money was weighed out in the streets, to save on counting the digits.[9] The dizzying whirl of devaluation continued until the autumn of 1923, when first a possible communist revolution and then a Nazi coup in Munich both failed. Yet as Antonio Gramsci wrote (in a paraphrase of Marx's *Critique of Political Economy*), 'no social formation disappears as long as the productive forces which have developed within it still find room for further movement'.[10] By the end of the year the crisis had passed, and the German economy had won a reprieve which would last until the Wall Street Crash in 1929.

The cartoonist George Grosz's 1923 collection *Ecce Homo* provides many of the most distinctive visual images of early Weimar. Take, for example, Grosz's famous watercolour *Evening Party*. A bourgeois lady with red hair and a face like a poodle welcomes her husband to her table. Already ensconced in her company are two more bourgeois men; one nods into his drink, the other watches the woman with the lusting expression of a red-faced bulldog pup. Even as her lover stares at her, the woman strokes his calf with her shoe. In the background officers smoke, waiters perform their duties, and polite society drinks itself into oblivion.[11] In this one scene you can trace the classic themes of Grosz's art, fleshy sexuality, opulence, bourgeois lust and greed. The faces of *Ecce Homo* are the faces of the complacent and decadent rich. Yet the retrospective fame of this collection is ironic, for the Communist Party member George Grosz was accused by the German government of 'defaming public morals, and corrupting the inborn sense of shame and virtue innate in the German people'. For this medieval crime, Grosz was found guilty, the collection confiscated and destroyed.

If George Grosz's art lay in exposing the faces of the bourgeoisie, this stands at some remove from the democratic theatre of Erwin Piscator's 'people's stage'. There are several ways in which Piscator attempted to push the stage beyond anything that had been achieved before. One innovation was the use of film, which could be used as a source of figures and statistics, or to highlight simultaneous events. A further change was the use of moving platforms, making vertical action possible. Another new technique was the use of non-theatrical media, including musical bands and cartoons. In all these changes, Piscator's guiding spirit seems to have been a rejection of the mannered artifice of the classical theatre, which he associated with the German bourgeoisie. But more than this, Piscator made his theatre accessible to working-class people. Slogans were used, also banners and non-naturalistic sets. Gerda Redlich was one of the young Communists who took part: 'There was a different electricity when you worked in front of a working-class audience. Even before the audience came in, the atmosphere was different. Less refined. The feel of the company, the relationship to the director were different. The plays were different, also. There were discussions with the audience, and plays could actually be whistled down, which was unheard of elsewhere.'[12]

One playwright who attempted to explain the significance of Piscator's innovations was his collaborator Bertolt Brecht. According to Brecht, Weimar theatre originated in the agitprop street troupes formed by left-wing supporters of the revolution in 1918. While traditional or 'dramatic' theatre had employed various conventions in order to suspend the audience's disbelief, Piscator's 'epic' theatre asked the audience to take part in the performance, not relaxing but thinking, not believing but asking questions of the play. The narrator would take part in events. Non-naturalistic settings encouraged the audience to consider the present-day relevance of historical theatre. The spectator of dramatic theatre was encouraged to think of drama in a certain way. In Brecht's words, the spectator would say 'Yes, I have felt like that too – Just like me – It's only natural – It'll never change – The sufferings of this man appal me, because they are inescapable – That's great art; it all seems the most obvious thing in the world – I weep when they weep, I laugh when they laugh.' By contrast, the epic theatre's spectator would leave thinking, 'I'd never have thought it – That's not the way – That's extraordinary, hardly believable – It's got to stop – The sufferings of this man appal me, because they are unnecessary – That's great art; nothing obvious in it – I laugh when they weep, I weep when they laugh.'[13] In the same essay, Brecht distinguished between the dramatic 'theatre for pleasure', and the epic, 'theatre for instruction'. In the latter, human thought and human agency were restored.

It is impossible to reconstruct the theatre of Piscator and Brecht. We know what the sets and the actors looked like, but their relationship to their audience cannot be renewed. For new generations which are not familiar with the older forms of cabaret and agitprop, the Weimar dramatists' synthesis of these traditions is less accessible. Yet some of the distinctive quality of Brecht's theatre can be observed in the 1932 film which he directed, *Kuhle Wampe*, subtitled 'To whom does the world belong?' Two scenes in particular are typical of Weimar art. One takes place at a workers' sports festival. This ends with the successful athletes and their audience singing together. This is a crowd scene, but one wholly unlike the crowd scenes of Nazi art. Men and women stand together. Anyone has access to the stage, no one possesses the right to demand other people's obedience. No leader is singled out for special attention. The final scene takes place on a train. One passenger reads in his paper that 24 million kg of coffee are being burned to keep prices high. This news encourages a number of young Communists, returning from their festival, to engage the other members of the train in heated discussion. Yet each time the youngsters establish a point it is immediately lost, as other passengers throw in their own meaningless objections: don't boil coffee, don't use a tin kettle. The director encourages a gentle mocking even of the Communist message of the film; then at the end the youngsters predict that the world will be changed by 'those who don't like it the way it is'.

The Weimar spirit also informs Brecht's poems, the most accessible and underrated of all his art. Even when events compelled Brecht towards didacticism, his poetry remained marked by a relentless humour. In exile in America in 1935, Bertolt Brecht criticised the New York Theatre Union's attempt to produce one of his Weimar plays, *The Mother*. Believing that the director had mauled the play's politics, Brecht responded in verse:

> Comrades, I see you
> Reading the short play with embarrassment.
> The spare language
> Seems like poverty. This report, you reckon
> Is not how people express themselves. I have read
> Your adaptation. Here you insert a 'Good morning'
> There a 'Hullo, my boy'. The vast field of action
> Gets cluttered with furniture. Cabbage reeks
> From the stove. What's bold becomes gallant, what's historical
> normal.
> Instead of wonder
> You strive for sympathy with the mother when she loses her
> son.[14]

In this poem, Brecht chided the actors for patronising their working-class audience. It was their distrust of their audience which caused them to misunderstand epic theatre. 'Comrades, the form of the new plays / Is new, but why be / Frightened of what's new?' Clearly what the American company lacked was the revolutionary spirit of Weimar art.[15]

Elsewhere in his poetry, Bertolt Brecht attacked Hitler's fascism in the same spirit. It would have been easy to expose the Nazis for their false revolutionism, doing deals with the conservative Prussian order, even while claiming to stand for change. This was the approach of the German Communist Party, whose members were urged into heroic acts of armed resistance, motivated by class and class demands alone. Instead of this direct approach, Brecht attacked his enemy with humour. The refrain of his poem was to think what was possible, 'but for the Jews advising against it'. 'The French Assembly has / Long harboured the desire to bestow the mineral resources of Lorraine / On our Chancellor, whose / Moustache it so admires.' England would offer its empire to Germany – 'only the Jews would not allow it'. Brecht continued:

> Until the Führer told us, we had no idea
> What a clever and powerful people the Jews were
> Though there are only a few of them scattered across the earth's
>   face
> It seems that they control everything because of their genius . . .
> This being so, the entire world asks itself with a shudder
> What would happen to the global structure
> If the Führer had chosen for his lofty purposes
> Not the relatively talented Germans, but
> The Jews.[16]

Such an attack mocked the dull-witted pomposity of fascism. It was a charge not from the front, but from the side, and where his enemy was at his weakest.

Another distinctive characteristic of the Weimar cultural milieu was its fascination with sex. At the front of this movement was Dr Magnus Hirschfield, whose Institute was established in 1919 to campaign for the rights of the 'Third Sex'. The Institute operated both as a museum of erotica and as a campaigning centre for sex-law reform. Hirschfield was frequently attacked by members of the right – one assault in Munich in 1921 left his skull fractured and the professor feared dead. Yet in Berlin, the mood was for toleration. By 1929 a law to legalise homosexuality was passed through the Reichstag – only to be dropped following the 1929 Wall Street crash. Sexual freedom was one point at which Weimar libertarianism was well ahead of the other urban cultures of western Europe. Christopher Isherwood's first novel of Berlin life was published in England on 17 February 1932. Its many gay characters made the book almost unintelligible to an English audience: 'I remember how one reviewer remarked that he had at first thought the novel contained a disproportionately large number of homosexual characters, but had decided, on further reflection, that there *were* a lot more homosexuals about, nowadays.'[17] What our dull English reviewer understood as a change in his dining company, a more perceptive German witness might have explained as the first signs of an organised movement.

So far, this chapter has described the art of the Weimar period, commenting on its vigour, its humour, and its contempt for pomposity in all its forms. What though of Gramsci's theory of passive revolution? The argument here is that the art of Weimar was forged out of the incomplete rise of the German workers' movement. The culture was at its most optimistic when Germany itself seemed on the verge of profound change. The art critic Ernst Fischer was one product of Weimar. He argued that the role of art in all societies was revolutionary, in the sense that it hinted at man's ability to transform the world, whether or not the victory of change was inaugurated in a single moment of transformation. The symbols he chose of such revolutionary practice were the British silent-film actor Charlie Chaplin and the Russian director Sergei Eisenstein. These were artists widely discussed in Weimar and widely imitated: 'One of the great functions of art in an age of immense mechanical power is to show that free decision exists and that man is capable of creating the situations he wants and needs. Chaplin, too, in his grotesque parodies of everyday life, hints at this victory: not a revolutionary event like Eisenstein's but a victory all the same, the victory of man enslaved by the machine over the machine itself.'[18] Fischer's hope for socialist transformation was real, but the absence of revolution in Weimar Germany was not accidental, and the failure could not be shrugged away.

It seems that the rebelliousness of Weimar art was not fixed but changed and developed over time. At the moment of revolution in 1918–23, very many artists believed that it would be possible to make a living connection between the revolutionary working class and the revolutionary avant-garde. The plays of Piscator and the cartoons of Grosz were both shaped in this moment of revolutionary upturn. The dominant themes of the hour were anger and hope. Yet after the failure of the German October of 1923, the dreams of revolution began to fade. According to one French Communist: 'In September, October and November, Germany lived through a profound revolutionary experience, which is hardly known about and understood. The armed vigil was long, but the hour did not sound.'[19] Afterwards, nothing was as hopeful again. In addition to the old revolutionary elan, new themes became more important: cultural pessimism, and a certain defensiveness, a fear that the working-class citadels could themselves be overthrown.

As early as 1919, a woodcut by Hans Baluschek showed *Berlin in revolution: two studies*. On the left, in the proletarian districts, workers bravely resisted the onslaught of the army and the state. On the right, in affluent Berlin, radical paper-sellers shouted against the outrage but found no audience to purchase their newspapers.[20] After 1923, George Grosz began to move away from the radical left. His art exposed the greed of the rich – but what could he do when these corpulent faces were no longer challenged from below, and hence no longer funny?[21] The new atmosphere of pessimism is also reflected in the very decadence of cabaret. Alongside the old exaggerated and satirical humour grew a new desperation and restlessness. This change saw the old music-hall-style singers begin to make way for dancers and elaborate striptease acts. One such show was led by the hyperactive cocaine addict Anita Berber. In the words of one contemporary lament:

> What interests the audience:
> Hunger, misery, suffering millions,
> Thousands, rotting away in jail?
> Does that interest the audience?
> Alas, the naked bottom of Anita Berber:
> That interests the audience.[22]

Yet even the introduction of nude acts could not guarantee the interest of the audience. In Max Beckman's woodcut *Nude Cabaret*, an audience pointedly ignores the naked women gyrating on stage. One officer stares, but otherwise the entire crowd, composed of the out-of-hours bourgeoisie shows little enthusiasm.[23] According to Beckman's pessimistic vision of Weimar, this was a society in which even sex had lost its traditional marketing appeal. And once sex had gone, what was there left to sell?

The dissident socialist Victor Serge was now living in Berlin, working for the Communist press. Writing after the failed October of 1923, he told the French journal *Clarté* that even Weimar culture was in decline: 'The book trade is one of the industries worst hit by the crisis. Thinkers and artists are silent. Nothing is heard but the voices of the demagogues.' What evidence did Serge find of this cultural defeat? He mentioned inflation, the pauperisation of the middle classes, the development of prostitution, begging and crime. There was no money to print books or sheet music, it was no longer possible to keep public museums open or to maintain a private artist's studio. Serge quoted one composer: 'In a few years, nothing but the memory of the rich musical culture of Germany will survive . . . Now musicians can no longer be trained; the best pupils from the Academy of Music have to play in expensive restaurants in the evening in order to survive . . .' Serge dubbed this process of cultural loss 'Stinnesation', after Hugo Stinnes, the plutocrat who bought up Germany (and German intellectual life) as the state went bankrupt.[24]

With cynicism came a new defensiveness, which intruded into all aspects of German cultural life. Even the montages of George Grosz's friend and collaborator John Heartfield, were shaped by the left's need to maintain ground lost since 1923. Nowadays Heartfield is remembered for his committed Dada images, many of which appeared for the Communist *Arbeiter-Illustrierte-Zeitung* (Workers' Illustrated Newspaper) or on covers for the left publisher Malik-Verlag. In 1929, Heartfield collaborated with the radical satirist Kurt Tucholsky, in producing a book-length onslaught against the 1920s, *Deutschland, Deutschland über alles*. The art was pure Weimar, democratic and scornful. Anonymous worker-photographers contributed images of the republic, while Tucholsky mocked the assembled generals, Nazis and plutocrats. *German sports* showed men with footballs instead of brains, while crowd scenes of protesting workers sat uneasily beside images of slum homes and prosperous churchmen. The front cover showed a ridiculous overlap of images – an icon composed of a capitalist's suit, a general's uniform, helmet and top-hat, Dada eyes, a German flag and a reindeer's nose.[25] Such was German nationalism, the vice of German social democracy since 1914. Such also was the new spirit of the Weimar left: the jokes remained, but they were sullen and bitter now.

When Kurt Tucholsky was condemned by middle-of-the-road socialists for his failure to support the moderate republic against its opponents, his response was to condemn the failure of German social democracy to defend itself. Meanwhile, John Heartfield's anti-fascism showed itself in such famous images as *Fascist memorials* (on the left a sphinx's head, on the right a pile of skulls from Mussolini's adventure in Abyssinia) and *As in the Middle Ages . . . So in the Third Reich* (a worker broken on the rack of the swastika). The best known of all John Heartfield's montages, though, is *Millions stand behind me . . . the meaning of the Hitler salute*. Based on Adolf Hitler's boast that the Nazis had the support of millions of ordinary Germans, this montage shows the Nazi leader with his arm seemingly outstretched in the fascist greeting, but the purpose of the movement is actually to take a bribe from the Nazi industrialist Thyssen. The millions were not people but cash.[26] Certainly after the elections of 1930, the priorities of anti-fascism dominated Heartfield's art.

According to Alain Steinweis, the limits of Weimar's artistic revolution could be seen most clearly after 1933. Traditionally the Nazis had found difficulty in recruiting artists and musicians. It was as late as 1928 that the party formed its first cultural organisation, the Combat League for German Culture (*Kampfbund für Deutsche Kultur*). Yet between January and October 1933, the membership of the Kampfbund grew from 6,000 to 38,000. This was just one side of a dual process of coercion and consent which culminated in the coordination of the arts within the regime's general policy of propaganda, administered by Goebbels under the aegis of the Reich Chambers of Music, Theatre and the Visual Arts. Steinweis gives examples of security police (SD) complaints aimed against 'art Bolsheviks' from as late as 1939, but he makes clear that most artists cooperated with the regime: 'Degenerate jazz musicians and "art-Bolshevik" painters were not as prominent by late 1939 as complaints lodged with the SD might indicate, and to the extent that they did exist, they were the exception rather than the rule. Notable instances of defiance should not overshadow the co-operativeness of the vast majority of German artists.'[27]

In this context, as in so many others, 'totalitarian rule corrupted the Germans'.[28] Once the German working-class movement had failed to rise against fascism in the decisive winter of 1932–3, then any action of resistance could only be the act of a minority. Fear of repression combined with a perception of popular apathy. Between 1933 and 1936 the German left continued to operate against the state in a heroic, underground manner, before being broken apart by a series of raids and defections. After 1936, there was no collective resistance by artists to Hitler – as indeed there was no collective resistance by workers or by women, by gypsies, the disabled or Jews. Individual acts of dissidence were legion, but mass protests were almost unknown.

Yet it would be wrong to end on this downbeat note. Even after 1933, the radical art of Weimar continued, if only in exile. The cultural anti-fascism of Ernst Bloch, Walter Benjamin and Wilhelm Reich continued to be produced after the defeat of 1933 – in line with Hegel's dictum about the owl of Minerva which flies only at dusk. The tasks which these writers set themselves included not only the negative goal of explaining their defeat, but also the positive task of generating a democratic art which would assist in completing the unfinished revolution of 1918. Thomas Mann's *Doctor Faustus* (1947) explained the rise of the Nazis, this 'monstrous national perversion', as a collective act of national insanity, epitomised by the rise and subsequent fall of the brilliant composer Adrian Leverkühn.[29] Georg Lukács attempted a similar 'national' explanation at the level of philosophy, blaming the right-turn taken by the nineteenth-century Young Hegelians for the rise of fascism.[30] Several of Bertolt Brecht's best-known works were first produced in exile in America, while John Heartfield was able to continue producing his art from exile in Prague.

It is in this context of defeat that Walter Benjamin's well-known description of fascism as 'the aestheticisation of politics' should be understood.[31] Properly speaking, fascism was not *the* aestheticisation of politics, but rather *an* aestheticisation of politics – one society in which the spectacle and imagery of the right had defeated the cultural politics of the left. This was a terrible defeat, but not a permanent one. While millions were condemned to death, humanity survived, and a different society could be built anew. Out of the tragedy that would engulf his own life, Benjamin drew an activist's conclusion: 'Only that historian will have the gift of fanning the flames of resistance, who understands that if his enemy wins even the dead will not be spared. And that enemy has not ceased to be victorious.'[32] Given the many crimes of Hitler's regime, this must be the right spirit in which any history of fascism should be written – as a thorough-going critique. Indeed, the anti-fascism of Weimar culture represents one of the first and finest critiques on which later generations can draw.

NINE

The Anti-fascist Politics of Albert Einstein

Albert Einstein (1879–1955) is the most famous physicist of the twentieth century. The founder of general relativity, Einstein did more than anyone else to break down the mechanistic view of nineteenth-century science. Since Einstein, a new world view has emerged which emphasises the fluid and related nature of physical concepts. Time, energy and matter are each now seen as dynamic. Einstein's special relativity, and his famous equation $E=mc^2$, showed that time and space were related; that matter *was* motion and motion *was* energy. His theories are credited today as the starting point of nuclear physics, modern cosmology and quantum mechanics, as well.[1] Not surprisingly, the events of Einstein's life have generated an enormous literature. Just between 1919 and 1929, more than 5,000 books were published in dozens of languages on the theory of relativity alone. Einstein's collected works have since been published, as have his love letters to his first wife. Soon his entire collection of working papers and manuscripts will be available in a single edition. Already the subject of biographies, several novels and plays, religious tracts, films and comic strips, Einstein's life is one of the best-mined seams in world literature. The obvious question to ask is: what is there left to say?

Albert Einstein's ideas can be understood by comparing the man to his milieu and friends. He was born in 1879, the year in which Wilhelm Marr founded the first modern racist party, the League of Anti-Semites. Einstein's friends at university included Friedrich Adler, the prominent Austrian socialist who would be jailed during the First World War. His earliest paper on relativity was published in 1905, the year of the first Russian revolution. In Prague before the First World War, Einstein moved in a Jewish literary circle, whose members included the writers Franz Kafka and Max Brod. Brod's novel *The Redemption of Tycho Brahe* includes a sketch of Brahe's collaborator Johann Keppler that was clearly based on the young

Einstein.[2] Following the 1918 German Revolution, Einstein lectured at the Marxist Workers' College, organised by the German Communist Party in Berlin. Einstein won the Nobel Prize in 1921, the year of the March action in Germany, when the Communist Party attempted an insurrection without mass backing, and even its own cadres failed to support the planned general strike.

Now a world-famous scientist, Albert Einstein moved in the most glittering circles of the League of Nations. He was friendly with liberal and social democratic politicians, including the British Labour Prime Minister, Ramsay MacDonald. Yet this happy period of his life would quickly come to an end. Einstein's life was increasingly shaped by the rise of anti-Semitism. He was close to Walter Rathenau, the German liberal Jew assassinated by the far right in 1922. As early as 1920, an anti-Einstein organisation was set up in Germany, and attempts were planned on his life. In response, Einstein raised money for Zionist organisations. After 1933, he was attacked by the German authorities as a Jew and an *Obersozi*, a top-rank red.

Forced into exile in America, Einstein addressed a series of public meetings. He toned down his earlier pacifism, and now spoke as the representative of an exiled community, demanding that something be done to stop the rise of fascism. Like many other public figures of this generation, Einstein moved in circles influenced by the Communist Party's notion of the Popular Front. He was friendly with the left-wing film star Charlie Chaplin, and spoke fondly of the pacifist Mahatma Gandhi and the playwright George Bernard Shaw. His stepdaughter married Dimitri Marianoff, a Soviet citizen, and Einstein was drawn into the controversy over Stalin's show trials. He also corresponded with political leaders, from Queen Elizabeth of Belgium to President Franklin Roosevelt of the United States. His 1939 letter to Roosevelt was a decisive moment leading to the development of the atom bomb. Later, Einstein was a critic of the politics of the state of Israel. His was very much a life carried out in the public view.

Many of the physicists and other scientists who have written about Einstein express surprise at the man's keen interest in political affairs. In some accounts, these are the years of his decline and old age. Having made his most important scientific breakthroughs by 1916, it is suggested that Einstein floundered when he entered into the world of politics. Albrecht Fölsing, author of one of the best recent biographies, talks of Einstein's 'confusion in political matters'. Stephen Hawking quotes the physicist's own phrase, that his life was 'divided between politics and equations'. Einstein continued: 'Equations are more important to me because politics is for the present, but an equation is something for eternity.'[3] Yet these words should not be taken as evidence of the physicist's final preference. He was an aggressively shy man, who had little desire to take part in public life. He did not choose to live in a world of war and exploitation, but having been born into this society, he saw no reason to keep quiet in the face of misery. Albert Einstein took to politics because politics took to him. The best way to understand his life is as a totality. His life was devoted to both science and politics. Neither was subsidiary; both formed part of a single whole.

Although I have stressed the unitary nature of his physics and his philosophy, this chapter can only address one half of Albert Einstein's life. It is a study in his political philosophy, discussed as an prominent example of the general anti-fascism of the interwar years. If Albert Einstein was a child of the 1880s and '90s – the years of the great depression – he was a man of the 1920s and 1930s – the age of fascism and war. This was the period in which his scientific discoveries were popularised and, as a consequence, this was also the time in which he first came into public view. In this chapter, three areas of particular controversy are addressed: Einstein's pacifism, his Zionism, and also his socialism. At each stage, his ideas are compared to those of his contemporaries. Albert Einstein's biography makes most sense if the physicist is understood as one member of a generation of European intellectuals. His philosophy can then be compared to the ideas of his time.

EINSTEIN'S METHOD

Before coming to the heart of the chapter – the discussion of Albert Einstein's politics – it is worth saying something about his general philosophical method. In his 1933 lecture on 'The Method of Theoretical Physics', Einstein argued that scientific breakthroughs were achieved by intuitive methods. The great physicists examined concept first, and then integrated the facts into their new theoretical models. Although purporting to describe the general approach of working scientists, Einstein was clearly describing his own methods of work.

> Our experience hitherto justified us in believing that nature is the realisation of the simplest conceivable mathematical ideas. I am convinced that we can discover, by means of purely mathematical constructions, those concepts and those lawful connections between them which furnish the key to the understanding of natural phenomena. Experience may suggest the appropriate mathematical concepts, but they most certainly cannot be deduced from it.[4]

One thing which this passage reveals is a general familiarity with German idealist philosophy. Einstein's teacher here was Ernst Mach, a nineteenth-century physicist and polymath whose book *Science of Mechanics* absorbed him when he first read it as a student in Zurich in 1897. Many of Albert Einstein's closest friends – then and later – were convinced Machists, including Friedrich Adler and later Besso, who worked with Einstein in the Swiss patent office.

Mach argued against all physical laws. Only that was true which could be confirmed by direct observation. 'No one is competent to predicate things about absolute space and absolute motion,' Mach wrote, 'they are pure things of thought, pure mental constructs, that cannot be produced in experience.' Such an approach was thoroughly idealistic; Ernst Mach argued that there was no reality independent of human experience. Clearly, Mach's philosophy could make no sense of the world before human beings inhabited it. Yet combined with the idealism was a devastating scepticism. Thus in his vigorous rejection of all absolute categories, Mach pointed the way towards Einstein's theory of special relativity, with its rejection of the assumed categories of classical physics. Mach was also important in the evolution of general relativity. In particular, Einstein took from his predecessor the argument that the direction of causality did not matter. What was important was the interaction of all bodies in relation to all others. Although Einstein later turned decisively against Ernst Mach's idealistic method, describing it as a sterile approach which 'cannot give birth to anything living', Mach's philosophy did help to shape Einstein's view of the universe as a closed process with no beginning or end.[5]

There are certain similarities between the dialectical method which Karl Marx took over from the German philosopher Frederick Hegel, and Albert Einstein's theory of relativity, mediated through the work of Ernst Mach. Both Marx and Einstein shared a belief that the world is a dynamic totality in which change occurs through violent processes of rapid transformation. Both were convinced sceptics, with Marx adopting the motto, 'doubt everything'. Both Marx and Einstein picked the best of the German idealist tradition, taking the dialectical method but welding it on to a materialist philosophy. Each elaborated a general method of intellectual enquiry. In the *Grundrisse*, Marx's economic manuscripts which later formed the basis of *Capital*, Marx defended a method of 'rising from the abstract to the concrete'. Those empirical thinkers, he argued, who began with empirical facts, ended in abstraction. Yet those who began with abstractions ended closer to the truth: 'Along the first path [of empiricism] the full conception was evaporated to yield an abstract determination; along the second, the abstract determinations lead towards a reproduction of the concrete by the way of thought.'[6] If this quotation is compared to the earlier passage from Einstein's 1933 lecture, what comes out is a common interest in the relationship between fact and concept. There is a clear family resemblance between the two thinkers.

The point in stressing the richness of Albert Einstein's general philosophical method is to reinforce one of the arguments of this chapter, that there is a continuity between Einstein's physics and his general approach to life. The thinking behind the general theory of relativity was materialist, in the sense that Einstein believed that there was a real world which was governed by rational laws. And it was also sceptical, meaning that Einstein was aware that the rules were far more complex and contradictory than classical Newtonian physics had allowed. This method of sceptical, dialectical materialism can be seen to have shaped Einstein's theory of relativity. Meanwhile, it also influenced his approach towards the pressing political issues of his day.

FASCISM VERSUS EINSTEIN

Following the 1920 proof of his argument that the movement of light was bent by gravity, Einstein quickly became a household name. For the next fifteen years, he stood at the height of his international reputation. He was the first scientific celebrity, as famous as Charlie Chaplin or Picasso. Yet Einstein was never welcome in Germany. Leaving aside for a moment his fame, and his known left-wing sympathies, there were many other reasons for jealousy. Some practical physicists objected to the exaggerated interest given to this theoretical man whose discoveries seemed to them to be little more than tricks of speculation. Working in the capital, Berlin, Einstein was also the victim of provincial intrigues. Finally, he was a Jew, and his racial identity became the key issue around which a powerful anti-Einstein lobby was organised.

One key player in this milieu was the 1905 Nobel Prize-winner Philipp Lenard. During the First World War, Lenard supported the most militarist statements coming from the German court. He became increasingly resentful of British scientists – one published letter complained 'that they had never quoted him decently'. Lenard came to support Houston Chamberlain's doctrines of biological racism. When Einstein was awarded the Nobel Prize in 1921, Lenard wrote a letter of protest to the committee, and to the press as well. He maintained that relativity was a 'Jewish fraud'. Later, when anti-Semites murdered Walter Rathenau, the Foreign Minister, Lenard refused to fly the flag of his institute at half mast. Finally, following the Beer Hall putsch Lenard joined the Nazis, announcing that Hitler and his comrades 'appear to us as the gifts of God'.[7] Lenard was joined in the Nazi Party by another Nobel Prize-winner, Johannes Stark. Unlike Lenard, Stark did not attempt to deny relativity. For his part, Stark maintained that the idea had been invented by a patriotic German soldier during the Second World War, and later stolen by Einstein.

Albert Einstein was quickly made aware of this hostile current within German physics. At first Lenard and Stark kept themselves at a distance, simply writing articles and speeches, and not confronting Einstein directly. Then at the 1920 meeting of the German Physical Society, Einstein found himself the victim of organised interruptions. Max Planck in the chair chose to end the meeting, rather than risk violence. On other occasions, Einstein presented himself in person at meetings of the anti-Einstein society. Doing so, he put himself in some danger. But before 1933 the state, at least, was on his side.

The crisis of the interwar years increasingly forced itself into Einstein's life. Following Hitler's rise to power in 1933, he was forced to flee his home in Germany, along with Walter Benjamin, Bertolt Brecht, Karl Korsch and many others. Nazi militia seized his house and raided his bank account. German newspapers announced Einstein's departure and followed that story with the odious headline 'Good News – He's Not Coming Back.' German scientists attempted to create a racially pure physics, one which would not be corrupted by the revolutionary idea of relativity. Their determination set back the Nazi war effort – how were they supposed to build the bomb without the physics expressed in Einstein's formula, $E=mc^2$? Several of Einstein's friends and colleagues died in the Holocaust. Pressed by events, Einstein became an active anti-fascist. But how was his anti-fascism expressed?

EINSTEIN'S ZIONISM

The starting point for Albert Einstein's politics was his recognition of his insecure position within German society, as a Jew. He was part of a left-Jewish milieu and this identity was more fundamental to his world view than anything else. Einstein spent his adolescence living in Munich in the last decades of the nineteenth century. His father owned a small factory manufacturing dynamos and electrical instruments. This was a time of enormous industrial and military expansion. Following German unification during the Franco-Prussian War of 1870–1, industry grew at an enormous rate. By the end of the nineteenth century, Germany was one of three economic superpowers. Huge cartels were formed, bringing together industrial and finance capital. The state was strongly involved in supervising the economy.[8] Einstein's later scientific career was only made possible by the extraordinary growth of big business. The German state sponsored technical education in the hope that it would reap the rewards through advances of technology. Meanwhile, between 1870 and 1890 the arms budget tripled. Threatened by the growth of the German Socialist Party, the SPD, the state encouraged popular nationalism and anti-Semitism. The young Albert Einstein attended a Catholic school, and was the one Jewish student in the class. As an adolescent, he witnessed a number of anti-Semitic demonstrations. These parades were enough to give him a strong identity as a Jew:

'If relativity is proved right the Germans will call me a German, the Swiss will call me Swiss, and the French will call me a world citizen. If relativity is proved wrong, the French will call me Swiss, the Swiss will call me German, and the Germans will call me a Jew.'[9]

Einstein defined himself as Jewish. What did he mean by this self-identification? Over many years, writers have debated what it means to be a Jew. One answer has been that Judaism is a religion, and hence that the Jews are only those who follow this faith. Such an approach made little sense to Einstein. Although he often spoke of God, he did so frequently in a very nebulous and vague manner. In his famous saying, 'God does not play dice', God was a code for the laws of physics, which were rational, simple and open to human understanding. His divinity was the God of the seventeenth-century Dutch philosopher Spinoza, 'the God who is nature'. Apart also from his occasional admiration for the Old Testament prophet Moses, Albert Einstein was otherwise a life-long agnostic. In his autobiographical 'testimony', he described his early reading, and the disdain which it encouraged in him towards all forms of authority:

> Through the reading of popular scientific books I soon reached the conviction that much of the stories in the Bible could not be true. The consequence was a positive orgy of free thinking coupled with the impression that youth is intentionally being deceived by the State through lies. It was a crushing impression. Suspicion against every kind of authority grew out of this experience, a sceptical attitude towards the convictions which were alive in any specific social environment – an attitude which never left me.[10]

In the absence of a religious definition of Jewishness, Einstein fell back on the common sense and 'cultural' treatment that many others of his generation also adopted. Jews were those who shared a common culture, originating in religion but transcending it. At moments of crisis, a Jew was simply anyone who was considered by his enemies to be a Jew.

Not surprisingly, Albert Einstein sided with those forces in society which opposed anti-Semitism. He had a natural sympathy for the socialist left, and he also supported plans to create a homeland, where Jews would be liberated from persecution. In *Ideas and*

Opinions, a collection of Einstein's many speeches and articles, there are a number of pieces which articulate his support for Zionism. Einstein's argument was simple and logical. No one should have to live in a place where they would experience persecution. It was an idea he would express himself in exile from Germany after 1933: 'As long as I have any choice, I will only stay in a country where political liberty, tolerance and equality of all the citizens before the law prevail.'[11] Yet such a simple idea contained within it all sorts of contradictions. It was true that German Jews faced the most horrendous oppression, but why should Jews respond to persecution by fleeing from it? In Russia, Poland and Germany, many socialist Jews responded to anti-Semitism by struggling for a world free of racism. At times, Einstein recognised the quality of their vision. For example, he wrote to celebrate the heroism of the 1944 Warsaw Ghetto uprising, a movement against fascism led by Bundists, Communists and socialist Jews.[12] Although torn by conflicting principles, for most of his adult life Einstein was identified with Zionism. He worked for the World Zionist Organisation in the 1920s, raising money on a number of tours across Europe and America, and in 1952, he was even offered the presidency of the new state of Israel.

In his eclectic response to anti-Semitism, Einstein can be compared to his younger contemporary, Walter Benjamin. Born in 1892, Benjamin shared Einstein's liberal upbringing, avoiding the synagogue. Like Einstein, he also left Germany for Switzerland, before returning to his mother country. Benjamin began a career in academia, finishing his doctorate on 'The Concept of Art Criticism in German Romanticism' at the University of Berne in 1919. Yet he was drawn away from the university system. Like Einstein, he was the victim of anti-Semitism and had difficulty in holding down a regular post. Instead Benjamin turned towards politics. He was a friend of the Bolshevik Asja Lacis, and learned his Marxism from her. He also was influenced by Zionism, and encountered Zionist ideas as early as 1912; he later considered moving to Israel. Walter Benjamin's friendship with Lacis was balanced by a parallel friendship with the prominent Zionist, Gershom Scholem. Yet Benjamin turned decisively away from nationalism, writing to Ludwig Strauss: 'If you say: school, the question of the women, socialism: none of these have anything to do with Judaism, these are human questions; then I would say that a nationalism that does not examine everything – above all the most human and important questions – is quite worthless, is nothing more than a dangerous force of sloth.' The conclusion of this letter rejected the Zionist solution to anti-Semitism. Benjamin wrote, 'everything Jewish that goes beyond the self-evident Jewishness in me is dangerous'.[13]

Albert Einstein also turned away from Zionism, although more equivocally, and without the public declaration that Benjamin chose to make. Even before 1948, he recorded his dream that Israel should be a multinational society like his beloved Switzerland: 'I am afraid of the inner damage Judaism will sustain, especially from the development of a narrow nationalism within our nation against which we have already had to fight strongly even without a Jewish state.' Another article from *Ideas and Opinions* expressed Einstein's concern at the triumphalism of the Jewish state. 'Palestine', he reminded his readers, 'is not primarily a place of refuge for the Jews of Eastern Europe, but the embodiment of the reawakening corporate spirit of the whole Jewish nation.' His conclusion was that sovereignty must be shared. Israel should be ruled under a system of joint Arab-Israeli government.[14] Einstein never lived in Israel, and he turned down the offer of the Israeli presidency. He died in 1955, suffering an aneurysm as he worked on a memorandum to build more friendly relations between Israel and Egypt.

EINSTEIN'S PACIFISM

Along with Zionism, pacifism was in the 1920s Einstein's most public concern. But the content of Einstein's hostility to war is hard to pin down. Another pacifist, Hem Day, has described Einstein's 'relative pacifism', and this phrase is apposite.[15] Einstein's public views changed, during the First World War and again before the Second. During 1914–18, Einstein was no supporter of the war, yet he added his name to a relatively even-handed petition which called on the state to fight for victory but to eschew territorial expansion. He was not rewarded for this moderation. In 1918, Einstein's name was added to a list of thirty-one prominent pacifists banned from travelling abroad. Later he identified the League of Nations as the most important means to achieve international peace. Yet his opinion of the League varied. In 1923, he resigned from the League of Nations Committee of Intellectual Co-operation, in protest at the League's inefficiency; in 1924, he rejoined. At times, Einstein spoke in defence of pacifism as an absolute virtue. All wars were bad. The military system was 'that worst outcrop of herd life'.[16] At other times, Albert Einstein would defend the logic of the just war. This was his position in the 1930s when he argued for military opposition to Hitler's Nazi state.

Occasionally, Einstein would support pacifism as an absolute good. In 1939, Mahatma Gandhi enjoyed his seventieth birthday. Einstein expressed his admiration for Gandhi's values of peaceful struggle: 'Generations to come, it may be, will scarce believe that such a one as this has ever in flesh and blood walked upon this earth.'[17] Yet like most pacifists, Einstein was aware that militarism could not be defeated by good wishes alone. What should pacifists do when faced by an armed and aggressive enemy? In 1934, he elaborated his vision of 'Active Pacifism': 'As long as armies exist, any serious conflict will lead to war. A pacifism which does not actively fight against the armament of nations is and must remain impotent.' Such doctrines led directly to Einstein's 1939 famous letter to Franklin Roosevelt. With three other scientists, Joliot Curie, Enrico Fermi and Leo Szilard, Einstein encouraged the US government to develop nuclear arms:

> Sir: Some recent work . . . leads me to expect that the element uranium may be turned into a new and important source of energy in the immediate future . . . It is conceivable that extremely powerful bombs of a new type may . . . be constructed. A single bomb of this type, carried by a boat or exploded in a port, might very well destroy the whole port together with some of the surrounding territory. However, such bombs may very well prove too heavy for transportation by air.[18]

Thus it was Albert Einstein the committed pacifist who gave the American state a strong push in the direction of atomic war. After the war, he is said to have declared, 'If I knew they were going to do this, I would have become a shoemaker.' He later returned to pacifism, and during the Cold War Einstein helped to found the Pugwash peace movement along with Bertrand Russell, the mathematician and philosopher.

Albert Einstein was not the only pacifist who trod this route at a time of crisis from absolute pacifism to a partial defence of anti-fascist violence. This chapter has already mentioned his friendship with Friedrich Adler, who followed his father Victor into the leading ranks of social democracy, becoming the editor of *Das Volksrecht* (People's Justice), the main Swiss socialist daily paper. Adler was a junior lecturer in physics at Zurich when Einstein was a student there. He published studies of the physicists Mach and Ostwald, two nineteenth-century scientists who are often seen as formative influences on Einstein's theory of relativity. During the First World War Frederick Adler was horrified by the Austrian workers' apparent support for the slaughter. His small group of socialist war resisters was going nowhere. Adler responded to his isolation by taking arms against the war and, in October 1916, he assassinated the Austrian Prime Minister Count Stürgkh. On trial, Adler refused to plead for his life. He defended his action as a deliberate gesture against the war: 'While we still live in an age of barbarity which recognises the necessity to kill and to be killed, while the age of humanity has still not arrived, then murder must not be a privilege of the rulers; then force shall at least serve the idea of humanity.'[19] Albert Einstein undoubtedly had access to the text of Friedrich Adler's speech. He submitted testimony on Adler's behalf, while Adler used Einstein's theory of relativity as one justification for his actions! Sentenced to seventeen years' imprisonment, Friedrich Adler was eventually released under a general amnesty following the collapse of the Austrian empire in 1918.

Albert Einstein's pacifism was more consistent than that of his 'old friend'. He was less of a protagonist in events, and more of a commentator by temperament. There is no suggestion that Einstein ever considered taking up the armed struggle himself against war. Yet he had no more belief than Adler in the moral power of non-violence. For this reason, Einstein's doctrine of 'Active Pacifism' amounted to a decisive rejection of the principle of non-violence. He had no more fundamental belief in pacifism than he did in Zionism. Faced by the rise of fascism in the 1930s, Albert Einstein came to the conclusion that if fascism and war were to receive any significant challenge then something more than words would be required. Aggressive militarism could only be defeated by an anti-militarist war.

EINSTEIN'S SOCIALISM

Like so many others of his generation, Albert Einstein found that he was forced to choose in a world which was hurtling towards the extremes. In his character, in his beliefs, in his friendships and in his temperament, Einstein found himself on the left. He was for the workers against the bosses, for culture against ignorance, for free-thought against the weight of tradition, and for the communists (always) against the fascists. Although less well known than other aspects of his philosophy, Einstein's socialism was as consistent as the other pillars of his world view. In 1918, he welcomed the German revolution which brought an end to the war. Following the declaration of the republic, Einstein wrote to his sister in Lucerne, 'A great thing has happened . . . To think that I have lived to see it! No bankruptcy is too great that one wouldn't gladly accept it for the sake of this compensation. Here, militarism and the Privy Councillor nonsense have been thoroughly liquidated.' Because of his pacifism, Einstein had already acquired a reputation as a socialist. He spoke to communist students, who set up a council modelled on the soldiers' and workers' councils of 1918. Einstein also showed no regret in lecturing in the 1920s at the Communist Party's Marxist Workers College, on 'What a Worker should know of the Theory of Relativity'.[20]

In *Ideas and Opinions*, there is an early attack on the values of contemporary capitalism. 'Can anyone imagine Moses, Jesus or Gandhi armed with the money-bags of Carnegie?' The book also contains an important article which Einstein wrote for the American magazine *Monthly Review* in 1949. 'Why Socialism?' began by emphasising the destructiveness of capitalism: 'It is only a slight exaggeration to say that mankind constitutes even now a planetary community of production and consumption. The economic anarchy of capitalist society as it exists today is, in my opinion, the real source of the evil.' Einstein explained man's alienation in terms of workers' exploitation at the point of production:

> The owner of the means of production is in a position to purchase the labour power of the worker. By using the means of production, the worker produces new goods which become the property of the capitalist. What the worker receives is determined not by the real

> value of the goods he produces, but by his minimum needs and by the capitalists' requirement for labour power in relation to the number of workers competing for jobs . . . The result of these developments is an oligarchy of private capital, the enormous power of which cannot be effectively checked even by a democratically organised political society.[21]

The article concluded by arguing that 'there is only one way to eliminate these grave evils, namely through the establishment of a socialist economy'. Einstein's thinking was clearly influenced by Karl Marx's *Capital*. For such an unorthodox physicist, his was a surprisingly orthodox socialism.

Over the years, a number of Marxists have returned the compliment, expressing their sympathy for Einstein's revolutionary approach to science. The Russian revolutionary Lenin famously addressed issues of contemporary physics in his book, *Materialism and Empirio-Criticism* (1908), a critique of Mach's followers Lunacharsky and Bogdanov.[22] In the 1920s, Lenin observed that the academic enthusiasm for Einstein was no proof that Einstein was wrong: 'The theory of Einstein . . . has already been seized upon by a vast number of bourgeois intellectuals of all countries; it should be noted that this applies not only to Einstein, but to a number, if not the majority, of the great reformers of natural science since the end of the nineteenth century.' His article followed a piece by Leon Trotsky in the philosophical journal *Pod Znamenem Marksizma* (Under the Banner of Marxism). In this earlier article, Trotsky had noted that Einstein's work had been used to defend philosophical notions of idealism, the argument that consciousness comes before matter. This interpretation Trotsky saw as incompatible with the strong realism implied in Einstein's approach. Trotsky encouraged Marxists to study and defend Einstein's theories.[23] His support for relativity was echoed by Lenin. In 1936, the Communist philosopher Tommy Jackson stressed the similarity between Marx's dialectic and Einstein's belief that there is nothing fixed in the cosmos: 'What Einstein has proved herein is simply what the Dialectical Materialist has always contended – that human knowledge is knowledge of things from the human point of view and that any pretension to absolute knowledge, to "final truths of the last instance", is only an absolute pretence.'[24] At about the same time, the British scientist John Haldane emphasised the similarity between relativity and Engels's comments on physics. 'Had [Engels's] books been known to my contemporaries,' he concluded, 'it was clear that we should have found it easier to accept relativity and quantum theory.'[25] More recently, Paul McGarr has explained Einstein's theory of relativity as part of a general process whereby 'science itself' pushes scientists towards dialectics as the most convincing basis on which to construct a dynamic understanding of the world.[26]

However, the question of Einstein's socialism is overshadowed, as it was for many others of his generation, by the related question of what he made of Russian society. For most of Albert Einstein's adult life, socialism was equated with the state system in the Soviet Union. Yet to say that the left and Stalinism were the same thing was to lose the crucial socialist vision of a workers' society, and to reduce socialism to another brand of totalitarianism, a vicious form of state capitalist rule. Those activists who defended the Soviet Union submitted themselves to a form of self-censorship. Not thousands but millions of committed Marxists deliberately closed their eyes to the crimes that were being committed in the name of the working class. We can understand why they did so. The Soviet Union seemed at the time to be the sole obstacle to the terrible threat of German fascism. It is not surprising that many socialists in the West attempted to justify individual Soviet actions. Yet the effect of this self-censorship was disastrous. Many thousands of militants, discovering the true nature of the Soviet system, turned their back not just on Stalinism but on all forms of socialism. The moral standing of the left was reduced – and has not been fully recovered since.

Einstein corresponded with Russian physicists and was drawn into the debates over the condition of Russian society. Yet the quality of his judgements varied. In 1930, he signed a petition to allow Leon Trotsky to emigrate to Germany. In that same year, he also supported a letter against the show trials. Yet in 1931, Einstein rescinded his criticisms and in 1937 he publicly defended the Moscow trials. Later, in his *Monthly Review* article, Einstein addressed the relationship between the Soviet state system, and the socialism that he wanted to see: 'It is necessary to remember that a planned economy is not yet socialism. A planned economy as such may be accompanied by the complete enslavement of the individual. The achievement of socialism requires the solution of some extremely difficult socio-political problems.'[27] For Einstein, this was unusually opaque language.

He said nothing here which was incompatible with the position of a fellow-travelling supporter of the Soviet Union.

In his uncertain attitude towards the Russian state system, Albert Einstein can be compared to another contemporary, the socialist playwright Bertolt Brecht. Like Einstein, Brecht was an unorthodox thinker, profiting from the tolerant atmosphere of Weimar Germany. Brecht learned his socialism from the most diverse of sources, in particular from the dissident Marxist Karl Korsch.[28] In conversation with Korsch, Walter Benjamin and others, Bertolt Brecht expressed on many occasions his misgivings as to the nature of the Stalinist system. Later, he was in no way pacified by the Russian takeover of East Germany. His poem, 'The Solution', was written in response to the uprising of 1953, and gives a clear sense of his own private support for the protests against Stalinist rule:

> After the uprising of the 17th June
> The Secretary of the Writers Union
> Had leaflets distributed in the Stalinallee
> Stating that the people
> Had forfeited the confidence of the government
> And could win it back only
> By redoubled efforts. Would it not be easier
> In that case for the government
> To dissolve the people
> And elect another?[29]

Despite these important expressions of private dissidence, Bertolt Brecht allied himself with the German Communist Party. Faced with the reality of Nazi rule in Germany, Brecht decided that the most important responsibility was to play down his criticism of Stalin's regime. Later, during the 1953 crisis, Brecht failed to support the workers' uprising. At no time did he publish any declaration on behalf of the protests, nor did he make this poem available. Much like Einstein's equivocal pacifism, Brecht's was only a relative anti-Stalinism.

Albert Einstein remained, like Bertolt Brecht, a fellow-traveller of the Communist Party. Having made public announcements of faith in the 1930s, he undoubtedly rose in the estimate of the Stalinist state. In 1937, he attempted to cash in on his high standing, by appealing on behalf of the German exiles, Alexander Weissberg and Friedrich Houtermans. His appeal had no effect. In 1938, both men were part of a group of 800 German, Austrian and Hungarian anti-fascists who were handed over to Hitler, as part of the renewal of diplomatic ties between Moscow and Berlin.[30] Despite such setbacks, Einstein did not at any stage retract his support for the show trials. The space for a dissident socialism, independent of the great-power rivalries, was closed by the events of 1933. Einstein was unable to comprehend that his own support for Stalinism diminished his socialism.

CONCLUSION

This chapter has examined Albert Einstein's politics, as a man of the 1920s and 1930s. At each stage his beliefs – his Zionism, pacifism and socialism – have been compared to those of his contemporaries. Some readers may feel that the picture has been simplified. There is no doubt that inside Einstein's writing and speeches there are statements which complicate the picture here. For example, on his arrival in America, Einstein made a number of claims about the wonders of American capitalist society, which sit uneasily with the account given here of his socialism.[31] Yet if these gestures are placed in context, then the impression given is of someone thanking his hosts on his escape from Nazi Germany. A generous turn of phrase can be forgiven in a man fleeing for his life. Once these speeches are placed in their historical situation, and Einstein's life is seen as a whole, there can be no doubt that these three themes were the most important recurring messages of Einstein's public life.

The picture which emerges is of a man trapped by the contradictions of his age, and unable to find a clear route through the claims of conflicting loyalties. One conclusion might be to see Einstein as a political failure. This is the approach of Albrecht Fölsing and Stephen Hawking, who describe Einstein's 'confusion' in political affairs. This chapter has seen the contradictions in Einstein's thinking as the contradiction of the times. Of the political writers mentioned here, neither Walter Benjamin, nor Friedrich Adler, nor Bertolt Brecht, managed better solutions to the problems which tormented Einstein's life. In his physics, Einstein was ahead of his contemporaries. In his political philosophy, the man was no better and no worse than his milieu. We can remember Albert Einstein today as one of the world's great scientists and a lifelong opponent of discrimination in all its forms.

TEN

The Battle of Cable Street

The battle of Cable Street which took place on the boundary between central and East London on 4 October 1936, has entered popular memory as the decisive moment at which British fascism was stopped. On the day, a crowd of up to 150,000 people prevented Sir Oswald Mosley's British Union of Fascists (BUF) from marching east through the crowded Jewish and working-class residential areas of the East End. This victory has been celebrated not only as a moment in the history of anti-fascism, but also as a key juncture in the history of the working-class movement in Britain. The purpose of this chapter is to explore the phenomenal interest which still surrounds this event. First, the chapter will describe briefly what took place on the day; second, it will discuss the overlay of myth and memory, which is said to have distorted the historical memory of the event; and third, the chapter will consider the contemporary relevance of Cable Street.

CABLE STREET AND GARDINER'S CORNER

The immediate background to Cable Street lay in a previous defeat suffered by the BUF. At Olympia in June 1934, Mosley's fascists had attempted to stage a major public meeting, in order to establish their respectable credentials. Yet Olympia proved in practice to be a major reverse. Several hundred anti-fascists forged tickets, or sent letters, to get in. There they heckled the fascist speakers, and were violently ejected for their pains. Many people were badly injured, and these scenes discredited fascism before its audience. After Olympia, the BUF went into near-critical decline. Such prominent supporters as Robert Forgan (a long-standing Mosley loyalist) and Lord Rothermere (owner of the *Daily Mail*) withdrew their support. BUF membership fell from 40,000 to 5,000 by the summer of 1935. Eventually, the BUF was rescued by a successful change in tactics.

After Olympia, the fascists gave up on their previous desire to win a significant middle-class audience, and reoriented their organisation towards London's working-class East End. The fascists aimed now to recruit workers who were ground down by years of unemployment, and who were attracted towards anti-Semitism as an explanation for their own misery. One result of this new tactic was that from 1935, the British Union of Fascists came to rely much more heavily on naked racism. Helped by the success of its latest approach, the BUF established new branches in Stepney, Limehouse and Bethnal Green. Indeed by spring 1936, the fascists claimed to have 4,000 members in Shoreditch alone. It was in the context of this seeming revival of fortunes that Oswald Mosley announced a huge demonstration that would march from the Royal Mint to Aldgate and then Limehouse, to take place on 4 October 1936.

Anti-fascists determined to oppose this march. At the heart of the resistance was a generation of East End Jews who aligned themselves with the Communist Party of Great Britain. The Communist-led Jewish People's Council (JPC) launched a monster petition to have the march banned. Individual members of the Labour Party, the Labour League of Youth, the Independent Labour Party, and the many local trade unions, all backed this demand. Yet it was the support of the London Committee of the Communist Party that proved decisive to the success of Cable Street. Despite its policy to support a rival Aid Spain rally in Trafalgar Square, the committee came under increasing pressure from the many rank-and-file communists in the JPC, and agreed to back the protests – with just two days to go. As barricades were established and chalk notices went up urging people to turn out, the leaders of the Labour Party and the Jewish Board of Deputies grew worried and called on local people to avoid the protest. George Lansbury, MP for Poplar, former leader of the Labour Party and one-time council activist, urged East Enders to stay at home.

Despite these warnings, on the day at least 100,000 people showed up to block Gardiner's Corner, the hub of any route from the City eastwards. There, they were attacked by around 6,000 mounted and foot police who attempted to fight a way through for the 1,900-or-so members of the British Union of Fascists. These figures are the police estimates – the real disparity between the sizes of the two camps was probably even greater on the day. At one point, a tram

1. British fascism (I): the 1930s, Mosley's supporters guard their headquarters in Durham. Several local offices were shut down during the fascist crisis that followed the defeat at Cable Street. (Durham University Library)

2. British fascism (II): post-1945, a Union Movement street-stall. British fascism failed to take off in the postwar years. When the tradition recovered, the Union Movement was overtaken by a rival fascist party, the National Front. (*Searchlight*)

3. British fascism (III): the National Front parades through Wood Green in North London, 1977. At this demonstration supporters of the Front were pelted with running shoes. (*Searchlight*)

4. John Heartfield, *As it was in the Middle Ages . . . So in the Third Reich*, 1934. The visual comparison between the swastika and the medieval rack was used in both Socialist and Communist posters at this time. (Photo: AKG, London)

5. Tom Mann Centuria, early British volunteers for the International Brigades in Spain. (*Searchlight*)

6. Rock Against Racism stickers: Love Music, Hate Racism. RAR was the forerunner of the Anti-Nazi League and was launched in the winter of 1976/7. (Private Collection)

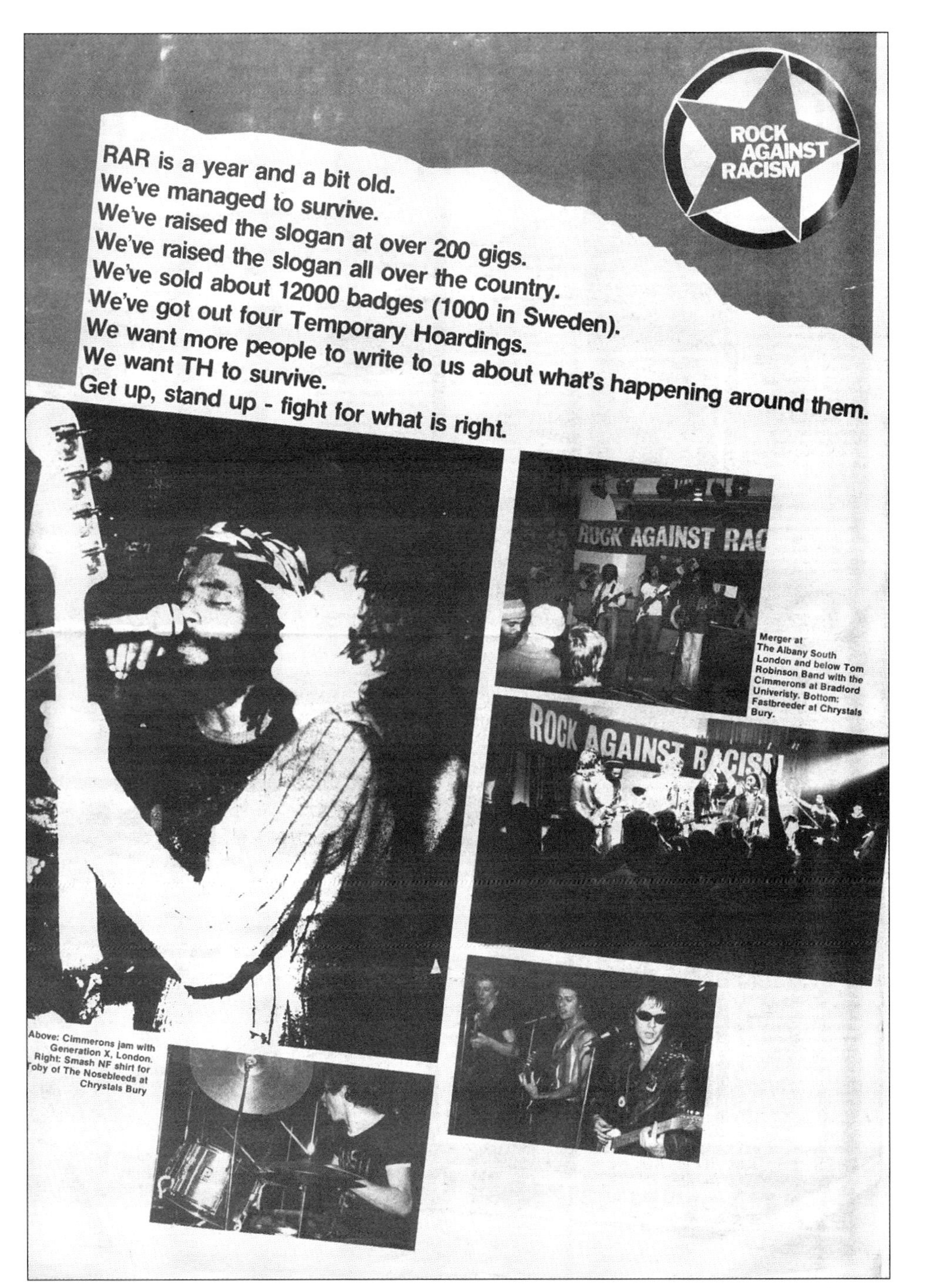

ROCK AGAINST RACISM

RAR is a year and a bit old.
We've managed to survive.
We've raised the slogan at over 200 gigs.
We've raised the slogan all over the country.
We've sold about 12000 badges (1000 in Sweden).
We've got out four Temporary Hoardings.
We want more people to write to us about what's happening around them.
We want TH to survive.
Get up, stand up - fight for what is right.

Merger at The Albany South London and below Tom Robinson Band with the Cimmerons at Bradford Univeristy. Bottom: Fastbreeder at Chrystals Bury.

Above: Cimmerons jam with Generation X, London. Right: Smash NF shirt for Toby of The Nosebleeds at Chrystals Bury

7. *Temporary Hoarding*, winter 1977/8. *Temporary Hoarding* was the magazine of Rock Against Racism. (Private Collection)

8. 'Southall Kids are Innocent', Rock Against Racism leaflet, April–May 1979. This leaflet was produced following the Southall demonstration at which Blair Peach was killed by members of the Metropolitan Police Special Patrol Group. (Private Collection)

driver brought his vehicle on to the scene. Encouraged by the protesters, he left his tram in the middle of the junction, blocking the road and preventing the police from using horses to clear it. When the police charges failed to make headway, they turned their attention instead towards Cable Street. This was a much narrower, residential working-class street. In aiming for there, the police hoped to circumvent the main blockade and force a new way through for the fascists. Yet the problem that police officers faced was that anti-fascists had rumbled the police's plan. Barricades were established all along Cable Street. As the police charged, people living in the adjoining houses began to throw projectiles down on to the police. Local legend describes the flurry of missiles, beginning with water and rags, then bric-a-brac, clothes, bricks, possibly a piano, clearly anything at all that came to hand. Blocked in the road, knocked off their feet, the police were unable to advance. Several officers were witnessed vainly attempting to surrender to the anti-fascist crowd. When the police failed in Cable Street, and there was no longer any possibility of allowing the fascists to advance, Sir Philip Game of the Metropolitan Police ordered the fascists to turn round. They then marched westwards to the Embankment and dispersed.[1] For the many anti-fascists assembled at Gardiner's Corner, victory celebrations began that evening.

CABLE STREET: NECESSARY MYTH OR COLLECTIVE TRUTH?

In a 1997 article for the journal *Changing English*, Harold Rosen has examined the ambiguous nature of memory. Starting from his own recollections of Cable Street, Rosen considered both the fictitious nature of memory and also its truthful content. In his words, 'a constructed narrative is designed to deliver meaning and dramatic closure is a crucial part of the process . . . [but] Cable Street happened and thousands of ordinary folk did actually stop a fascist march'. This chapter will argue that Harold Rosen was right to stress the ambiguous and subjective nature of personal memory. But to describe memory as myth is to suggest that memory is primarily an artificial and retrospective conduct:

> If you are lucky, there are moments in your life which are especially and uniquely illuminated. They stand out from the rest

> of your life as bright icons, huge representative symbols which give meaning to how you have lived, which is why we purify such moments, polish them, and in our heads, play them over again and again. Cable Street was one of those moments for the Left in the Thirties. We gave it a mythological and heroic dimension.[2]

It seems to me that if such an account is to be taken as an example of the general process of memory then the result may be off-balance. Memory is not predominantly mythic. Individuals' memories may have this character, but collective memory, the contested memory of the majority, has a truthful content.

What is 'collective memory'? The writer who first coined the term was the French writer Maurice Halbwachs. A follower of Emile Durkheim's collectivist sociology, Halbwachs was writing to challenge what he considered the excessive individualism of academic psychology. Halbwachs addressed the role of family, religion and social class in generating the memories that individuals believed were their own. His argument was that society shapes individual memory. In the absence of individual memory, present-day concerns fill the gap: 'An individual who does not find in his memory the remembrance of a case similar to the one that is the source of confusion would look to the people in his midst.' Writers influenced by Halbwachs have tended to describe collective memory as an arbitrary phenomenon shaped by the interplay of social forces. His use of the term was perhaps less optimistic than the use here. My argument is that the creation of collective memory is a process, and that there is a limit to the distorting influence played by latter-day concerns.[3]

The important point is that memory is shared. By exchanging memories and also by comparing our own memories to alternative accounts of the past we come to a different and more complete account. What takes place is a process. Memory is compared to collective memory, and in this way memories are revised. False memories are demonstrated to be false, and for this reason they come out of circulation. More accurate memories are retained. Although individual memory may be mythic, to focus on the individual is to miss the collective experience. Out of the total process of remembering, memory becomes history. The direction of this process is towards a more accurate account of what actually took place. Collective memory approximates towards a correct, if often partial, account of events which actually took place. For this reason it is inappropriate to describe memory as myth. Memory, especially collective memory, can be just as much truth as myth. Following the example of Harold Rosen's article, it is appropriate to use the memory of Cable Street as an example to demonstrate this more general point.

In the immediate aftermath of Cable Street there was a spontaneous process of remembering and retelling. Initially this was no more than individuals telling their own stories. These stories did have a mythic content, but they also possessed a great deal of truth. One participant, Phil Piratin, later the Communist MP for Stepney, described the men and women of the East End showing their friends where they had fought. For the most part, Piratin suggested, these stories were told by the people who were actually there:

> The people were changed. Their heads seemed to be held higher, and their shoulders were squarer – and the stories they told! Each one of them was a 'hero' – many of them were. In the barber shops there was only one topic of conversation for the next fortnight. Even the racing lads slipped up on placing their bets in time for the races while in keen conversation as to the part they played on that Sunday. People from the docks and the factories would take their workmates who had not been in Stepney to show them the scenes, and where they had played their part.[4]

Very quickly the story of Cable Street ceased to be simply the private property of the individuals who took part. There was, for example, a 'Communist' story of 1936. This can be traced through the Communist Party's newspaper, the *Daily Worker*. On 5 October, the day after Cable Street, the paper led with the banner headline: 'Mosley Did Not Pass: East London Routs The Fascists'. The *Daily Worker* rejoiced that the British Union of Fascists had been defeated: 'Sir Oswald Mosley's challenge to East London yesterday resulted in the most humiliating rout of the Blackshirts.' The paper insisted that Cable Street was a popular mobilisation. It described the 'hundreds of thousands' who took part: 'the whole of East London's working class rallied as one man (and as one woman) to bar the way to the Blackshirts. Jew and Gentile, docker and garment worker, railwayman and cabinet maker, turned out in their thousands to show that they have no use for Fascism.' The success of the blockade was put down to the work of the Communist Party: 'the Fascists were due to assemble at Royal Street at 2:30, while the Communist Party had appealed to the workers to throng Aldgate and Cable Street at 2 pm'.[5]

Phil Piratin's book, *Our Flag Stays Red*, was published in 1948 and quickly became the fullest statement of the Communist history of Cable Street. By this time, Piratin was the Member of Parliament for Stepney – one of just two Communist MPs in Britain. The book was written as a celebration of the events of 4 October, and also as a response to what was then a revival of fascism and anti-Semitism in Hackney and the East End. The revival is described elsewhere in this book. Given the moment at which it was published, Piratin's account was only likely to be celebratory. It stressed the huge numbers of people involved in Cable Street, and the success of their action. In his words, 'The fascists lined up, saluted their leader, and marched through the deserted City to the Embankment, where they dispersed. The working class had won the day.'[6] Again and again Phil Piratin highlighted the role of the Communist Party in presiding over and organising the events of that day: 'The Communist Party had shown itself capable of leading the working class in keeping the fascists off the Stepney streets when the Government and the police, ignoring the requests of the London citizens, had attempted to foist the fascists upon them.'[7]

Such a memory was contested. Most obviously, fascists had their own recollections of 4 October 1936. The two main fascist newspapers, *Blackshirt* and *Action*, both attempted to present an alternative fascist story of Cable Street. In the fascist press the actual events of 4 October faded out of sight. The BUF endeavoured to ignore the defeat at Cable Street by making the rival claim that East End fascism survived beyond 1936.[8] The issue of *Action*, for example, which came out on 10 October 1936, featured a front-page article by William Joyce: 'The Organisation of Terror'. Joyce maintained that Cable Street was an act of outsiders: 'the Oriental mob', 'Red Terror', 'Jewish Communists', 'the Church-burners International', 'Red Barbarism', 'the few thousand Communists employing methods of terror'. Inside *Action*, there was a special four-page supplement with articles by E.D. Randall, H. Sheppard, and John Beckett. Beckett followed Joyce's line, arguing that using 'Moscow Gold', the Communist Party had paid for 'up to 10,000 imported hooligans'. But Beckett also put a second argument, that Cable Street was a fascist victory. The publicity following 4 October, he suggested, had helped the British Union of Fascists: 'the banning of the demonstration . . . has secured the greatest amount of publicity yet given to Fascism in this country.' Beckett claimed that the fascists recruited 5,000 new members within 48 hours.[9]

The articles in *Blackshirt* followed Beckett's lead. They insisted that popular support for fascism after 4 October had reversed the defeat which took place at Cable Street itself. The *Blackshirt* of 10 October 1936 ran a headline, 'For Alien or for Briton?' It claimed that 'indignant crowds of working people have swept away Communist orators from the streets, while the most intense enthusiasm has been shown at every National Socialist meeting'. At this stage the *Blackshirt* was both hyperbolic and vague: the paper could not give a single concrete example to demonstrate this claimed spontaneous wave of popular support. Later in the month, however, the paper did have a success to trumpet. On 14 October, Mosley staged a large rally in Shoreditch, with up to 10,000 supporters present. The *Blackshirt* of 17 October described the rally as 'the greatest Blackshirt march ever seen'. It claimed that 100,000 fascists were there. Even one week later the Shoreditch rally remained the lead story: now it was claimed that 30,000 people had been present, still enough, the paper believed, to prove that the East End was really Mosley's.[10]

The important point is that the fascist memory of 1936 did not, and does not, cut. Cable Street was a fascist defeat. By stressing fascist success *after* 4 October, the fascist newspapers were tacitly accepting their defeat on the day. They lost and they admitted it. To blame this defeat on outsiders, as Joyce did, was equally risible. Of the 150,000 or so people who congregated at Gardiner's Corner, the great majority came from the East End. Many of them were Jewish, although some were not. Many were Communists, although many more were not. What is clear is that the great majority of people at Cable Street were local. Joyce's attacks were little more than the staple fictions of fascist imagination.

As Cable Street was in reality a fascist defeat, so it has been seen ever since. One would be hard pressed to find a non-fascist who agreed with the fascist account of 4 October 1936. On the other hand, the Piratin version of Cable Street was, and has been, broadly accepted. It has been used as the basis for a whole series of commemorative activities: in several plays, including Arnold Wesker's play *Chickensoup With Barley*; in poetry and television documentary; in Alan Gibbons's children's book, *Street of Tall People*; from the anniversary celebrations in 1986 and 1996, to the large wall mural on Cable Street itself.[11] Much as the anti-fascists 'won' on 4 October, so their history of 4 October has become the one which 'won' inside society. The failure of the fascist memory of Cable Street can be explained in all manner of different ways. It is important that fascist parties were small and marginalised after 1945. They did not have the influence to spread their memory of 1936. However, it is also important that the fascist account of 1936 was inconsistent and dishonest. It dodged the question of 'who won at Gardiner's Corner?' As a result, it was simply not convincing. A memory existed, but it contradicted known fact, and was dropped.

There has been a parallel process inside and within the left-wing account of 1936. In the late 1970s, and in response to the successes of the National Front, a new generation of anti-fascists emerged, often in competition with the anti-fascists of the Communist Party. These new anti-fascists generated their own memories of Cable Street. In the magazine *International Socialism*, for example, Colin Sparks suggested that the leaders of the Communist Party were initially hostile to the demonstration at Cable Street. According to Sparks, 'they tried a very sordid compromise'. He pointed out that as late as Wednesday 31 September 1936, just four days before Cable Street, the Communist Party's 'line' was to call for unity with the Labour Party. The means to achieve this was through a 'Popular Front' demonstration in Trafalgar Square. Sparks quoted the *Daily Worker* of 30 September, insisting that Trafalgar Square must come before the occupation of Gardiner's Corner: 'A call has been sent out by the London District of the Communist Party for workers to go in their thousands to Trafalgar Square, and after the demonstration to march through East London's streets to show their hatred of Mosley's support for the fascist attack on democracy in Spain.'[12] Sparks's account of Cable Street has since been confirmed by the memoirs of Joe Jacobs, in 1936 a leading member of Stepney Communist Party. Jacobs described the actual arguments within the local party branches in the run up to 4 October. He suggested that the party's decision to back the demonstration was taken on the evening of 30 September. The crucial turning-point, Jacobs suggested, came when Harold Cohen, a member of the Party, and the leader of the Ex-Servicemen's Anti-Fascist Association, insisted that the Communist Party take full part.[13]

The result has been a transformed left-wing memory of Cable Street. Published accounts of 4 October stress the role of spontaneous local anger. Most histories of 1936 now downplay the role of the Communist Party as an organised body. Instead, they emphasise the extent of local feeling. The demonstrators are seen to have been fighting not only against the police and the fascists, but also against leaders on their own side who were unwilling to lead militant action. The commemorative pamphlet *The Battle of Cable Street*, produced by the Cable Street Group for the 60th anniversary, revolves around a series of interviews with local activists: Piratin, Jacobs, Bill Fishman, Charlie Goodman, Jim Wolveridge, and so on. The format is fragmented, but celebratory. The typical story is somewhere between Joyce Goodman's, 'Now a few years later I met Charlie, my husband. And one of the first questions he asked me was: "Where were you on October 4th?" Everybody laughs at this, but this is what East Enders asked themselves in those days',[14] and Sam Berkowitz's, 'Without the Communist Party there might have been a mêlée and a riot but it wouldn't have been a disciplined riot which is the difference between a riot and an achievement.'[15] Similarly, in D.S. Lewis's *Illusions of Grandeur*, the real 'heroes' of Cable Street are the Jewish People's Council and the Ex-Servicemen's Movement, ad hoc local groups sympathetic to the Communist Party, but less concerned about alliances with Labour, closer to the actual fears of East End Jews, and more radical as a result.[16]

In short, then, there has been a process. Memories have arisen, been contested and accepted, modified or rejected. The result is a fuller memory of the past. And this collective memory comes to shape the memory of the individual. Having interviewed a few of those who took part in Cable Street, it is clear to me that many exaggerate their own importance to the events which took place that day. One witness was then a member of the Labour League of Youth. He told me that he had been central to the events of the day. His account was implausible, his own role and significance were clearly exaggerated. He insisted that he had stopped the police attack at Gardiner's Corner. He also told me that he had stopped the tram and thus built the crucial barricade:

> The week before I spoke at eight outdoor meetings. Our group had enormous numbers of people at Gardiner's Corner . . . Standing next to me was a young woman. The police caught her on the side of her face, left her bleeding. I got round the other side and pushed him out of the stirrup. Then everyone got round him, kicking and punching. That's when the police withdrew . . . The old fashioned trams came round here. I took a few people and went up to the driver. I said to him, 'If you was to stop the tram here, it could cause complete confusion.' He said, 'I'm a trade union man.' He stopped the tram.

But it is also clear that personal accounts of the past have been shaped by rival memories. They are enriched, and more accurate. The same man, who was in real life probably standing bored among the crowds at Gardiner's Corner, described to me the events at Cable Street itself. He 'remembered' the barricades. He knew that the Metropolitan Police Commissioner instructed the fascists not to march. He pointed to the feelings of the Irish dockers, the organised workers who stood beside the East End Jews.[17] This man 'knew' events which he could not have witnessed. His account was more complete, more truthful and accurate to the day as a whole because it included experiences which were not his own. Perhaps he had talked to other witnesses. Maybe he had looked at the large mural now erected on Cable Street itself. For whatever reason his memories of 4 October 1936 had been shaped by other people's recollections, and were more complete as a result.

So then, was Cable Street a myth? Was it even a 'necessary myth'? Cable Street was an event. It actually happened. It was a fact. When individual participants remember Cable Street they do not have a total and accurate image of the whole event. But their memories are stories of something which did happen. And even though these stories can be distorted over time, the process of change and correction can also lead to more accurate accounts. When memory ceases to be the act of a lone individual and starts to become something collective, something contested, then the result comes closer to what actually happened in the past. Individual accounts remain partial, and often obscured. But collective memory is more truth than myth.

CABLE STREET: CONTEMPORARY LESSONS

Having described what I see as the fundamental truth of Cable Street, expressed as it is in private memories and in the collective memory of the event, it is appropriate to conclude by restating the lessons of that event – as they would have occurred to the activists who took part. The first striking point is that fascism did not emerge from individuals, from a failure of education, or from an abundance of individual prejudice. The battle of Cable Street took place towards the end of the Depression. The reason why Mosley targeted the East End was that in the aftermath of the Wall Street crash, this was an area of poverty, unemployment and despair. Around one-fifth of the populations of Shoreditch and Stepney were living in absolute poverty. Having briefly observed a fascist march through the East End, Phil Piratin observed that Mosley's supporters were the poorest of the poor: 'These people, like most in the East End, were living miserable, squalid, lives. Their homes were slums, many were unemployed. Those at work were often in low paid jobs.'[18]

A second conclusion to make from these events is that no matter how desperate things seem, fascism can always be beaten. For trade unionists living in Europe in the 1930s, life seemed to be a story of ongoing defeat. The German workers were crushed without resistance in 1933. Austrian workers rose against fascism in Vienna in 1934, but were slaughtered. Cable Street itself took place at the very beginning of the long defeat of the Spanish left in the civil war. Within a general picture of working-class defeat, British fascism enjoyed the additional advantage of patronage from wide sections of the British establishment. Oswald Mosley's backers included Lord Rothermere, William Morris of Morris Motors, and Sir Leonard Lyle of Tate & Lyle. The threat of fascism seemed very powerful, very real, and it would have been easy for anti-fascists to lose heart. Yet the victory at Cable Street provided the opening to an ultimately successful four-year struggle to drive fascism out of the East End.

A third lesson is that the secret to beating fascism is in the numbers. At Hyde Park in 1934, 100,000 anti-fascists turned out to oppose 3,000 fascists. At Cable Street, around 150,000 anti-fascists outnumbered fascists by more than fifty to one. At Bermondsey, one year later, the numbers were weighted once more against the fascists. This was not just important in terms of the strategy of confrontation, but also in terms of show and confidence. Each time the effect of the huge numbers was to give heart to anti-fascists, and to further demoralise the right.

The overriding image of Cable Street is of working-class solidarity, expressed in the common visual image of the Orthodox Jew and the Catholic docker, arm in arm for the fight. This is how one activist described that day's unity: 'South Wales miners, the slate workers, they sent contingents, Sheffield steel workers, Tyneside shipbuilders, and from London docks of course, a lot of seamen jumped ships and joined the anti-fascists. Also the nurses and dockers of London hospital, the Whitechapel hospital turned out . . . White-collar workers, blue-collar workers, some from further afield. They were saving democracy.'[19] But such unity could not be forged simply in the last few days before the battle of Cable Street happened. Instead, it was the product of fifty years of agitation by socialists in the East End. As John Charlton has argued, when the dockers were on strike in 1889, their most consistent support came from Jewish garment workers.[20] Solidarity was reforged before the war, when working-class men and women campaigned together for the vote.[21] No doubt dockers and Jews campaigned together again in the general strike of 1926. So fascism was pushed back, on the basis of solidarity and class politics.

A further point to stress is the need for a political struggle against fascism. When it came to opposing Mosley on the streets, the most important organisation was the Communist Party of Great Britain. And yet the Communist Party was a strange, hybrid organisation, which came close to missing out on the day's events. The Communist Party represented the fate of the Russian Revolution in Britain, sharing the brief high and steady decline of its parent. In 1936, the main obstacle was the party's support for the Popular Front, which took the Communists away from their long-held belief in street politics. Although the Communist Party was on a detour rightwards, it was not a spent force. The party retained a link, especially to the Jewish workers of the East End.

The Communist Party retained some form of radical politics. It continued to understand the need to win people away from fascism. Indeed, the quality of British Communism was perhaps most evident in the agitation launched after October 1936, especially the housing campaign which began at Paragon Mansions in 1937. Two families with members in the BUF approached the fascists for support in their campaign against evictions. Having suffered a rebuff there, the families turned instead to the Communists to launch a defence league. With its success in preventing bailiffs from turning the families out, the word of Communist success spread. Between 1937 and 1939 the party took part in literally hundreds of housing campaigns. As Piratin records, 'the lessons did not require to be pressed home. BUF membership cards were destroyed voluntarily and in disgust . . . We were now supplementing our propaganda with positive action. The kind of people who would never come to our meetings and had stranger ideas about Communism and the Jews, learned the facts overnight and learned the real meaning of the class struggle.'[22]

The last conclusion to draw is that Cable Street is not simply a moment in past history. There are still fascist organisations in both Britain and Europe. The economic and social conditions which enabled such parties to grow in the 1930s still exist, if not in the exact same forms they took in the past. Cable Street stands as the most practical symbol possible of successful unity in the fight against fascism.

ELEVEN

The British Left and Spain

The last chapter described the battle of Cable Street, one of the proudest moments in the history of the British left. The one party which took most credit for organising this protest was the Communist Party of Great Britain, whose best face was clearly on show. If the party's intervention was shaped by the Popular Front, then this distortion was not yet decisive. The party provided organisation and leadership on the day; without the Communists, Cable Street simply could not have happened. Yet the contradictions in the party's anti-fascist politics were much more evident in the campaign on behalf of Republican Spain, which began at about the same time. What is true of the Communists is indeed true for the British left as a whole. The Spanish Civil War was a bitter, fractious defeat, and the questions over what went wrong continue to the present day.

The Spanish Popular Front began when two liberal parties – the Spanish Socialists, the Spanish Communist Party (PCE) – the Catalan Communists (PSUC) and the independent Marxist Workers' Party of Marxist Unification (or POUM), came together in an alliance to win the elections of February 1936. Five months later, in July, General Franco began his military uprising against the elected government. The outcome of his eventual victory was to turn Spain into an authoritarian and militarised state. Hundreds of thousands of workers were killed, during and above all after the left's defeat. Indeed, following his victory Spain remained a dictatorship for the next thirty-five years.[1]

Yet it would be wrong to concentrate only on the murderous consequences of Franco's coup. One positive result of his attempted coup was that it liberated the best and most generous instincts of the Spanish working class. In the first few days of the conflict, Franco's troops were pushed back by successful workers' uprisings, most famously at Barcelona in northern Spain. Two-thirds of the land in

Spain was controlled by republicans. The question of tactics then came to the fore, and revolutionary Spain divided into two camps. On the right stood the liberal parties, sections of the Spanish Socialist Party, and the Spanish Communist Party (initially a minor player on the left, whose significance grew rapidly as the war went on). This group followed the logic of the Popular Front in arguing that victory in the war required that the left should end the revolution, disarming the workers' militia and seeking an alliance with Britain and France. On the other side were the POUM and the anarchists, who insisted that the revolution was the very life-blood of the government. They argued that the republic should offer Morocco its independence, which would separate Franco's colonial troops from their leaders. The left insisted that to disarm the workers' militias would undermine the revolution, and would cause the war to be lost.

This dispute over tactics was not a gentle controversy. From the start of 1937, the Communists called for their opponents to be suppressed. In May 1937, following several months of clashes in Barcelona, the police moved in to occupy buildings held by anarchists and the POUM. Workers organised mass strikes and street battles broke out between the left and supporters of order (many of which took their lead from the Spanish Communist Party and representatives of the Communist International). Some 900 people were killed in the fighting, and in its aftermath many more were arrested and shot. Although this incident has generally been seen as a conflict between Stalinists and Trotskyists, both sides involved broad alliances. At the moment of conflict the republican right included both Social Democrats and Communists, both of which were able to build on significant middle-class support. Meanwhile, the left included both the POUM, which despite its reputation was attacked by Trotsky in exile as 'centrist', and also some anarchists, including notably the Friends of Durruti, who were critical of the main FAI-CNT syndicalist leadership.[2]

In the end, the argument was won by the republican right, which disarmed the workers, and imposed its politics on the revolutionary camp. Whatever the moral logic of the left wing in the revolution, the right-wing republicans had the backing of the Spanish Communists, and they in turn controlled the arms and supplies coming to Spain from Russia. The PCE and PSUC acted as a Trojan horse in the workers' movement. They were a 'left-wing' voice calling for the most conservative strategy. Indeed, they were able to impose their politics by their weight of arms. The great symbol of the Communists' hostility to the Spanish left was the murder of Andreas Nin, one of the leaders of the POUM. This event was later described by Jesús Hernández, at the time a leading member of the Spanish Communist Party. The PSUC claimed to have found correspondence between Nin, a lifelong anti-fascist, and Adolf Hitler! Nin was murdered without protests from any allies of the Communists.[3] Thus the government of anti-fascist unity saw its enemies among the most resolute anti-fascists, and having imprisoned or killed them, was itself destroyed by Franco.[4]

The argument here is not primarily concerned with the activities of the Spanish left, which have been examined in detail by many other writers.[5] Instead, this chapter will look critically at the activities of the several British left-wing organisations which took part in the Spanish Civil War, including the British Communist Party, its literary fellow-travellers, the Independent Labour Party (ILP) and finally the International Brigades. Quite rightly, the brigaders have gone down in left-wing history as the most extraordinary of men. Volunteers who fought for socialism and democracy, they are recognised today as heroic symbols of working-class solidarity. Yet as this paper will argue, the genuine heroism of the brigades served to legitimise a Stalinised Communism, a socialism which was hostile to the cause of revolution in Spain and elsewhere. One effect of their bravery was that the volunteers provided cover for a cause that was not their own.

BRITISH COMMUNISTS ABROAD

In every country, Communists claimed credit for the campaign to Aid Spain. The British party boasted that its work formed 'the proudest pages in our party history; it had saved the honour of the British Labour Movement'. The Communist Party certainly campaigned on behalf of the communists in Spain, but its agitation reflected both the strengths and the weaknesses of the Popular Front. Beneath such headlines as 'Neutrality is Treason', the *Daily Worker* rightly exposed the perils of non-intervention. At the 1936 Trades Union Congress, Bill Zak of the Furnishing Trades Association warned that appeasing Spanish fascism would only 'increase the audacity of the fascist powers'. An Aid Spain campaign sent medical facilities and food to the embattled republican North. The Communist Party also contributed to the formation of a British battalion of the International Brigade. As George Matthews records, 'About half of the 1,500 members of the British Battalion [were] members of the Communist Party or the Young Communist League.' Half again of the 533 who were killed were Communists. Prominent Communists among the International Brigaders included Bill Alexander, Bob Cooney, Peter Kerrigan, Will Paynter, William Rust and Sam Wild.[6]

In Oxford anti-fascists raised £1,000 for the cause. They held solidarity marches, plays were organised, and refugees provided with shelter. Although such bodies as the local Trades Council acted as official sponsor to the Aid Spain campaign, it was the local Communist Party which provided the initiative, and organised the six local volunteers who served.[7] Again, in Liverpool, the Communist Party played a key role. Some 128 people from Liverpool volunteered to fight in the Spanish Civil War. Generally, industrial workers made up the largest group of volunteers, with working-class Communists and unemployed dockers providing the largest groups of volunteers. Of the 128 volunteers, 28 were killed, including 17 in one day at Jarama. As Dave Auty records: 'The local Aid Spain movement was an alliance between the Communist Party and Young Communist League, Labour supporters and a few prominent Liberals. The Conservative Party was invited to give its support, but no Conservatives took part. Bob Tissyman was a leading supporter of the campaign. In mid-1937, a food ship was sent to Spain, for which £6,000 was raised in just two months. Collections were taken all over working-class Liverpool, and outside many factories workers handed over their pay packets unopened. Money was also raised for Spanish orphans, even after the war ended.'[8]

Yet for all the important work carried out by local Communist activists, there was a second side to the party's intervention in Spain. In January 1937, even before the suppression of the Spanish left, the English language edition of *International Press Correspondence* (distributed in England by the British Communist Party) printed an article by Michael Kolzov, on 'The Trotskyist Criminals in Spain':

> The adherents of this organisation [the POUM] were a handful of persons who had been expelled from other parties for disruption,

> swindling and theft. They collected troops of their own, and at first all went well. Then a remarkable thing became apparent. Three commanders, leading the three POUM columns, made a practice of leaving the front with their troops at the moment when fighting began . . .

The article continued for several pages, compounding accusation with slander and lie.[9] Nor was this only a matter of official Comintern sources. In May 1937, after the POUM had been banned, Claud Cockburn ('Frank Pitcairn') of the *Daily Worker* defended the action of the republican government: 'In the past, the leaders of the POUM have frequently sought to deny their complicity as agents of a Fascist cause against the People's Front. This time they are convicted out of their own mouths as clearly as their allies, operating in the Soviet Union, who confessed to the crimes of espionage, sabotage, and attempted murder against the government of the Soviet Union.' His criticisms of the so-called 'Catalonian rising' were also picked up by the British left weeklies, *Tribune* and the *New Statesman*.[10]

For the historian of anti-fascism, Claud Cockburn is a fascinating character.[11] Born in 1904, he worked for *The Times* for three years in America, and then arrived in Britain in 1933 to found a one-man satirical weekly, *The Week*. Small, poorly duplicated and printed in a near-illegible dark-brown ink, *The Week* was an unlikely success. Yet in practice it revolutionised the medium of investigative journalism. As Cockburn was later to record: 'This small monstrosity was one of the half-dozen British publications most often quoted in the press of the entire world. It included among its subscribers the foreign ministers of eleven nations, all the embassies and legations in London, all diplomatic correspondents of the principal newspapers in three continents, the leading banking and brokerage houses in London, Paris, Amsterdam and New York, a dozen members of the United States Senate, twenty or thirty members of the House of Representatives, about fifty members of the House of Commons, and a hundred or so in the House of Lords, King Edward VIII, the secretaries of the leading Trade Unions, Charlie Chaplin and the Nizam of Hyderabad.'[12] Even this impressive list neglects to mention two of *The Week*'s most prominent subscribers – Joseph Goebbels and von Ribbentrop, the German ambassador to London.

What ultimately 'made' *The Week* was Cockburn's 1936 discovery of the 'Cliveden Set', a social circle composed of affluent English Conservatives committed to peace with Germany. Cockburn's friends on *The Times* proved invaluable in creating the story, since Geoffrey Dawson, the editor of that newspaper, was said to be one of the key members of the set. A typical Cockburn report described the desire of Lords Londonderry and Lothian to send Hitler a telegram congratulating him on his occupation of the Rhineland, while other scoops condemned Halifax's winter 1937 visit to Berlin.[13] Although few historians would now see the Cliveden Set as a determining influence on the British Establishment's policy of appeasing Hitler, it does appear that this group were symptomatic of a wider malaise within their class.[14] Certainly Hitler's response to Halifax's visit was to inform his generals that the British would not oppose German expansion eastwards. The subsequent 'Hossbach Memorandum' has been described as the moment when Hitler decided to go to war.

Given Cockburn's evident left-wing politics and also his proud role as a radical journalist, it is no surprise that Harry Pollitt of the Communist Party invited him to work as a reporter for the Communist Party-backed *Daily Worker* in Spain. Whatever the eventual outcome of his journalism, it is clear that Cockburn left Britain in 1936 with a desire to write sympathetically and honestly about the struggle of the Spanish people for democracy. Indeed, his early articles are superb war journalism, conveying the life and the anger of the Republican struggle against Franco. The first began, 'By July you did not need to enter Spain to know that "something was going to happen". Ticker-tape carried news of murder by day and bombs by night, as tommy guns, automatics and bombs registered the violent answer of the Right to the February election victory over the democrats.' Cockburn's dispatches captured the mood of Spain: perfumed fascist colonels, the sad and pointless suicide of José Castillo of the Assault Guards, revolutionary artists, meetings of syndicalist railwaymen, murders by Franco's snipers, and the victory of workers' power in Barcelona.[15]

Yet by the time of the events in Barcelona of May 1937, Cockburn's language had lost its vitality. His journalism appears falsely optimistic and evidently propagandist in a way it had not been previously. His discussion of the Barcelona events is written in the lifeless prose of a Stalinist hack:

> Today, the people of Spain are discussing one thing: the message of the Communist Party radioed from a Valencia meeting of the Party to every town and village in the country on Sunday morning.
>
> This meeting will mark a stage in Spain for freedom as important and decisive as the meeting of the Communist Party in the Monumental Cinema in Madrid in the summer of 1935, when the Communist Party announced their appeals for the People's Front; as important as the manifesto issued in December 1936, when the Communist Party called for the final constitution of the regular army and of the people and the introduction of compulsory service.
>
> The actions of the Communist Party changed the course of the history of Spain. Yesterday's meeting was in the same category.

Having announced the success of Spanish Communism, Cockburn went on to convey the real substance of his report:

> There is a specially dangerous feature about the situation in Catalonia. We know now that the German and Italian agents, who poured into Barcelona ostensibly in order to 'prepare' the notorious 'Congress of the Fourth International', had one big task. It was this: They were – in co-operation with the local Trotskyists – to prepare a situation of disorder and bloodshed, in which it would be possible for the Germans and the Italians to declare that they were 'unable to exercise naval control on the Catalan coasts effectively', because of 'the disorder prevailing in Barcelona', and were, therefore, 'unable to do otherwise' than land forces in Barcelona.[16]

One excuse that could be made in Claud Cockburn's defence is that there are times when a small lie must be made in order to combat a greater evil. Yet what was the evil which the Communists prevented? The slaughter of the POUM and the destruction of working-class democracy in Spain created a cynicism and passivity among the republicans, paving the way for Franco's victory. The fact that it was a superb journalist who was made to do a hack's work only makes their decline more shocking.

FELLOW-TRAVELLERS

Claud Cockburn was just one of a generation of intellectuals attracted towards Communism in the 1930s. Indeed these were years of profound change for British Communism; from mid-1935, the British Communist Party grew at a breakneck speed. Party membership rose from 6,500 in February 1935, to 12,250 in May 1937, and 17,750 in July 1939. The Communist Party built up an impressive periphery of fellow-travellers and other supporters: 'In the year 1937–8, the Party's Central Propaganda Department issued 17 penny pamphlets of which 300,000 were sold; this was in addition to others sold by the districts.' The politics of the Popular Front implied alliance with members of the 'progressive bourgeoisie'. A number of literary organisations were established, to raise money for Spain and to win support for the Popular Front in Britain. The most important achievement in Britain was the formation of the Left Book Club. By April 1939, there were 1,200 local groups with 57,000 members. In its first ten years, the club published 6 million books – an extraordinary number.[17]

This was an impressive era of growth for the British left, but the new line also had its critics. Writing in 1938, Leon Trotsky was contemptuous of these middle-class recruits to Communism: 'A whole generation of the left intelligentsia has . . . turned its eyes eastwards and has tied . . . its fate not so much to the revolutionary working class as to a victorious revolution, which is not the same.' In a similar vein, Hugo Dewar observed that the party grew at the time of the Popular Front, and suggests that there was a connection between the dilution of the party's politics and the character of the new members who joined. Noreen Branson has replied that professional support was needed if the British Communist Party was to respond to the urgent threat of fascism.[18]

The strong pressure on authors was reflected in a famous pamphlet, *Authors Take Sides on the Spanish War*, published by *Left Review* in 1937. Instigated by Nancy Cunard, a letter was sent to several hundred British writers: 'Are you for, or against, the legal Government and the people of Republican Spain? Are you for, or against, Franco and Fascism?'. Of the 149 replies published in the pamphlet, 127 were 'FOR the Government', and only 5 'AGAINST'. The division between these two figures may be misleading. Among those counted 'NEUTRAL?' included the distinctly fascistic Vita Sackville-West and Ezra Pound.[19] There was also no place for George Orwell, who returned from witnessing the defeat of the Spanish revolution at first hand, to find that such left-wing publishers as Victor Gollancz would not print his *Homage to Catalonia*.

The two best-known literary figures associated with the Popular Front were W.H. Auden and Stephen Spender. Auden was influenced at different times by Freud (like Strachey) and Christianity, as well as the ideas of Karl Marx. On his departure for Spain in December 1936, he wrote to an old teacher, extolling the need for individual acts of conscience in the face of a powerful enemy, but also admitting some confusion as to what he should expect on his journey of self-discovery: 'I feel I ought to go; but O I do hope there are not too many surrealists there.' Auden's subsequent poem, 'Spain 1937', did not suffer from the vice of surrealism, but expressed instead an unfelt and unpersuasive existentialism: 'I am your choice, your decision: yes I am Spain.' Auden's utopia looked rather more like Edwardian England than the USSR of the Five Year plans. Communism, for Auden, was no more than a rhetorical device that he could use to highlight his personal discontents. At the same time, Stephen Spender was travelling on his own route towards Marxism. His book, *Forward From Liberalism* (1937), defended Communism as the only means to achieve a historic goal, the replacement of politics with aesthetics: 'The final aim of the civilised man must be an unpolitical age, where conditions of peace and security are conducive to a classical art, rooted not in a small oligarchy but in the lives of the whole people.'[20]

For its critics, the Communist Party's celebration of literary celebrity during the late 1930s marked a sharp turn from the earlier habits of the British party. Doctrinaire intellectuals looking only for national unity, pacifists at a time of class war, Auden, Spencer and their like packed the Popular Front platforms. Indeed, in retrospect it appears that the turn towards a new generation of liberal writers and intellectuals (occasioned by events in Spain) represented for the British party a distortion of its original politics, as significant a corruption as the demands of loyalty to Moscow. Hugh MacDiarmid's 'Third Hymn to Lenin' represents the hostile verdict of a fellow poet: 'Michael Roberts and All Angels! Auden, Spender, these bhoyos / All yellow twicers; not one of them / With a tithe of

Carlisle's courage and integrity / Unlike these pseudos I am of, not for, the working class.' Leaving aside the question of MacDiarmid's own politics (which had their own distance from the Communist Party's early and more creative Marxism) his criticism of late 1930s British Communism hits the mark. In Britain as in Spain, official Communism rapidly became a rightwards-moving force.[21]

'TROTSKYISTS'

The point has already been made that – contrary to myth – the Marxist left in Spain was not simply 'Trotskyist'. Indeed, the number of people in Spain who actually considered themselves Trotskyists in the mid-1930s was tiny. Many of these were foreigners, including the Czech Erwin Wolf, who wrote a scathing report to the International Secretariat of the Fourth International, criticising the abstract character of Trotskyist propaganda. Around fifty foreign Trotskyists fought in the POUM's 'Lenin Brigade', alongside supporters of the Italian leftist Bordiga.[22] Most of the 'Trotskyists' who were condemned so vociferously by the Spanish Communists came from a rival political tradition. It is true that one of the leaders of the POUM, Andreas Nin, had previously been a co-thinker of Trotsky's, but the gap between the two men was now vast. Leon Trotsky himself did little to bridge the divide, with his French organisation publishing articles critical of Nin for supporting the Popular Front, even after the war had begun.[23] Andreas Nin's party, the POUM, was established in 1936 out of an alliance between several currents including the Catalan-based Workers and Peasant Bloc (BOC) and the Communist Left (ICE). This was an impressive body. Having campaigned energetically for unity against fascism, the BOC-inspired Workers Alliance led the Asturian Commune of 1934, an extraordinary revolutionary alliance of Marxists and Anarchists which paved the way for the events of 1936.[24]

Rather than being simply 'Trotskyist', the POUM was far more of a heterogeneous, left-centrist organisation. Its ancestor, the BOC, had refused to take any line on international questions. Meanwhile, the POUM itself was affiliated to the so-called London Bureau, along with groups in Germany, France and Holland. It was linked in British politics to the Independent Labour Party, formerly the membership section of the British Labour Party, now inhabiting a political space on the spectrum somewhere between reform and revolution. Ironically, one of the most vivid and critical sources for the politics of the Independent Labour Party is George Orwell, who was later to champion the ILP's interpretation of events in Spain. Prior to his arrival there, Orwell's opinion of the British independent left was very low. Published after he departed for Spain, his *The Road to Wigan Pier* maintained that Socialism had become a magnet for 'every fruit-juice drinker, nudist, sandal-wearer, sex-maniac, Quaker, "Nature Cure" quack, pacifist and feminist in England'. While hoping that an 'effective Socialist Party' would emerge, presumably out of the bowels of the ILP, Orwell was pointedly pessimistic. Later, of course, his views would change.[25]

Orwell travelled to Spain in the winter of 1936–7, having first offered his services both to the British Communist Party and the ILP. He had followed events from Britain, and initially took a position close to the Communist Party line, that the revolution should be ended if the war was to be won. Yet having arrived in Barcelona, Orwell rapidly changed his mind. The society he found was one in ferment, where the working class was in control of cities, and even the cafés had been collectivised. Reading Orwell's memoir of the conflict, *Homage to Catalonia*, the reader feels that he has access to a moment of self-discovery. George Orwell, the heroically unsystematic socialist, is increasingly convinced by events that a different and revolutionary order is possible.[26]

> Up here in Aragon one was among tens of thousands of people, mainly though not entirely of working-class origin, all living at the same level and mingling on terms of equality . . . Many of the normal motives of civilised life – snobbishness, money-grubbing, fear of the boss, etc. – had simply ceased to exist. The ordinary class-division of society had disappeared to an extent that is almost unthinkable in the money-tainted air of England . . . One had been in a community where hope was more normal than apathy or cynicism, where the word 'comrade' stood for comradeship and not, as in most countries, for humbug. One had breathed the air of equality.

One of the qualities of *Homage to Catalonia* is its unfinished tone. The writing of the book appears to the reader as a moment of progression; even as he writes, the author still needs to convince himself of the truth of the events he has witnessed.

Like Claud Cockburn, Orwell wrote about the events which took place in Barcelona in May 1937. The protests began with the police occupation of the CNT-controlled phone exchange. Working-class Barcelona responded by declaring a general strike. George Orwell immediately decided to back the protesters: 'The issue was clear enough. On the one side, the CNT, on the other side the police . . . when I see an actual flesh-and-blood policeman, I do not have to ask myself which side I am on.' Orwell helped to guard POUM buildings in case of attack. He took part in no offensive action. Orwell refused to gloss over this incident. Nor, like Cockburn, would he apologise for the counter-revolution in Spain. Through the rest of his life, this episode would inform Orwell's politics, explaining the acute anti-Stalinism of his later writing career.[27]

Although *Homage to Catalonia* is the great document of ILP involvement in Spain, Orwell was not the only independent Marxist to serve at the Spanish front. About thirty members of the ILP fought on the Huesca front, including Orwell, John McNair, Bob Edwards and Staff Cottman. Cottman shared Orwell's innate hostility to questions of doctrine – he was a member of the Young Communist League (YCL) and, like Orwell, he would have been happy to serve as part of the British Communist section, but the ILP (unencumbered by the requirements of Russian security), replied to his letter first. Having served with distinction, Cottman contracted tuberculosis, and is described as a co-resident with Orwell of the POUM sanatorium. On his return home after the events of May 1937, Cottman discovered that he had been expelled by his comrades from the YCL, while his mother's house was picketed by Communists accusing him of being a fascist and an 'enemy of the working class'.[28] Cottman was not the only member of the ILP to face the charge of Trotskyism from the right. Bob Smillie, grandson of the Scottish miners' leader, was less fortunate – he was arrested and killed by the Spanish police.

INTERNATIONAL BRIGADES

The last group to mention are the International Brigades. Some 60,000 foreign volunteers served, 2,000 of them from Britain.[29] Of this British delegation, roughly one-quarter died on the battlefield. Their action was the most remarkable sacrifice – ordinary men and women choosing to fight in the cause of democracy. The leading Spanish Communist Dolores Ibárruri (La Passionara), who spoke at the farewell ceremony: 'They gave up everything, their loves, their countries, home and fortune; fathers, mothers, wives, brothers, sisters and children, and they came and told us, "We are here, your cause, Spain's cause, is ours – it is the cause of all advanced and progressive mankind." You can go proudly. You are history, you are legend.'[30] Even George Orwell, who often criticised the official war effort, refused to criticise the members of the brigade. He always praised the heroism of the volunteers, who were 'in some sense fighting for all of us'.[31]

Later generations can only admire the generosity of spirit and heroism of such volunteers as Felicia Browne, Harold Fry and the others who died. Yet the recruitment to the brigades was organised on party lines, and they suffered from the same flaws as the democracy they chose to defend. It is not surprising that the conventional parties were concerned about the presence of so many revolutionaries in Spain. The chief culprit, once again, was Spanish Communism. Its behaviour legitimised on the left a method of spying on fellow socialists. According to Orwell's biographer, John Newsinger: 'Within the Brigades themselves the Communist secret police assiduously hunted down "traitors" and dissidents, and reputedly in the region of 500 volunteers were executed by their own side.'[32]

The International Brigades began as a spontaneous movement of foreign volunteers, following the Franco uprising in July 1936. They included 200 athletes in Barcelona for the People's Olympiad, a sporting event planned as an alternative to the Olympic Games in Berlin. The first British presence appears to have been two East London garment workers and Communists, Sam Masters and Nat Cohen, who were cycling near Spain at the moment of the revolt and helped to form a Tom Mann Centuria, whose early members included Tom Wintringham, Jack Barry and Dave Marshall.[33] Initially, the volunteers attached themselves quite arbitrarily to anarchist, communist or POUM militia – it was only once the war had been underway for several months that the political dividing lines became more clear. A decision to form International Brigades was taken at the executive of the Communist International in September 1936. The expressed hope was to build an alliance between liberals and communists, in a mirror image of the Spanish Popular Front. Military advisers were sent from Russia, such as General Emilio Kleber, the first commander of the brigades, and previously a military adviser to the Chinese Communists. Around 600 brigaders had been in the USSR. The French Communist André Marty acted as Chief and First Commissar.

The high point of the brigades seems to have begun with the siege of Madrid in November 1936. Indeed, Communist newspapers suggested that the brigades saved Madrid. This claim is probably exaggerated; Andy Durgan argues that the fascist advance had already been checked on the day before the brigades went into battle. Yet there is no doubt that the presence of these troops added enormously to republican morale. The anarchist press in the capital reported that on the Brigaders' arrival 'The people ran out to cheer them . . . the cry rang out from many a balcony – Long live the Russians!' British participants in the rescue of Madrid included a group of machine-gunners, led by Fred Jones and John Cornford, who were attached to the Commune de Paris battalion. Yet despite the triumph at Madrid, by March 1937 the brigades had suffered major losses at Guadalajara. Here, Italian anti-fascists clashed with Mussolini's troops. Leaflets were printed in Italian and every attempt made to persuade fascist troops to defect. As Madrid, so Guadalajara was a victory for the republican side. Yet after Guadalajara, the brigades were barely used, and they were removed from September 1937. The British and French policy of non-intervention contradicted the presence of foreign troops in Spain. Meanwhile, in the paranoid atmosphere that followed from events in Barcelona, all foreigners were subject to suspicion.[34]

Back in England, the Communist Party's Harry Pollitt was the man most associated with the brigades. Having visited Spain on four occasions himself, Pollitt was the man who received correspondence from the families of the volunteers. Clem Beckett, the motorcycle champion, was known to feature among the dead. Soon many other families also feared the worst. Some correspondents pleaded for more detailed information about their loved ones. Others were more stoic. Parents who came themselves from socialist backgrounds were more likely to understand the nature of their child's sacrifice.

A typical letter came from a Mrs McWhirter, a Glaswegian, a long-standing Communist and mother to a serving brigader:

> I am proud that he is there fighting for a cause that is just. Now I see by the *Worker* that they want books sent on. I have about six of Upton Sinclair's I would only be too glad to send off if you can let me know how to go about it. I have also three volumes of the *Russian Revolution* by Trotsky, I would let you have for a raffle for funds for the brigade if they would be any use to you. Please write and let me know.

To his credit, Pollitt replied in temperate language even as he declined to handle such subversive, Trotskyist literature: 'We are quite literally "up to the eye" in one thing and another and just could not take a raffle on.'[35]

Meanwhile, another correspondent was less friendly. Marion Teasdale demanded to know what had happened to her comrade, Frank Whitehead, whose surviving friends (including a young soldier named Bloom) had told the family that Whitehead had been killed. 'We had to tell Mrs. Whitehead that Frank was dead, even while we had nothing officially from your organisation to show her. This inefficiency on the part of your organisation is in my own opinion, and that of our friends, very bad. You are the only persons that receive authentic information yet you fail to notify relations and leave young boys like Bloom, who have already gone through enough, to tell second hand news to us . . .' Again Pollitt's response was diplomatic:

> To explain to you the difficulty of our position. Three comrades have been reported as killed, their parents have been informed and it has subsequently turned out not to be true. You yourself will appreciate how distressing this naturally is. It is not a question of inefficiency, it is a question that there are factors operating over which we have no control, and in one of the most difficult and distressing times it is possible to go through in connection with comrades who have been killed and wounded, we have at all times tried to act in such a way, that no undue anxiety or sorrow would be caused to their relatives.[36]

Sent the day that Teasdale's letter arrived, as part of a hand-drafted letter of about 1,000 words in length, this was probably the best that could have been said.

It seems that there were two sides to the Spanish Civil War. On the one side, working-class people flocked in their thousands to support a cause of justice and solidarity. Rather than dismissing Spain as a far-away country of which they knew little, ordinary British workers understood that their class interests could not be separated from events elsewhere. Their heroism stands as a powerful symbol of unity in the face of fascism. Yet the other side of the conflict cannot be ignored. For all the extraordinary spirit of the volunteers, theirs was a tarnished cause. The only way that the suppression of the POUM and the anarchists could be justified was with lies. Those journalists, including Claud Cockburn, who praised the International Brigaders, used the genuine courage of these volunteers to justify the imprisonment and murder of the Spanish left. Nor has the distortion been restricted to the writers of past decades. When Ken Loach's film *Land and Freedom* came out in 1995 a number of writers and former activists attacked it in the spirit of the communists in May 1937. Santiago Carrillo, the former General Secretary of the Spanish Communist Party, blamed the POUM for their own destruction. Jack Jones, the pensioners' activist and former member of the International Brigade, claimed that 'there is now little doubt that Fascist agents were used to stir up the revolt' in Barcelona.[37] The habit of deceit, once learned, is clearly hard to shed. More optimistically, we can say that the memory of the past is turning in favour of the POUM and the marginalised voices of revolutionary Spain.

TWELVE

Interviewing Anti-fascists: 1945–51

An earlier chapter in this book drew a contrast between the impression of postwar fascism which appears in the work of conventional historians, and the memory of fascism as it was experienced by non-fascists and anti-fascists at the time. This chapter will take that insight further, through a discussion of anti-fascism in 1940s Britain. For the purpose of this chapter fifteen anti-fascists were interviewed, all of whom had been active in the years 1945–51, and many of whom had been members of one particular organisation, the militant anti-fascist 43 Group. Martin Savitt worked for the Jewish Board of Deputies, while Gerry Ross had been a Labour councillor. Duncan Hallas, Frank Henderson, and Chanie Rosenberg had been supporters of the Trotskyist organisation, the Revolutionary Communist Party (RCP). Monty Goldman had been too young to join anything in 1945–51, but had known members of the 43 Group, and regarded himself at the time as a supporter of theirs. Morris Beckman, Morris Block, Stanley Marks, Len Rolnick and Len Sherman had been members of the 43 Group, while Chimen Abramsky, Mark Garland, Royden Harrison, and John Saville were active in the Communist Party of Great Britain. Of these last nine, two had been members of both the Communist Party and the 43 Group. Stanley Marks had been in both organisations at different times, while Len Rolnick had been an active supporter of the Communist Party within the 43 Group.

Many of the interviewed anti-fascists were eager to place themselves near to the centre of events. Each of the interviewees had read Morris Beckman's book, *The 43 Group*, a stirring participant's account of the campaigns of the time.[1] Almost all defined themselves and their role in 1945–51 in relation to the material in this book. Some, including Beckman himself, wanted to defend the detail of his account. Others, often members of rival anti-fascist parties, tended to see his book as having stressed the importance of the 43 Group at the expense of their own former organisations. Several of the former members of the 43 Group also criticised Beckman's account. More than one interviewee suggested that Beckman, a founder member of the 43 Group, had not been an eyewitness to all of the events he described. Some interviewees felt that his account was placed too definitely in the thick of events, while other members of the group, notably Gerry Flamberg and Jeffrey Bernerd, the formal leadership of the group at the time, had played a more important role in the campaign than Beckman's account would suggest. Conducting the interviews, I was also aware that I, as the interviewer, was playing a role in the creation of memory. Several of those interviewed wanted to know if I had a Jewish or left-wing background. It was hard not to feel that they were structuring their accounts around their expectations of what I would like them to say.

At an early stage of my research, I considered whether or not to interview surviving fascists, in order to ask what had been their experience of anti-fascism. It is relatively easy to find and interview such people, and it is something which has been done several times in the past. A group of ageing fascist disciples, the Friends of Oswald Mosley, publish a journal, *Comrade*, dedicated to putting forward the British Union of Fascists' version of events. These Friends are happy to provide material to sympathetic listeners. A.W.B. Simpson drew extensively on their help when writing his book on the internment of fascists in 1940, while Tom Linehan used their evidence to analyse the membership of the BUF in East London in the 1930s.[2] Stephen Cullen borrowed from their testimony in writing a sympathetic account of women in British fascism.[3] Cullen, the historian who has spent most time with surviving fascists, has also written an obituary for *Comrade*,[4] and has elsewhere argued that fascists were largely the innocent victims of street aggression from Jews and communists in the 1930s.[5] It seems to me that those historians who have approached the Friends of Oswald Mosley, and conducted interviews on their terms, have in the process (and often despite their intention) been influenced by the fascist understanding of events. Consequently, the decision was taken not to interview any surviving fascists.

Before discussing what was learned in the interviews, it is worth summarising the history of the anti-fascist campaigns, in so far as it can be constructed from other non-oral sources.

WHAT ACTUALLY HAPPENED: ANTI-FASCISM 1945–51

The anti-fascist campaign was a response to a brief revival in the fortunes of British fascism, which took place between 1945 and 1951. First, Oswald Mosley, the pre-war leader of British fascism, published a long programme, *The Alternative*. Then he brought out a newspaper, the *Mosley Newsletter*. Next, a network of Mosley book clubs were set up, to provide a forum to discuss the leader's ideas, and also with the intention of recruiting a new layer of respectable fascists.[6] Meanwhile, Mosley, Jeffrey Hamm, Alexander Raven Thomson and other well-known fascists, did the rounds of the several small fascist groups, encouraging even renegade anti-Mosley fascists to join the new organisation.[7] By autumn 1947, the largest fascist party, Hamm's British League of Ex-Servicemen, was holding weekly public meetings with up to 3,000 people present at the largest rallies. Finally, in November 1947, Mosley staged a meeting, attended by Hamm, the British League, the book clubs, and about fifty organisations all told, where he announced that he would soon form a new political party, the Union Movement.[8]

The Labour Party was in government for most of this period, and many anti-fascists expected it to take action against the Union Movement. Between 1945 and 1951, however, there were no Labour-sponsored demonstrations against fascism, no speaking tours, and no campaign. There was no change in the law, either to ban fascist parties or to outlaw anti-Semitic propaganda. The Home Secretary, J. Chuter Ede, actively argued against using the law to stop fascism, and his position was adopted by the rest of the cabinet. Not surprisingly, this stance was criticised from within the Labour Party. There were various amendments calling for the fascist parties to be banned at the 1946, 1948 and 1949 Labour conferences.[9] In addition to these conference motions, a small number of Labour MPs, including L.J. Solley and the left-wing lawyer John Platt-Mills, did speak out against fascism, supporting anti-fascist demonstrators in court, and calling for a change in the law, to ban fascism.

The failure of the Labour Party to take a lead in the campaigns against Mosley meant that there was a vacuum; this was largely filled by the Communist Party, which formed the bedrock of the anti-fascist movement in many areas.[10] For example, the party was the largest organised anti-fascist force active in Bethnal Green from

1945 to 1951.[11] At a national level, however, the Communist Party did not lead an all-out campaign against Mosley. There were leaflets, but no national coordination. Anti-fascism was left to the branches and, in certain areas, especially south Hackney, the party simply did not have the resources to stop fascism alone. The tended to work alongside the National Council for Civil Liberties (NCCL), an alliance whose members included Tory MPs, Liberals, Church groups, and other often unaffiliated individuals. The NCCL had either anti-fascist groups or contacts in Bethnal Green, Brighton, Bristol, Crewe, Derby, Hackney, Hendon, Glasgow, Liverpool, Manchester, Oxford and Scunthorpe.[12] The rest of the left was also involved in the anti-fascist campaigns, as far as resources permitted.

Alongside the working-class parties, there were also Jewish groups which organised against the fascist threat, although they did so in different ways. At one end of the scale were middle-class Jews living in the areas furthest from the anti-Semitic flashpoints. Their social position was reflected in the anti-fascist work of the Board of Deputies. Because it was the most middle-class of the Jewish groups, so the board was the least determinedly anti-fascist. The board rejected calls for a law against anti-Semitism, while the *Jewish Chronicle* did not oppose Mosley's release from internment in 1943. At the other end of the spectrum was the 43 Group, which was founded by Jewish ex-servicemen in 1945, and had at its peak a membership of around 2,000. Members of the group linked up with left-wing anti-fascists, and early sponsors of 43 Group literature included the Labour MP Tom Driberg, Frederick Mullally, and the Communist fellow-travellers, D.N. Pritt MP and Hewlett Johnson (the so-called 'Red Dean' of Canterbury).[13] The 43 Group published its own newspaper, *On Guard*, and sent infiltrators into the Mosley Book Clubs and the Union Movement. The group seems to have specialised in turning over fascist platforms. A typical activist might close down thirteen fascist meetings in one Sunday's work.[14]

At first, the military methods of the 43 Group brought clear success. According to Beckman, at the start of their campaign a 43 Group spy heard Alexander Raven Thomson say, 'You know, if we don't find a way to finish off those bastards, they'll do for us.'[15] There was, however, one obvious weakness with the group's tactics, which quickly became apparent. The 43 Group could mobilise a maximum of 200 or 300 commandos for any one stunt. They were not enough to close down Jeffrey Hamm's meetings, once his average audience had grown to 2,000 or 3,000 a week. At this stage, groups such as Hackney Trades Council and the London Communist Party came much more to the fore, opposing and sometimes closing down the Union Movement's larger meetings, in Hackney, Lambeth and elsewhere.

The organised activity of the anti-fascists is not a complete explanation of the failure of the Union Movement. Clearly, there were other factors which contributed to its defeat. The awful legacy of the war and the Holocaust forced fascism on to the defensive. The ending of the British presence in Palestine in 1948 meant that there was no longer a wellspring of popular anti-Semitism in Britain for the fascists to draw on. Added to this, Britain enjoyed full employment between 1945 and 1951, and there was no economic crisis in sight. However, it is clear that at a time when the fascists were already experiencing major difficulties, the intervention of anti-fascists was extremely important. Their hostility effectively reduced Mosley's potential support; by reinforcing the political isolation of the Union Movement as a whole, it exposed the weakness of the fascists to their audiences and to themselves.

MEMORIES OF A CAMPAIGN

Many of the anti-fascists were ex-servicemen. The Second World War set the way in which they understood fascism, and it also shaped the way in which they perceived their own anti-fascist campaign. Martin Savitt wondered what exactly the war had been for: 'I thought, "This is crazy", I'd just given six years of my life fighting fascism'. Even those who had not served in the war understood their anti-fascism in light of what had happened there. Royden Harrison, a former member of the Communist Party, remembered heckling Jeffrey Hamm. One of the policemen protecting Hamm turned round to him and said, 'You know, that man was a member of the Army.' Harrison replied, 'Which one?' Other anti-fascists used overtly military language and metaphors; some described themselves as intelligence officers or commandos. It is clear that some anti-fascists, especially members of the 43 Group, modelled their anti-fascist practice on the military campaigns in which they had fought. Given that there was a broad situation in which Jewish men and women were being attacked by fascists in the streets, anti-fascists believed that any successful anti-fascism would have to include some amount of defensive violence. According to Len Sherman, 'You have to defend yourself. There was no other way.'[16] Sometimes, however, anti-fascist violence had a much more offensive character. Bill Moore, a former member of the Communist Party, remembered the time that Jeffrey Hamm attempted to speak in Sheffield:

> The meeting was an open-air one outside the City Hall, the top side of the City Hall in those days was a Speakers' Corner. Hamm mounted a platform they brought and was surrounded by 10 or a dozen local fascists. A couple of policemen stood by. We all surrounded the platform and shouted him down, asking questions especially, 'What did you do in the war?', all of which he ignored. Then suddenly Bill Ronskley asked us quietly to let him through. He made a dash, broke through the platform and knocked Hamm clean off the platform.[17]

Morris Beckman argued that such tactics were necessary and frequently used:

> In the large meetings, our commandos would form three solid wedges of very hard men . . . At a given signal, sometimes a whistle, they would start to move slowly towards the fascist platform . . . And then they would pick up speed. When they hit fascist cordons, then they would hit them at speed. Our boys . . . went through to the platform. When the platform went over, the meeting was finished.[18]

Although several of the interviewed anti-fascists were ready to stress the necessarily violent character of their work, it was clear from the interviews that most anti-fascist activity was less brutal, less glamorous, and more mundane. The most common form of confrontation was to disrupt fascist meetings by heckling the speakers, while another of the main tasks for anti-fascists was to grab the important meeting platforms and prevent the fascists from speaking. According to Chanie Rosenberg:

> At Ridley Road, there was always a battle, at the end of every Saturday, to get the platform. The market would pack up and the first people there got the platform. It was either us or Mosley. If you got the platform, you had to stay with the platform till Sunday. If you left it the other lot would come in.[19]

For the members of each of the different anti-fascist groups, the most common forms of anti-fascist practice involved educating non-fascists about the dangers of fascism. In the words of Len Sherman, 'We wanted to expose the fascists, and to give the people the truth.'[20] Anti-fascists distributed leaflets, held meetings and demonstrations, and sold their newspapers and pamphlets. They went canvassing and petitioning and removed fascist graffiti. Martin Block described this activity: 'We would paint over their slogans. "Mosley speaks here" would become "An insult to our dead".' Martin Savitt suggested that the routine of anti-fascism was the routine of all democratic politics: 'It was not glamorous, it was hard, dirty work.'[21]

For a number of reasons, anti-fascists frequently came into conflict with the police. Monty Goldman, then a young boy living in Hackney, remembered that 'Hackney police were vicious against the anti-fascists.' According to Royden Harrison, 'We were not favourably regarded by the police. The police protected the fascists.'[22] When asked how the fascists survived the hostility of the watching crowds, Chanie Rosenberg replied:

> The police did it. There was Mosley and a small little coterie and the police kept the others away. People would be squashed against the shop walls and the shop windows. And the police would come and to get through was very difficult. If they saw some small poor-looking Jewish youngster then they'd put their leg up so that he fell over and then they'd arrest him for obstruction or attacking the police or something. That was regular.[23]

Many of the anti-fascists who had been active around Ridley Road shared a particular dislike of Superintendent Satterthwaite, in charge of the Dalston police force. Len Rolnick remembered him with particular venom as 'a first class anti-Semite who would have done a good job at Belsen'.[24] Stanley Marks also suggested that the police took the side of the fascists, although he was prepared to put this down to the situation the police found themselves in: 'The trouble was the police. The magistrates were quite good. They were more on our side. The police, there were definitely anti-Semitic police. But the real trouble is that we always had the initiative. So we were the ones causing trouble.'[25]

For the interviewed anti-fascists, organisation was a key expression of their politics. Typically, they would date the moment at which they became anti-fascists from the moment at which they joined an anti-fascist group. Again and again, those interviewed would describe a moment of conversion, at which the decision was taken to play an active part in the anti-fascist campaign. Phrases recurred throughout the interviews: 'the first thing I *did*'; 'what made me want to join'. This is how Martin Block explained his motives in joining the 43 Group: 'We'd had the news of the Holocaust. It wasn't all revealed, but what we had learned was bad enough. And then these bastards came along with their arms up, giving the fascist salute . . . Our minds boggled.' Martin Savitt claimed to have been motivated by fear: 'The whole of the period was frightening. The fascists were really tough, violent people, armed to the teeth with their knuckle-dusters.' Monty Goldman 'felt Dalston was a no-go area. I used to look over my shoulder.' According to Stanley Marks, to understand the mood of the anti-fascists, 'You've got to be in 1945 where we were. It was only when we came back from the war that we saw the pictures. A lot of people that would have been in Burma or wherever didn't know what was going on. It dominated your feelings. Even in France where they co-operated. It was all very frightening.'[26] Other anti-fascists, while also describing a process of conviction, portrayed their emotions in terms of positive hopes rather than negative emotions of anger or fear. Len Sherman of the 43 Group claimed that, 'the only thing we wanted to do was get better conditions for the people'. According to Martin Block, 'Our sole purpose was to get them banned.' Martin Savitt from the Board of Deputies also described a coherent anti-fascist movement, with a single aim: 'We wanted it to be an offence for anyone to stir up or incite race hatred.' In the words of Morris Beckman, 'The man in the street turned out in force to do what the government failed to do. We were defending democracy.'[27]

Because anti-fascism was so much a story of organisation, surviving anti-fascists were generally keen to defend the legacy of the group in which they had taken part. However, there were exceptions to this rule, as when former members of the 43 Group disagreed with parts of Morris Beckman's history of it. For example, Stanley Marks, then the Director of Intelligence within the 43 Group, was critical of the decision to launch a paper, *On Guard*. According to Stanley Marks: 'The more [the fascists] knew about us the worse, the more we struck quickly and secretly the better . . . Also it revealed that we had information . . . All groupings make mistakes.'[28] Marks also made the point that Beckman exaggerated the military character of the Group. He suggested that most of its work was clerical, involving tasks of surveillance and education: 'I don't like references to commandos. We weren't commandos'.[29] Similarly, although most of the former members of the 43 Group felt that the decision to send infiltrators into the fascist parties 'worked'; other members pointed to the occasional failure of the tactic, as when one spy, Wendy Turner, was caught and then very badly beaten up by members of the Union Movement. This incident was omitted from Beckman's book.[30]

The biggest potential source of tension within the 43 Group was the presence of several members of the Communist Party. The police at the time believed that the entire group was simply a front for the Communists. Sir Harold Scott, then the Commissioner of the Metropolitan Police, described the group in his memoirs as 'a body of young Jewish Communists'.[31] When I interviewed him, Morris Beckman argued the opposite, that the Communists were just another small faction within the group:

> We all had politics. We had Communists. We had Conservatives. We had Socialists. We had Unionists. We had Scottish Nationalists. But, inside the group, our chairman Jeffrey Bernerd laid down some ground rules, which we all had to adhere to . . . Politics was taboo inside the group . . . We had tunnel vision. We wanted to knock out the fascists. The other discipline was that anybody involved who said they would take part in an action, had to turn out, and they did.[32]

Contrary to this account, however, it became clear from the number of interviewees who mentioned it, that a number of prominent members of the Communist Party, including Maurice Essex and Jack Perry, had taken part in the discussions leading to the formation of the 43 Group. Indeed, there was a party cell within the group. The key activist was Len Rolnick. By 1946, he had been a Communist for some years and was friendly with Harry Pollitt, a leading figure within the party. When Rolnick heard about the formation of the 43 Group, he approached Pollitt: 'Pollitt gave me a choice. If you want to continue, try to organise a cell within the group.' Officially, Rolnick tore up his party card, 'we didn't want the party to get a bad name', but in reality, Rolnick remained in regular contact with leading members of the party, including Wolf Arnold and Abe Lazarus, of the party's National Jewish Committee. Rolnick was quickly invited on to the executive of the group. He held regular meetings with other former party members, including Wolf Wayne and Tony Clayton. This 'cell' enjoyed the tacit support of Jeffrey Bernerd, one of the chairs of the group, who Rolnick believed shared the party's broad politics.[33]

As well as the 43 Group, there were other Jewish and left-wing organisations active in the struggle against fascism. One was the Board of Deputies of British Jews, which was broadly aligned with the Jewish ex-servicemen's organisation, AJEX. Martin Savitt was a member of AJEX at this time. At first, his main task was to observe fascist meetings, to take down notes, and to then pass on the information to anti-fascist speakers: 'The idea was to find out what the hell they were talking about . . . so we could evaluate their propaganda so that we could then counter it with our own leaflets and propaganda . . . If for instance they said the press was controlled by the Jews, we could come back and say *The Telegraph*, *The Express*, who they were owned by.' The board was then critical of the 43 Group, and accused this younger body of creating a spiral of increasing violence. Savitt believed that there was an alternative, to lobby the government and to call for legislation that would outlaw racism, 'It is the duty of the government to protect its citizens and to create a harmonious relationship between the different groups.' He insisted that 'violence created a lot of publicity which never did anyone any good'.[34] Surviving members of the 43 Group were, however, equally critical of the Board of Deputies. Len Rolnick accused them of shying away from the real battle, which took place on the streets. 'Their policy was similar to that of the German Jews before 1933. There was no way we could work with the Board.'[35] Martin Block was 'disgusted' with the official leaders of the Jewish community: 'They didn't understand. The war had demonstrated that the best way to deal with the fascists was to kill them.'[36]

Inside the working class left, the most important organisation was the Communist Party. Chimen Abramsky and Monty Goldman both described the role which its members had played in the original formation of the 43 Group. Malcolm Garland remembered fighting between the Communist Party and the Union Movement in Nottingham and Derby.[37] Royden Harrison recalled turning over fascist platforms put up on Sundays on Hampstead Heath. In Hampstead, he suggested, the lead was taken by younger members of the Communist Party: 'We were young. We hadn't fought in 1939–45. We wanted to catch up.'[38] On the other hand, the Union Movement's greatest successes all took place within a small area of East London. Consequently, there were whole regions of the country where anti-fascism was unnecessary. Several interviewed anti-fascists, including members of the Communist Party then living in Hull, told me they felt at the time that Mosley was an irrelevance, and that there was no need for anti-fascist work in their area.[39] Fascism, they believed was a London problem. Chimen Abramsky, then a leading member of the National Jewish Committee of the Communist Party (NJC), argued that the NJC then took a very similar view. Anti-fascist work, he argued, was not a priority even for Jews within the Communist Party:

> They always had some articles on fascism, but by this time Mosley was a spent force. The British fascists had very minor leaders . . . You have to see it in a sense of proportion, the Communist Party did not devote many of its activities against the fascists. It was more important to formulate their policies against the Labour government. Certainly it was not a central issue. If you look at the *Jewish Clarion* [the paper produced by the NJC], it does not take on the central issue of the day.[40]

Other Jewish Communists felt differently. Presented with this quotation from Chimen Abramsky, Monty Goldman replied that most Hackney Communists would have disagreed. He referred to the views of other members of the National Jewish Committee: 'Perhaps you would have got a different answer from Lazar Zaidman.'[41]

Former supporters of the Fourth International in the Revolutionary Communist Party (RCP) recalled their organisation taking an active part in the struggle in Manchester and London. In Manchester, Duncan Hallas suggested, 'it was the RCP that stopped him, the RCP first, and the Communist Party second'. The 'one time', that 'the fascists showed up, we just chased them off, just a few hundred of us. There were only a dozen, maybe 18 of them.'[42] Chanie Rosenberg, then a Trotskyist living in Hackney, recalled walking around the small Jewish sweatshops that covered the area. 'People were so angry, and so glad to see us. We could collect £70 for the campaign in just one day.' Smaller organisations like the RCP could hardly claim the full credit for Mosley's defeat. Generally, they worked with other organisations, and contributed towards a joint effort against the fascist threat. Rosenberg remembers the first rumours that the 43 Group was about to appear and sweep Mosley off the streets. Although she had herself lived in Israel and was a staunch anti-Zionist who held no identification with Jewish organisations, Chanie Rosenberg was glad to hear that the 43 Group was playing its part: 'I thought "about time too" that the Jews began to organise themselves into a proper fighting organisation.'

I asked all the surviving anti-fascists what they had felt their contribution had been. All felt their activity had made a difference, although most qualified this, accepting that they had been working in a friendly context. Outside factors, including the legacy of the war, ensured that fascism was unacceptable. There was no danger that British fascism could have seized state power during 1945–51, but fascism could have grown. The Union Movement and other groups could have generated a new layer of cadres that might have held their organisation together. Even against such a limited and nuanced measure of success, however, fascism clearly failed. The fascist groups which seemed ascendant in 1947 and 1948 were divided and retreating by 1950 or 1951. Chanie Rosenberg put the success of the anti-fascists in this broader context: 'It was the fact that the boom was starting. Unemployment was receding rapidly. Within that we actually stopped them, although our numbers were so small. There was hope . . . There was a Labour government . . . Things did start getting better. And so it was quite possible to smash the Nazis quite easily.'[43]

Martin Block explained the dissolving of the 43 Group in terms of its success: 'We achieved what we wanted to achieve . . . It wasn't needed anymore.' Stanley Marks also saw the group as a triumph, 'We had the motivation and the passion. We were ex-servicemen continuing the battle against fascism, and we won.' Morris Beckman described the group's success in terms of changing the self-image of Jews: 'We unhinged the fascists . . . the fascists were indoctrinated into believing that the Jews were soft targets . . . They never believed that the Jews would out-violence them.'[44] According to Len Sherman, 'When Mosley saw that his power was slipping, even his own men started to desert him . . . You could see that he was a very beaten man. He knew that he was finished. Mosley had been beaten.'[45]

The purpose of this chapter, though, is not to examine whether or not the anti-fascists were correct in their evaluation of their success. The reason for interviewing surviving anti-fascists was to give them the opportunity to express themselves. It is to be hoped that the result is a more nuanced history, alive to the hopes and successes of anti-fascist activity, but also pointing to the tensions between and within different organisations. Contrary to the argument of Morris Beckman's book, it should be clear from this account that the 43 Group was neither the only, nor the most important, party of organised anti-fascism. A number of different groups took part in the campaign. The purpose of this chapter has been to study all the groups, in order to arrive at a sense of what each actually did. The history that results is more accurate, and truer to the struggles which were actually fought.

THIRTEEN

Sounds of Resistance: the Anti-Nazi League, 1977–82

Is there such a thing as an anti-fascist *tradition*? Certainly there are continuities. When a movement is required, it is surprising how often the high-points of previous struggles have been revisited – so that lessons learned by one generation come easier to the next. This process of relearning is true of anti-fascism in 1970s Britain – the activists combined the urban confrontations of Cable Street and the 43 Group with the cultural politics of 1920s Weimar Germany, to obvious effect. Yet in other ways the Anti-Nazi League (ANL) was a most unlikely success. It was set up in 1977, at a time when politics was shifting to the right, when the generation of left activists was moving largely towards cynicism, and when racist ideas were becoming more acceptable. Despite all these barriers, the Anti-Nazi League succeeded in its aim of isolating the National Front, which had acted as the main carrier of organised racism in Britain.[1]

The birth of Rock Against Racism (RAR)and the Anti-Nazi League needs to be placed within the broader context of the Labour government of 1974–9. The Labour Party won the two 1974 elections on the back of a left-moving mood, and its manifesto was the most radical in the party's history, promising increased taxes on the rich to pay for better public services. Tony Benn and Michael Foot joined the Labour cabinet, while TUC left-wingers, including Jack Jones and Hugh Scanlon, were brought into close contact with the government. Bitter struggles continued throughout the five years of Labour rule, but the overall result was to reduce the levels of militancy within society. The government cut spending on public services, closing hospitals, and demoralising many of its most ardent supporters. So the Wilson–Callaghan government was a period of popular disillusionment, in which society shifted to the right, preparing the ground for the Tories' election victory in 1979.

One party which gained from the failure of the Labour government was the National Front. First set up in 1967, the NF grew under Edward Heath's government, and claimed 17,000 members in 1973, but only really took off under Labour. In 1976, the NF received 15,340 votes in Leicester. The following year, it achieved 19 per cent of the vote in Hackney South and Bethnal Green, and 200,000 votes across the country in local elections. The real strength of the organisation was on the streets. By 1976 and 1977, the NF had more activist members than ever before. It was more visible, putting up graffiti and distributing leaflets. Its cadres waged a violent race war, committing dozens of racist attacks. Thirty-one black people were killed in racist murders in Britain between 1976 and 1981.

In August 1976, Eric Clapton, the rock guitarist, interrupted a Birmingham concert to make a speech supporting Enoch Powell, the Tory MP who held controversial views on immigration. The photographer Red Saunders wrote a reply, which was subsequently published in a number of papers including the *New Musical Express* and *Melody Maker*. The letter led directly to the formation of Rock Against Racism: 'When we read about Eric Clapton's Birmingham concert when he urged support for Enoch Powell, we nearly puked. Come on Eric . . . Own up. Half your music is black. You're rock music's biggest colonist . . . We want to organise a rank and file movement against the racist poison music . . . P.S. Who shot the Sheriff Eric? It sure as hell wasn't you!' Dave Widgery, Red Saunders, Roger Huddle and others followed up the letter by organising a series of anti-NF concerts. The message was angry, exciting and compelling, effective at reaching the young. This editorial in the first issue of *Temporary Hoarding* was RAR's manifesto, 'We want Rebel music, street music. Music that breaks down people's fear of one another. Crisis music. Now music. Music that knows who the real enemy is. Rock against Racism. Love Music Hate Racism.'[2]

JAZZ, FUNK AND PUNK

The first Rock Against Racism gig took place on 10 December 1976 at the Royal College of Art, with Carol Grimes headlining. Members of RAR made up a poster, spray-painted on to a massive white sheet, then photographed it, and reduced the image to normal size. In their enthusiasm, they originally forgot to put on the time of the gig. The organisers of the first concert felt that the gig had been 'very studenty'.[3] It was only after the second concert, with members of the black bands Aswad and Steel Pulse in the audience, that members of RAR saw the potential of the new movement. These, after all, were the years of punk, when the old millionaire stadium bands of the 1970s lost touch with their audience, and a new music sprang up, based on simple chord sequences, music that anyone could play. It was a musical style which was itself libertarian and anarchistic, in the best sense of those words. As Caroline Coon wrote in the *Melody Maker* in August 1976:

> The musicians and their audience reflect each other's street cheap ripped-apart, pinned-together style of dress . . . The kids are arrogant, aggressive, rebellious . . . Punk rock sounds simple and callow. It's meant to. The equipment is minimal, usually cheap. It's played faster than the speed of light . . . There are no solos. No indulgent improvisations . . . Participation is the operative word.[4]

By the middle of 1977, however, the early radicalism of punk had begun to wear off. As it became fashionable, even glamorous, punk antagonised many of its earliest followers, who felt cheated. Skinhead writer George Marshall describes the increasing bitterness that street punks began to feel towards bands like the Sex Pistols: 'When it became High Street fashion with High Street price tags, it also became the preserve of those who could afford it rather than those who could feel it. Buying a pair of ready made bondage trousers for thirty quid down the King's Road could hardly be chalked up as one in the eye for the system. And neither could paying a fiver for a ripped bin liner.' As early as 1978, the graffiti went up, 'Punk is Dead', a view seconded by Julie Burchill and Tony Parsons's *The Boy Looked At Johnny*, and confirmed when the famous punk fanzine, *Sniffin' Glue* printed its last issue.[5]

The birth and demise of bands like the Sex Pistols created a space which was partly filled by a revived skinhead subculture, which the NF attempted to tap into. Here it was helped by traces of ambiguity which punk displayed towards fascism. The style was anarchistic, but politically vague, individualistic and sometimes nationalist.

Members of the Sex Pistols and their entourage wore swastikas, while one of the band's last singles pronounced that 'Belsen Was A Gas'. The sound of punk, with its jagged three-chord repetitions, was the antithesis of 1970s reggae or dub; in Jon Savage's phrase, 'the style had bled Rock dry of all black influences'. The Front's Martin Webster promised to ban black music, claiming that reggae was for 'degenerates and monkeys'.[6]

Part of RAR's political radicalism lay in its total acceptance of skinhead punk's rough working-class sound, the music of bands like the UK Subs or Jimmy Pursey's Sham 69. Sham 69 in particular stressed their urban origins. Songs like 'I Don't Wanna' and 'The Cockney Kids Are Innocent' were written for an audience of aggressive, angry, often unemployed young workers, precisely the people that the NF and RAR were both fighting for. Sham 69 consequently had a reputation for being a band with a violent and racist following. In 1977 and 1978 their gigs at Kingston, the London School of Economics, Middlesex Polytechnic and their set at the Reading Festival all ended in mass brawls. At Middlesex Poly, members of the National Front stormed in through the lift shafts and briefly took the stage, but were repulsed, and the gig ended with Jimmy Pursey singing back on stage and alongside the rasta group Misty. In this way, the night ended on a note of real hope, as Syd Shelton recalls: 'There was an affinity, a wonderful moment of black and white unity.'[7]

While other bands may have understood the political theory better, and several did play more RAR gigs, Sham 69's contribution was crucial. The band gave anti-racists a route into the hearts of young skinheads, for whom Pursey was where life was at. The historian of the skinhead movement, writer George Marshall, pays testament to the power of Sham 69:

> Lyrics to songs like Borstal Breakout and If the Kids are United might look simple and naïve on paper, but they weren't being entered into a sixth form poetry competition anyway. And it's only when played live that they genuinely come into their own and sound as sharp as any Stanley blade. The pride and passion with which Jimmy belted out his three minute masterpieces, and the way every word was unanimously echoed by the crowd, is what it's all about. And going to Sham 69 was about being part of

> something, a part of probably the best band ever to tell it as it was on the streets.[8]

In adopting this street music as its own, Rock Against Racism grabbed it out of the hands of the white racists. Sham 69 did not play the first Anti-Nazi League carnival, but Jimmy Pursey did join the Clash live on stage to sing 'White Riot'. Writing afterwards, John Hoyland and Mike Flood Page stressed the presence of Sham 69 as crucial to the success of the event. Pursey's near fanatical hard-core following consisted of skinheads whose political allegiance had hitherto been to the National Front and the British Movement:

> They import the aggressive solidarity of the football terraces to Sham's gigs, and their NF chants formed a disturbing counter-point when Sham 69 played the Central London Poly for Rock Against Racism a couple of months back. Pursey has hitherto refused to take a stand on his followers' politics . . . [yet] the presence of Pursey and his erstwhile Front following on the march and at the gig could be a sign of something changing.[9]

Rock Against Racism did not simply adapt itself to the existing punk sound. Rather it sought to change and develop punk music. For this reason, RAR brought together white punk rockers and black reggae bands – Jimmy Pursey alongside Misty, Tom Robinson with Steel Pulse. According to John Rose of the Socialist Workers Party (SWP), this unity was best expressed in the Clash song 'White Riot', the finale at the first Anti-Nazi League carnival: 'White Riot by the way, was made after the riots at Notting Hill. For a while some skinheads who supported the National Front and the other more overtly Nazi British Movement believed that this was their song. They have been disappointed. Clash belongs to the same movement as Rock Against Racism – RAR. White Riot says that white kids riot in solidarity with black kids – not against them.' Chris and Clarence from Misty were active members of the London RAR Committee, travelling up from Brixton to Hackney for the weekly committee meetings. They gigged for Rock Against Racism, playing Carnival 2, the RAR tour, at Southall Park, with Jimmy Pursey, with the Ruts and the Mekons, 'more times than we can remember'.[10]

As Rock Against Racism developed, so did the sound of the main RAR bands. The Clash brought out a single, 'Police And Thieves', based on a Jamaican tune which was said to have blared out over the anti-racist riot in Lewisham. They also hired a black producer, Lee Perry, and wrote perhaps their greatest song, 'White Man in Hammersmith Palais'. 'White Man' describes attending a reggae night; the narrator is the only white man present, looking for an evening of authentic political music – he senses that everyone else is there for entertainment. The words of the song move to unease, even despair, while the music of the song takes up the pauses and missed times of reggae, subverting the message of the lyrics, and offering an alternative sense of hope.

The race was on to find a sound which could unite black and white. After the Clash, The Special AKA were the next to come up with a mix of their own. Having joined the senior band's 1978 'On Parole' tour, only to find themselves glassed off stage, the Specials decided that it was time for a subtle change. Rather than marrying punk with reggae, the band turned instead to an earlier Jamaican sound, ska. Keyboard player Jerry Dammers took the decision. The band's bass sound was strengthened. Meanwhile, The Specials promoted an entire new look, based on porkpie hats, wraparound shades, mohair suits and black loafers. The name of their label – 2 Tone – summed up the deliberate mixed-race appeal of the music. The two-tone family soon included Rude Boy and Rude Girl, Bad Manners, the Selecter and Madness.

The Ruts also tried to fuse reggae and punk styles, while Sham 69 mixed together South American protest music with football terrace chants to produce, 'If The Kids Are United', which was first played on an ANL platform. Siouxsie and the Banshees, having worn swastikas in 1976 and 1977, now wrote 'Metal Postcard', based on the collages of the German anti-fascist Johnny Heartfield. Elvis Costello's first single, 'Less than Zero', warned of a 'Mister Oswald', presumably the British fascist Oswald Mosley, who committed crimes, including murder, but had 'an understanding with the law'. The Slits sang about the blandness and boredom of ordinary women's lives. Meanwhile, the Gang of Four were another group that turned towards a funk-punk fusion. Their bassist, Andy Gill, describes their sound as the product of the crisis of its time:

> There was terrible violence, pitched battles between students and British Movement members on the University campus. We could see the struggle between the SWP and the B[ritish] M[ovement] capturing the stray youth. We were sympathetic to the SWP, we had done some benefits, but we didn't make our own approach in those broad political terms. It was more to do with living in a late capitalist society, we were also very concerned about the spectre of Thatcherism, and what it was going to do to the people in this country.[11]

George Csapo, front-man for the two-tone band Bethnal, opened his gigs with anti-Front slogans, while his band reflected the anger of young blacks: 'It's a long time since we've been here / We're the second generation / You can talk on the phone / And you wouldn't even know / Who dat you talk to?' This is how Csapo articulated the band's anti-Front strategy: 'They're hitting at us so we've got to hit back. We're not going to go out with guns and try and stop 'em, but we can do it in our music.'[12]

The Tom Robinson Band was one of the most consistent of RAR acts. Old for the punk milieu, Robinson was twenty-seven at the time of the first RAR carnival. A member of the Campaign for Homosexual Equality, Tom Robinson was best known for his anthem, 'Glad to Be Gay'. Robinson's anti-fascist politics were expressed in several songs, including 'Up Against the Wall': 'Consternation in Mayfair / Rioting in Notting Hill Gate / Fascists marching on the high street / Cutting back the welfare state / Operator get me on the hotline / Father can you hear me at all? / Telephone kiosk out of order / Spraycan writing on the wall.' RAR music was a new, aggressive, urban and revolutionary sound. There had never before been a chart music which combined the energy of punk with the radical politics of songs like this.

The relationship between the music of punk and the politics of the RAR was at its most productive in the first six months of 1978. Rock Against Racism filled a musical gap created mostly by the big political crisis of the decaying Labour government, but partly also by the events of punk's death. The Sex Pistols were splitting, and the bands of the moment, the Clash and the Tom Robinson Band, were at the forefront of Rock Against Racism. According to John Savage, 'Early 1978 was the time of RAR, not only because some public show of solidarity seemed necessary to disassociate Punk and its culture from any taint of racism, but also because its amphetamined politics filled the black hole left by the Sex Pistols' demise.' New bands including the Mekons, the Ruts and the Gang of Four, started out at RAR benefits. Music and politics came together, as Steven Wells describes:

> Punk wouldn't have had so much impact outside London without the anti-fascist movement, but then the anti-fascist movement would not have had so much impact without Punk. In Leeds, where the Young National Front were really strong, some of the early Punks had formed fascist groups like the Dentists and the Vents. Punk was apolitical in that context, many people saw it as fascistic even though Martin Webster came out against it. RAR caused Punk to make real contact there, the time when most people see Punk as being diluted was the time when it was gaining substance.[13]

Keith Flett, who briefly organised RAR gigs as a young activist living in Middlesbrough, compares Rock Against Racism in its heyday to the Chartist practice of exclusive dealing. 'If a band or a musician did not support RAR then they were in serious trouble. They were deeply untrendy and people would not get their records.'[14]

The music magazines and fanzines were overwhelmingly friendly to Rock Against Racism. *New Musical Express* interviewed most of the major RAR bands, and ran two large plugs for the first RAR carnival, quoting Tom Robinson in their article, 'It's important to realise that you're not helpless. If people join together they become strong.' The *NME* covered Sham 69's central London gig, and a cartoon of an NF march summed up the paper's hostility to the far right. Beneath a drawing of an typical Front march, came the speaker's words, 'Friends, we've got to make England safe again – for psychopaths, morons, inadequates, sadists and power-mad bastards like ourselves.'[15]

The success of RAR, and later the ANL, was dependent – at least in part – on the radicalism of its music. This is what Widgery, Huddle and others argued in a letter to the SWP's magazine, *Socialist Review*, which they saw as having failed to live up to the mood of RAR: 'Atrocious articles on Carnival. Mr Calico Nickers wants to harness and channel the energy of "Youth" who have ten times more idea of what's going down than your pretty average

Marxist Editor . . . Working class kids NOW are political and fun without having to make five minute speeches to prove it.'[16] Gary Bushell, then a socialist, also denounced what he saw as 'Fossilised theoreticians who want to write skins and punks in on the page that says "the proletarian youth flocked to the party's leadership". As for the other sanitised slide-rule socialists – you can sit there with your logarithms writing these on the perfect revolution until they're ready to fumigate your cell at the next Belsen.'[17]

It is perhaps worth stressing just how new it was to see the far left taking guitar music seriously. Before the 1970s, the dominant approach on the left had been to look for socialist politics in the folk songs of earlier times. In Britain and America, left-wing artists modelled themselves on the nineteenth-century singing tramps. The socialist politics of artists like Woody Guthrie, Penny Seagar and Euan MacColl was used to support the belief that the only properly socialist music was folk music. Such conservatism was well established in the British left, but was not limited only to older British organisations like the British Communist Party. As late as July 1977, the Italian Trotskyist paper *Quotidiano dei Lavoratori* ran a 1,000-word article arguing that punk was inevitably fascist. The author, Nemesio Ala, linked punk to 'the acceptance of social repression', and insisted that 'it is a good thing that punk rock has so far taken only a limited hold in Italy'.[18] Rock Against Racism was the first successful attempt by the left to take pop music seriously.

Precisely because of its musical radicalism, Rock Against Racism was taken up by young punks, including those who were not socialist, or did not consider themselves political. Lucy Toothpaste remembers that 'Many people who came along didn't have political persuasion, but they responded to the statements made by musicians, that it was necessary to challenge people who were putting forward racist ideas.' Caroline Harper was then aged nineteen, and living in a squat in London. She heard about the first RAR gig, and was attracted by the music, and the anti-establishment feel of the event, although she described herself either as 'unpolitical', or 'an anarchist' and never identified with the full politics of RAR or the SWP: 'It was part of our culture, living in London as punks. We were getting harassed by the police. We naturally identified with other people getting harassed by the police. It was when the sus laws were at their height. It didn't matter if you had green hair or were black, you would be stopped by the police, for any reason . . . We felt like victims of an authoritarian state.'[19]

KEEPING ON . . . KEEPING ON

On 13 August 1977, thousands of anti-fascists, including large numbers of local black youths, prevented the National Front from marching through Lewisham. The original NF demonstration was publicised as an anti-mugging march, a crude attempt to intimidate the many Afro-Caribbean residents in the area. Angus MacKinnon, an *NME* journalist, took part in the counter-demonstration: 'Like a lot of people I didn't think the Front march was a good thing. On the day, I arrived at New Cross and couldn't get any further. It said in the press the next day that there were three thousand, but it must have been twice that number. They said it was the standard rent-a-mob. It wasn't. Many had come from all over the country, for the same reason as myself: enough was enough.'[20] After several hours of street fighting between the anti-fascists and the police, one thing was clear: the National Front had failed to pass.

After Lewisham, the media took the side of the police. Daily and weekly newspapers featured the 200 people arrested and the 50 policemen injured, ignoring the causes of the protest, and portraying the conflict as a senseless battle between two parallel sets of extremists. The *Daily Mail* ran with a front-page picture of a policeman holding a studded club and a knife, weapons supposedly found at Lewisham, and beside him was the headline, 'After the Battle of Lewisham, a question of vital importance: now who will defend him?' Several Labour Party voices claimed that SWP demonstrators amounted to 'red fascism', an equally despicable counterpart to the National Front. The *Daily Mirror* claimed that the SWP was 'as bad as the National Front', while Michael Foot, a Labour left-winger since the 1930s, insisted that 'You don't stop the Nazis by throwing bottles or bashing the police. The most ineffective way of fighting the fascists is to behave like them.'[21]

The Anti-Nazi League was set up in the days following Lewisham. There are different accounts of how and when exactly it was formed, but it is clear that Paul Holborow, the SWP's district organiser in East London, approached two prominent left members of the Labour Party, Ernie Roberts, the trade unionist, and Peter Hain, the anti-apartheid activist, and the three of them together agreed to launch a movement. Holborow then became National Secretary of the ANL. Although the Anti-Nazi League was originally set up on the initiative of members of the Socialist Workers' Party, the ANL did receive the support of the Communist Party and sections of the broader left. Prominent members of the Anti-Nazi League included Tariq Ali, of the International Marxist Group; Arthur Scargill of the National Union of Mine-workers'; Peter Hain the anti-apartheid activist; and Ernie Roberts, of the engineers' union and later a Labour MP. The ANL's founding statement was signed by Brian Clough, Arnold Wesker, Keith Waterhouse, Warren Mitchell, and several hundred trade unionists, community activists, footballers, musicians and other celebrities. Dozens of local ANL groups were set up, including Aardvarks Against The Nazis, Left-Handed Vegetarians Against The Nazis, and Football Fans Against The Nazis. Patrons of a Manchester pub, the Albert, even set up their own group, Albert Against The Nazis.

The largest RAR/ANL events were the huge carnivals. The first took place on 30 April 1978, and was fully publicised, not only by the left but also in the musical press. The carnival began with a march to Victoria Park, where the Clash, Tom Robinson, Steel Pulse, X-Ray Spex and others played to an audience of at least 80,000 people. Richard Buckwell was involved in the organising team, and remembers being 'flabbergasted' by the size of the event: 'We expected 10 or 20,000 people, which would have been excellent, a big rise in the numbers who came on the marches and the demos. But on the day there were tens of thousands of people there.' John Shemeld was also 'utterly amazed at how big it was. No one expected it to be so big.'[22] This first carnival was followed by local carnivals in many areas. Some 35,000 came to the Manchester carnival, 5,000 to Cardiff, 8,000 to Edinburgh, 2,000 to Harwich, and 5,000 to Southampton.

The second Anti-Nazi League carnival took place in Brockwell Park, on 24 September 1978, with Sham 69 as the headline band. It was a huge event, even larger than the first Carnival, with 100,000 people attending. Unfortunately, the events were partly overshadowed by a National Front mobilisation in East London. Called only after the carnival had been publicly announced, the NF march was simply intended to embarrass the organisers of the event. Some on the left took up this theme, insisting that the carnival should be called off, and that the 100,000 present should be sent to the East End. One small sect even told carnival-goers that they were 'SCABBING on the struggle'. Although there would not have been any point in sending the whole crowd against a small NF march, the leadership of the ANL was caught in a dilemma, and unable to decide how best to go ahead. On the day, confusion grew, and Paul Holborow admits that the leadership of the ANL failed to send enough people to stop the Front demonstration: 'We collectively bungled it.'[23] Some 250 NF marchers assembled in the East End, but the counter-marchers were badly organised, arrived late, and failed to disperse the NF group. So, although overall the second carnival was still a success, it does not seem to have enjoyed the extraordinary atmosphere of the first.

The Anti-Nazi League was as varied and colourful as the left at its very best. Ronnie Williams was then a furniture-worker on Merseyside. His memories of the Liverpool group give a sense of the diverse alliances involved:

> Maria [O'Reilly] started a Writers' Workshop which produced several booklets of poems and short stories. We affiliated with the Worker Writers Federation and teamed up with the Red Star writers workshop from the Communist Party social club in Shaw Street. They had a young Jimmy McGovern in membership. There was also the Liverpool 8 writers workshop who had Dave Evans. He had to leave South Africa after carrying out acts of sabotage . . . Eric Lynch was a CP member. One night, his son and his friends had been attacked by a group of fascists for no reason. A demo was organised quite quickly. The police near crapped themselves. The police estimate was 5,000 marchers, so draw your own conclusions about the real figure. The march ended at Pier Head with speeches from Bob Parry, Eric Lynch, Bob Wareing and a Chilean folk group who were in exile.
>
> We held a successful day school at Stanley House for ANL activists in the North West. Maurice Ludmer, who edited *Searchlight*, was a guest speaker. Several RCP members showed up to push their line. They would not join the ANL, fair enough, but unlike the Spartacist League, they wouldn't join in bashing the fascist either. They and the WRP were brilliant at sniping from the sidelines but useless if there was a chance of a bit of direct action. What they would have done in a revolution is anyone's guess . . .

> There were several International Marxist Group people involved in the ANL as well as the Socialist Organiser group from the Labour Party, although not Militant who did crap all . . .

As well as all these groups, the local Anti-Nazi League also involved Alf Cottrell and Colin McGuire from the Irish Republican Socialist Party, various activists from the Merseyside Anti-Racist Alliance, and members of the Indian Workers' Association. The ANL organised gigs and paint-outs, discos at the Caribbean centre, and showed several films – including a *World in Action* film about the NF, and another film about the Grunwick strike.[24]

This whole period, from 1976 to 1979, witnessed a succession of anti-fascist demonstrations. On 14 May 1978, following the racist murder of Altab Ali in East London, around 7,000 young Bengalis took part in a protest march against racism in Brick Lane, which was then the biggest demonstration by Asians that had been seen in Britain. On 18 June 1978, 4,000 supporters of the ANL and the Bengali Youth Movement Against Racist Attacks – a short-lived alliance between three major Bengali youth organisations – marched again through the East End. John Shemeld remembers these demonstrations, the first time he had seen large numbers of Sikhs taking part in a public protest: 'It was so different from the meek image of law-abiding Asians.' Tasaduq Ahmed, an educational worker in the East End, also commented on the growing self-organisation among young Bengalis living around Brick Lane: 'What is not being sufficiently stressed is the strong multi-racial response that these acts have evoked, in particular among the Bengali youth, who have joined enthusiastically with their white friends in combating a menace which in its ultimate form will spell the death knell of a democratic Britain.'[25]

The next conflict to turn violent was at Southall on 23 April 1979. Here the police Special Patrol Group brutally attacked Anti-Nazi League demonstrators, again failing to force a way through for the fascists. Their only success was in killing Blair Peach, a teacher, and a member of the ANL and SWP, who was walking away from the march when he was attacked. Some 15,000 people marched the following Saturday in honour of Blair Peach, with 13 national trade union banners taken on the demonstration, and Ken Gill of the TUC General Council spoke at his funeral.[26]

Between 1977 and 1979, at least 9 million ANL leaflets were distributed and 750,000 badges sold; 50 local Labour Parties affiliated, along with 30 AUEW branches, 25 trades councils, 13 shop stewards' committees, 11 NUM lodges, and similar numbers of branches from the TGWU, CPSA, TASS, NUJ, NUT and NUPE trade unions.[27] The cumulative effect of all this campaigning was that the National Front was forced on to the defensive, and thoroughly routed. Its activists were unable to put their message across, their graffiti was painted out, and they could not march. As early as the winter of 1978–9, Colin Sparks, one of the most acute observers of fascism, and also an active member of the ANL, felt confident to predict that the NF would not be the source of future reactionary developments within British capitalism. As important was the threat from right-wing Conservatism.[28] In the April 1979 general election, Thatcher's Conservatives won a forty-seat majority. Meanwhile, the NF received a mere 1.3 per cent of the vote. Demoralised, it split into three rival factions and the Front's support on the streets crumbled.

With fascism in retreat, there seemed to be less need for an anti-fascist movement. RAR and ANL campaigners took up different radical causes, including the Right to Work marches and Campaign for Nuclear Disarmament. Meanwhile, many of the RAR bands moved into the more glamorous and rewarding world of chart music. Thatcher's victory also had an effect, not only in further demoralising the NF, but also in confusing many left-wing ANL activists, who could see that the brief political moment of the ANL had now passed. The last RAR Carnival took place in Leeds in 1981, with 30,000 attending, while the ANL was officially wound down in 1982.

CONCLUSION

The strategy of the Anti-Nazi League was to focus on the most extreme expressions of racism, in order to demonstrate that racism of all sorts was wrong. In Dennis Potter's play, *Brimstone and Treacle*, there is an attempt to dramatise this method. A suburban couple, Mr and Mrs Bates, are visited by a stranger, Martin. Mr Bates dwells longingly on the England he used to know, and admits his membership of the Front. Martin responds by suggesting, it seems innocently at first, that blacks should be placed in special camps. Mrs Bates says 'like Butlins'. Then Martin continues:

> Camps. Any camps for the time being. Oh think of it! . . . Hundreds of thousands. Millions. Rounded up from their stinking slums and overcrowded ghettos. Driven into big holding camps, men, women, piccaninnies . . . You'll see England like it used to be again, clean and white. They won't want to go . . . They'll fight, so we shall have to shoot them and CS gas them and smash down their doors . . . Think of all the hate we'll feel when they start killing us back. Think of all the violence! Think of the de-gra-dat-ion and in the end, in the end, the riots and the shooting and the black corpses and the swastikas, and the . . .

Bates begs him to stop, and promises not to renew his membership of the Front. Uncomfortable, isolated, confronted by the end results of racism, he is compelled to rethink what he stands for.[29] This is exactly how the Anti-Nazi League tried to work.

Many of those involved in the ANL had been active for years in different campaigns: against the Vietnam War; in support of French students, or the miners; against unemployment and the Social Contract. Yet these same activists remember the ANL period as the one moment where their work, their intervention, was of decisive importance. Ian Birchall's account is typical:

> In the 35 years I've been in the IS [and then the] SWP the ANL period was the one where I am reasonably certain that the party's intervention did have some impact on the course of mainstream politics in this country, by preventing the far right from taking off in a situation that was favourable to them. There have been other times when I have had the sense of being part of a movement that was affecting the course of events – Pentonville Five, Poll Tax – but then the party was merely participating in a broader movement. In the case of the ANL I think our intervention as a party was crucial.[30]

Another activist, Mike Beaken, has a similar, positive memory of the ANL. 'It played a great part in reducing people's fear of the NF; the ANL made them look very small and insignificant. It also had a big role to play in making racism indefensible, especially to the young.'[31] Looking through the list of left-wing campaigns in recent British history, one could find no better example of success than the Anti-Nazi League of the 1970s.

Rock Against Racism and the Anti-Nazi League both intended to turn back the growth of the National Front. They achieved the goal they set themselves. In the mid-1970s, British fascism was powerful and growing. But by 1978 or 1979 the ANL had given the NF a defeat from which its successors have not yet recovered. As a by-product of their endeavours, the RAR also generated new musical styles which simply had not existed before, while the ANL showed the possibility of what mass radical politics could look like. Indeed, one effect of the ANL was that it established a tradition that anti-fascist work should be exciting, popular, bold and political.

The greatest innovations of the period were undoubtedly musical. For Roger Huddle (writing at the time), the whole point of RAR was that it converted music that was already revolutionary into an organisation which could live up to it. 'RAR's fight is amongst the youth whose life style is rebellious . . . Punk is not just the music. It was visual, it revolutionised graphics, it's anti-authority, anarchistic and loud. It has a lot to give RAR and RAR has a lot to give it.'[32] The Anti-Nazi League was the first modern movement to have been founded on the basis of radical music, or as John Hoyland and Mike Flood Page put it, the first to understand pop music 'from the inside'.[33] Dave Widgery's book, *Beating Time*, argues that it was the radical and cultural politics of RAR which enabled the ANL to succeed: 'It was a piece of double time, with the musical and the political confrontations on simultaneous but separate tracks and difficult to mix. The music came first and was more exciting. It provided the creative energy and the focus in what became a battle for the soul of young working-class England. But the direct confrontations and the hard-headed political organisation which underpinned them were decisive.'[34]

One last point; although the main lesson of the Anti-Nazi League is that unity works, it remains true that many other conditions exist before a campaign can win. Successful campaigns rely on their appeal and their timing at least as much as they do on their strategy. The task of the future cannot be to recreate the conditions of previous success but rather to take the spirit and the anger of the spirit and apply them anew.

Conclusion

One purpose of this book has been to criticise the way in which many historians have written about fascism. Rather than consigning fascism to the past, I have suggested that its politics remain a matter of present-day concern. But how to write about fascism (historic or present-day) if not in the idealistic manner which I have criticised? This book has argued that the only way to generate a consistently anti-fascist approach towards the history of the far right is by relating the ideas of fascism to its actions, and by grasping the two in their relationship to each other. This, I have suggested, is what the most interesting critical anti-fascists from the 1930s attempted to do. Such figures as Albert Einstein, Bertolt Brecht, Dave Wigery and Wilhelm Reich have been discussed, for their critical sense of what fascism was.

Part of my argument stems from a rejection of the philosophy behind fascism studies; one that treats myths, aspiration and ideology as if they were the only true reality. My feeling is that the people who are only interested in ideas are less able to understand the actual significance of these words. To focus all attention on reconstructing the fascist myths is to divert attention from the more interesting questions of communication and response. So the idealists see the grand myths, but not the ideas in practice, the lived experience of different approaches as they have been worked through in the real world. Just to take one example, all of us are familiar with the methods of marketing and communication, especially political marketing. We learn in our everyday lives to treat such 'ideas' with an appropriate degree of cynicism. Most of us know that when you hear a politician promising tax cuts, this is verbal wallpaper, and can be ignored. But if the same speaker announces plans to introduce capital punishment for pre-teens, then we know (by instinct or by experience) that this policy is distinctive, something new and different to observe, to remember, and to judge.

Even such basic insights into political communication are impossible for the historians influenced by fascism studies, who treat all fascist communication as an undifferentiated mass of 'ideas'. Every fascist sentence, poster, or speech is a fascist 'idea'; all are alike, indivisible and the same. Elsewhere in this book, I have already cited Roger Griffin's argument that fascism should be understood – like other movements – in terms of the claims made by its supporters.[1] Such a claim is immediately problematic. Clearly, any understanding of fascism conducted on the basis of fascism's own terms runs the risk of moving from comprehension to empathy. But Griffin and other protagonists of this approach have their reply to hand. Any movement (they argue) is based on myths and aspirations, which are subjective. So how else can we proceed except through the myths of the fascists?

This is certainly not the first historical school to have been founded on idealism. One of the greatest of the English idealist philosophers, R.G. Collingwood, is famous for saying that all history is the history of ideas.[2] What he meant by this phrase was that there is no way to reconstitute the past except through the choices taken by individuals. Such an approach deliberately understands the story of the past in terms of the choices of the most famous of the so-called 'great men'. In Collingwood's account, human history is understood as a succession of picturesque tableaux – Caesar crossing the Rubicon, Napoleon determining to attack Russia. Yet the trend of the past thirty years and more has been towards a different and more democratic way of writing about the past – where the activities of the great men are fitted into a general approach, which takes seriously the lives of all human beings. No one man built London, no one man alone determined the fate of the Roman or the French republics. To reduce the complex set of human behaviour and emotion to the actions of a few state-builders is to do a disservice to the unknown billions of people who have lived and worked and reshaped the world in their own image.

If the decisions of individuals only make sense when these people are displayed against the background of the time, then the ideas of the 'great men' must also be examined with thought and greater attention. Take the question of Hitler's role in German history. Any historian worth their salt will agree that the question of what made

Hitler a fascist is inherently less interesting than the question of what made Hitler's audience choose to vote for him. It surprises no one that pre-1914 Vienna contained a multitude of violent crackpots. Karl Lueger, the Mayor of Vienna, was a nationalist, a populist and an anti-Semite. Of course, he had supporters; this fact is generally known. What shocks is the speed with which one such racist was able to transform Europe after 1933. This was civilised Europe: Weimar Germany was the bastion of culture and social democracy – what factors then let Hitler in?

The approach of 'great man' history is necessarily limited. When the men were also fascists, the inappropriate nature of this historical method becomes doubly apparent. And what about the ideas of these men? The consistent argument running through this entire book has been that the ideas of fascism were connected to fascist practice. This point is true of all political movements – there is no practice without ideas, no ideas without practice. The fascist myths worked themselves out in the Second World War and the Holocaust; the flower of death and destruction was always present in the seed. Seen again in this new light, the fascist myths and symbols take on a new significance. The huge ritual marches become a prelude to war, the spring festivals accompany the terrible murder of the Jews. I have not argued that ideas of fascism are unimportant – quite the reverse, I have argued that the ideas were important, and can only be fully understood if the myths of the fascist programme and propaganda are connected to the practical steps by which these ideas were communicated and then carried out.

Many historians have learned to read the historical propaganda of fascism, but they have not found a contemporary source to explain the consequences of the fascist myths. It seems to me that a new emphasis on anti-fascism could resolve this false division between ideas and action. If we see fascism as a 'thing' then there is no way to step away from the problems of such intellectual history. But if we see fascism as a process, as a relationship between one movement and its opponents, then there is an alternative memory on which historians can draw. If the autobiographical novels of Primo Levi tell us at least as much about the experience of the Holocaust as we can learn from Hitler's *Mein Kampf*, then so also the memory of Cable Street or of the International Brigades in Spain can be used to explain the nature of fascism. In short, it is hoped that the experience of anti-fascism can become a lens through which to understand and judge fascism itself. The opinion of anti-fascists is certainly a more accurate lens than the camera obscura through which the fascists viewed themselves. Armed with the insights of contemporary anti-fascists, historians of fascism can come to a fuller understanding of fascism as well. That at its simplest is the approach which has been taken in this work.

At the end of this book, at least one point should be clear. My reason for emphasising the history of anti-fascism is the same as when I first became interested in these subjects and began to write about them; to write against fascism, to judge, to condemn and to warn – to describe events from which later generations can learn.

Notes

Introduction

1. D. Renton, *Red Shirts and Black: Fascists and Anti-fascists in Oxford in the 1930s* (Oxford, Ruskin College Library, 1996).
2. E. Nolte, *Three Faces of Fascism: Action Française, Italian Fascism, National Fascism* (New York and London, Weidenfeld and Nicolson, 1966).
3. For both criticism and defence of the fascism studies approach, see the series of articles, 'Understanding Fascism', published in the anti-fascism magazine *Searchlight*, between August and October 1999.
4. G. Watson, *The Lost Literature of Socialism* (London, Lutterworth, 1998).
5. G. Watson, 'Hitler and the Socialist Dream', *Independent on Sunday*, 22 November 1998; also see the correspondence in *Independent on Sunday*, 29 November 1998, and 6 December 1998. I am grateful to David Turner for drawing my attention to these articles.
6. M. Neocleous, *Fascism* (Buckingham, Open University Press, 1997), p. 9.
7. The same criticism can be made of Griffin. My own thoughts are contained in D. Renton, *Fascism: Theory and Practice* (London, Pluto, 1999), pp. 91–9; and in chapter eight, below.
8. D. Renton, *Fascism, Anti-fascism and Britain in the 1940s* (London, Macmillan, 2000); also Renton, *Fascism: Theory and Practice.*
9. K. Marx, *A Contribution to the Critique of Political Economy* (London, Lawrence and Wishart, 1971), p. 21.
10. In *Fascism: Theory and Practice*, I talked of 'three claims', which constituted points two to four here. In this book I have added point one to clarify an argument which was implicit in my earlier book.
11. N. Mosley, *Rules of the Game/Beyond the Pale: Memoirs of Sir Oswald Mosley and Family* (London, Pimlico, 1998).
12. Mosley, *Rules of the Game*, p. 568.

PART ONE

1. Fascism: a Brief History

1. A useful, if controversial, account of such early French fascism appears in Z. Sternhell, *Neither Right nor Left* (Berkeley, University of California Press, 1986).
2. Oswald Mosley's record was as poor as Mussolini's. By contrast, Adolf Hitler was decorated for bravely delivering messages under fire.

3. D. Horn (ed.), *War, Mutiny and Revolution in the German Navy: The World War I Diary of Richard Stumpf* (New Brunswick, Rutgers University Press, 1967), p. 75.
4. J. Hatheway, 'The Pre-1920 Origins of the German National Socialist Workers Party', *Journal of Contemporary History* 29/3 (1994), 443–62.
5. See chapter ten, below.
6. A. Raven Thomson, *The Coming Corporate State* (London, British Union, 1936), p. 7.
7. C. Levi, *Christ Stopped at Eboli* (London, Penguin, 1990 edn).
8. I. Kershaw, *The Nazi Dictatorship* (London, Edward Arnold, 1985).
9. For more on Spain, see chapter twelve, below.
10. J. Noakes and G. Pridham, *Nazism 1919–1945, Volume 3: Foreign Policy, War and Racial Extermination* (Exeter, Exeter University Press, 1995), p. 1208.
11. P. Novick, *The Holocaust and Collective Memory* (New York, Mariner, 2000).
12. The key source for this period is D. Renton, *Fascism, Anti-fascism and Britain in the 1940s* (London, Macmillan Press, 2000). Also see chapters six and thirteen, below.
13. M. Lee, *The Beat Awakens: The Chilling Story of the Rise of the Neo-Nazi Movement* (New York, Little, Brown and Co., 1997), p. 102.
14. *Searchlight* (July 2000), also chapter seven, below.
15. D. Renton and R. Rammeiser, 'Austria Erupts', *Jewish Socialist* 42 (2000), 10–11.

2. *One of the Causes of Fascism? German Exceptionalism Revisited*

A version of this chapter is due to appear in the *Journal of Peasant Studies* 28/4 (2001).

1. R. Dahrendorf, *Society and Democracy in Germany* (London, W.W. Norton, 1968); G.M. Luebbert, *Liberalism, Fascism or Social Democracy: Social Classes and the Peculiar Origins of Regimes in Interwar Europe* (New York and Oxford, Oxford University Press, 1995); H.-U. Wehler, *The German Empire 1871–1918* (Oxford, Berg, 1973); also A. Gerschenkron, *Bread and Democracy in Germany* (Berkeley, University of California Press, 1943).
2. This paper is focused simply on the relationship of German development to the general pattern. For those who are interested in linked questions of national identity, there is a substantial literature. Among the most useful of recent additions to this genre is Mary Fullbrook's discussion of German nationalism in the shadow of the Holocaust: M. Fullbrook, *German National Identity after the Holocaust* (Cambridge, Cambridge University Press, 1999).
3. G. Lukács, *The Destruction of Reason* (London, Merlin, 1962), p. 37.
4. B. Moore Jr, *Social Origins of Dictatorship and Democracy* (Harmondsworth, Penguin, 1966)
5. T.J. Byres, *Capitalism from Above and Capitalism from Below: An Essay in Comparative Political Economy* (London, Macmillan, 1996).
6. E.R. Wolf, *Envisioning Power: Ideologies of Dominance and Crisis* (Berkeley, University of California Press, 1999).
7. D. Blackbourn and G. Eley, *The Peculiarities of German History: Bourgeois Society and Politics in*

Nineteenth-century Germany (Oxford, Clarendon Press, 1984). For a similar perspective, G. Eley, 'What Produces Fascism: Pre-industrial Traditions or a Crisis of the Capitalist State?, *Politics and Society* 12 (1983); and J. Kocka, 'German History before Hitler. The Debate about the German *Sonderweg*', *Journal of Contemporary History* 23 (1988).

8. M.A. Karaömerlioglu, 'Elite Perceptions of Land Reform in Early Republican Turkey', *Journal of Peasant Studies* 27/3 (2000), 115–41.
9. P. Anderson, 'Origins of the Present Crisit', in R. Blackburn (ed.), *Towards Socialism* (London, New Left Books, 1965); T. Nairn, 'The British Political Elite', *New Left Review* 23 (1964), 19–25; T. Nairn, 'The English Working Class', *New Left Review* 24 (1964), 45–57; T. Nairn, 'The Anatomy of the Labour Party', *New Left Review* 27 (1964), 48–65 and 28, 33–62.
10. G. Comninel, *Rethinking the French Revolution* (London, Verso, 1987); E. Meiskins Wood, *The Origins of Capitalism* (New York, Monthly Review Press, 1999), pp. 54–7; also E. Meiskins Wood, *The Pristine Culture of Capitalism* (London, Verso, 1992).
11. K. Takahashi, 'A Contribution to the Discussion', in R.H. Hilton (ed.), *The Transition from Feudalism to Capitalism* (London, New Left Books, 1976), pp. 68–97.
12. A. Gramsci, *Selections from the Prison Notebooks*, eds Q. Hoare and G. Nowell Smith (New York, International Publishers, 1971), pp. 106–14; also P. Corner, *Fascism in Ferrara 1915–1925* (London, Oxford University Press, 1975).
13. W. Sombart, *Why is there no Socialism in the United States?*, ed. C.T. Husbands (New York, M.E. Sharpe White Plains, 1976); S. Lipset, *Political Man: The Social Bases of Politics* (London and New York, Johns Hopkins University Press, 1983), pp. 45, 346–7.
14. Wolf, *Envisioning Power*, p. 199.
15. Dahrendorf, *Society and Democracy*, pp. 52–3.
16. E.P. Thompson, *The Poverty of Theory and Other Essays* (London, Merlin, 1987), p. 47; A. Callinicos, 'Exception or Symptom?', *New Left Review* 169 (1988), 97–107; C. Barker and D. Nicolls (eds), *The Development of British Society* (Manchester, Manchester University Press, 1988).
17. Blackbourn and Eley, *Peculiarities*, p. 146.
18. A. Callinicos, 'Bourgeois Revolutions and Historical Materialism', in A. Callinicos and P. McGarr, *Marxism and the Great French Revolution* (London, Bookmarks, 1993), p. 153.
19. C. Hill, *England's Turning Point* (London, Bookmarks, 1997); B. Manning, *The English People and the English Revolution* (London, Bookmarks, 1991); G. Rudé, *The Crowd in the French Revolution* (Oxford, Clarendon, 1972); A. Souboul, *La Revolution Française* (Paris, Editions Sociales, 1982).
20. J.A. Perkins, 'The German Agricultural Worker 1915–1914', *Journal of Peasant Studies* 11/3 (1984), 3–27; also R.G. Tiedemann, 'Rural Change, Peasant Conservatism, and the Transition to Capitalism', *Journal of Peasant Studies* 9/1 (1981), 97–109.
21. K. Kautsky, *Die Agrarfrage, Eine Übersicht über die Tendenzen der modernen Landwirtschaft und die Agrarpolitik der Sozialdemokratie* (1902), pp. 106, 136, 138–40. There is a useful discussion of this essay in J. Banaji, 'Illusions about the Peasantry:

Karl Kautsky and the Agrarian Question', *Journal of Peasant Studies* 17/2 (1990), 288–307; also T. Cliff, *Marxism and the Collectivisation of Agriculture* (London, Bookmarks, 1980).
22. V.I. Lenin, *Collected Works, Volume 13* (London, Lawrence and Wishart, 1962), pp. 273–4.
23. Adapted from E. Hobsbawm, *The Age of Empires 1875–1914* (London, Peter Smith, 1987), p. 343.
24. V.I. Lenin, *Collected Works, Volume 4* (London, Lawrence and Wishart, 1964), pp. 133, 143–4.
25. Kautsky, *Die Agrarfrage*, pp. 174–93.
26. Ibid., pp. 92–105.
27. N. Koning, *The Failure of Agrarian Capitalism: Agrarian Politics in the United Kingdom, Germany, the Netherlands and the USA 1846–1919* (London, Routledge, 1994), pp. 65–6, 100.
28. Koning, *The Failure*, pp. 152, 173–4.
29. Renton, *Fascism*, p. 30.
30. Karaömerlioglu, 'Elite Perceptions'.
31. B. Mussolini, 'Fascism and the Countryside', in R. Griffin, *Fascism* (Oxford, Oxford University Press, 1995), pp. 41–3.
32. Griffin, *Fascism*, p. 7.
33. A. Bramwell, *Blood and Soil: Walther Darré and Hitler's 'Green Party'* (Kensal, Kensal Press, 1985); Griffin, *Fascism*, p. 127.
34. C. Fischer, 'The SA of the NSDAP: Social Background and Ideology of the Rank and File in the Early 1930s', *Journal of Contemporary History* 17/4 (1982), 651–70.
35. G.A. Craig, *Germany, 1866–1945* (Oxford, Oxford University Press, 1978), pp. 609–10.
36. Renton, *Fascism: Theory and Practice*, pp. 33–8.
37. J. Herf, 'The Engineer as Ideologue – Reactionary Modernisers in Weimar and Nazi Germany', *Journal of Contemporary History* 19/4 (1984), 631–48.

3. *Women and Fascism*

A version of this chapter is due to appear in *Socialist History* 20 (2001).

1. The only author singled out for criticism in this chapter is Martin Durham. Yet I would suggest that Steve Cullen and Julie Gottlieb's recent work shares many of the arguments present in Durham. See S. Cullen, 'Four Women for Mosley: Women in the British Union of Fascists 1932–1940', *Oral History*, 24/1 (1996), 49–59; also J. Gottlieb, 'Women and Fascism in the East End', *Jewish Culture and History* 1/2 (1998), 31–47; and J. Gottlieb, *Feminine Fascism* (London, I.B. Tauris, 2000). The controversy here bears a family resemblance to the older controversy over the reception of Claudia Koonz's work on Nazi Germany. See C. Koonz, *Mothers in the Fatherland: Women, the Family and Nazi Politics* (London, Jonathan Cape, 1987); and L. Gordon, 'Nazi Feminists?', *Feminist Review* 27 (1987), 97–106.
2. M. Durham, *Women and Fascism* (London and New York, Routledge, 1998); also M. Durham, 'Gender and the British Union of Fascists', *Journal of Contemporary History* 27/3 (1992), 513–29; and M. Durham, 'Women and Fascism', *Searchlight* (January 2000).
3. Durham, *Women and Fascism*, pp. 165–6.
4. Ibid., pp. 165–7.

5. Ibid., p. 182.
6. Ibid., p. 4.
7. This is precisely the approach of Miriam Poya's study into the gender dynamics of post-revolutionary Iran, *Women, Work and Islamism* (London, Pluto, 2000).
8. Durham, *Women and Fascism*, pp. 13, 20, 64.
9. A. Alexander, 'Daughters of the Century, The Politics of Women's Liberation 1900–1999', in K. Flett and D. Renton (eds), *The Twentieth Century: A Century of Wars and Revolutions?* (London, Rivers Oram, 2000), pp. 54–79.
10. Many of the key documents in this context are published in English in J. Noakes and G. Pridham (eds), *Nazism 1919–1945, Volume 2: State, Economy and Society 1933–1939: A Documentary Reader* (Exeter, University of Exeter Press, 1984), pp. 448–70.
11. R. Evans, *Comrades and Sisters: Feminism, Socialism and Pacifism in Europe 1870–1945* (Brighton, Wheatsheaf, 1987), p. 13.
12. S. Berger, *Social Democracy and the Working Class in Nineteenth and Twentieth Century Germany* (Harlow, Longman, 2000) pp. 148–9.
13. L. Caldwell, 'Reproducers of the Nation: Women and the Family in Fascist Policy', in D. Forgacs (ed.), *Rethinking Italian Fascism: Capitalism, Populism and Culture* (London, Lawrence and Wishart, 1986).
14. P.R. Wilson, 'Women in Fascist Italy', in R. Bessel (ed.), *Fascist Italy and Nazi Germany: Comparisons and Contrasts* (Cambridge, Cambridge University Press, 1996), pp. 78–93.
15. V. de Grazia, *How Fascism Ruled Women: Italy 1922–1945* (Berkeley, University of California Press, 1992).
16. Durham, *Women and Fascism*, pp. 16, 21, 30, 168, 180.
17. The classic example of this literature is Tim Mason's two-part study of women and German fascism: 'Women in Nazi Germany' which appeared in issues 1 and 2 of *History Workshop Journal* (1976).
18. For a chronology of women in the anti-racist movement, D. Renton, 'Can the Oppressed Unite? Women and Anti-fascism in Britain 1977–1982', in C. Barker (ed.), *Conference Proceedings: Alternative Futures and Popular Protests 2000* (Manchester, Manchester Metropolitan University, 2000).
19. Women and Fascism Study Group, *Breeders for Race and Nation: Women and Fascism in Britain Today* (Birmingham, Women and Fascism Study Group, 1978).
20. Ibid., p. 3.
21. Holtby is cited in S. Rowbotham, *Hidden from History: 300 Years of Women's Oppression and the Fight Against It* (London, Pluto, 1974), p. 126; also in Durham, 'Gender and the British Union of Fascists', pp. 514–5.
22. Women and Fascism Study Group, *Breeders for Race and Nation*, p. 22.
23. Big Flame, *Sexuality and Fascism* (London, Big Flame, 1979), p. 5.
24. The return of British fascism generated a similar interest in socialist-feminist understandings of fascism; see V. Ware, 'Island Racism: Gender, Place, and White Power', *Feminist Review* 54 (1996), 65–86.
25. Big Flame, *Sexuality and Fascism*, p. 13.
26. *Women's Voice* (September 1977).
27. *Women's Voice* (February 1978).
28. L. Toothpaste, 'Sex Vs. Fascism', cited in Women and Fascism Study Group,

Breeders for Race and Nation, pp. 21–2.

29. 'The Dialectics of Liberation', in D. Widgery, *Preserving Disorder* (London, Pluto, 1989), pp. 110–14, esp. p. 112.
30. Women and Fascism Study Group, *Breeders for Race and Nation*, p. 18.
31. W. Reich, *The Mass Psychology of Fascism* (London, Souvenir Press, 1970), pp. 98–103; also W. Reich, *The Sexual Revolution* (London, Vision, 1951 edn).
32. Reich, *Mass Psychology*, p. xii, also Women and Fascism Study Group, *Breeders for Race and Nation*, p. 19.
33. D. Widgery, *Beating Time: Riot 'n' Race and Rock 'n' Roll* (London, Chatto and Windus, 1986), p. 43.
34. J. Caplan, 'Introduction to Female Sexuality in Fascist Ideology', *Feminist Review* 1 (1979), 59–66; and M.-A. Macciocchi, 'Female Sexuality in Fascist Ideology', *Feminist Review* 1 (1979), 67–82.
35. Macciocchi, 'Female Sexuality', pp. 68, 70, 77, 81.
36. G.L. Mosse, *Nationalism and Secuality: Respectability as Normal Sexuality in Modern Europe* (New York, Howard Fertig, 1985), pp. 153–81, esp. p. 161.
37. K. Theweleit, *Male Fantasies II: Male Bodies: Psychoanalyzing the Whiter Terror* (Cambridge, Polity, 1989). For a recent use of Theweleit's categories, A. King, 'The Postmodernity of Football Hooliganism', *British Journal of Sociology* 48/4 (1997), 576–93. King is criticised in T. Smith, 'MUFC Fans, Sex and Football Violence: A "Preferred" Postmodern Past', *North West Labour History* 24 (1999/2000), 55–69.
38. M. Attwood, *The Handmaid's Tale* (London, Vintage, 1996). I am grateful to Anne Alexander for this reference.
39. The arguments in this chapter have emphasised fascist appeals to female sexuality. One parallel approach has been to consider the appeal of the image of the white mother – a racist and sexist image, which has still appealed to many women. 'Disloyal to Civilization', in A. Rich, *Lies, Secrets and Silence* (New York, Norton, 1979); also V. Ware, *Beyond the Pale: White Women, Racism and History* (London, Verso, 1992).
40. Although there was, of course, a similar notion of false consciousness in Freud – and this overlapping area helped to create a space for writers like Wilhelm Reich.
41. This quote from Marx is taken from 'Contribution to the Critique of Hegel's Philosophy of Law', in K. Marx and F. Engels, *Collected Works: Volume 3* (London, Lawrence and Wishart, 1975), pp. 3–129, 175–87, esp. p. 175. There is a useful discussion of Marx's theory of ideology in A. Callinicos, *The Revolutionary Ideas of Karl Marx* (London, Bookmarks, 1983), pp. 97–100. Reich offers his own understanding of ideology as a 'material force', in Reich, *Mass Psychology*, pp. 3–33.
42. The relationship between the leader and the crowd in fascist propaganda is discussed in I. Kershaw, *The 'Hitler Myth': Image and Reality in the Third Reich* (Oxford, Oxford University Press, 1987). Similar themes also inform M. Stone, *The Patron State: Culture and Politics in Fascist Italy* (Princeton, Princeton University Press, 1998).

4. *Understanding Adolf Hitler*

Parts of this chapter first appeared in a short article for *Socialist Review* (December 1998).

1. W.C. Sellar and R.J. Yeatman, *1066 and All That* (London, Penguin, 1960 edn).
2. The hostility of (English) historians to what they perceived as 'Theory' is described in C. Parker, *The English Historical Tradition since 1850* (Edinburgh, John Donald, 1990), pp. 20–50 and passim.
3. E.H. Carr, *What is History?* (London, Penguin, 1964), p. 55.
4. K. Marx, 'The Eighteenth Brumaire of Louis Bonaparte', in K. Marx and F. Engels, *Collected Works: Volume 11* (London, Lawrence and Wishart, 1979), pp. 99–197, esp. p. 103.
5. G. Plekhanov, *The Role of the Individual in History* (New York, International Publishers, 1940). Plekhanov's short book has also been one of the influences on the interactionist approach of Ian Kershaw, whose biography of Hitler is discussed below.
6. L. Trotsky, *The History of the Russian Revolution* (London, Pluto, 1997), pp. 343–4.
7. A. Bullock, *Hitler: A Study in Tyranny* (London, Odhams, 1952; also London, Pelican, 1962 edn); J.C. Fest, *Hitler* (Harmondsworth, Penguin, 1974); I. Kershaw, *Hitler: 1889–1936: Hubris* (London, Allen Lane, 1998); I. Kershaw *Hitler: 1889–1936: Nemesis* (London, Allen Lane, 2000).
8. Bullock, *Hitler* (1962 edn), p. 13.
9. H.-U. Wehler, *The German Empire, 1871–1918* (Oxford, Berg, 1984), p. 5.
10. K.-D. Bracher, *The German Dictatorship* (Harmondsworth, Penguin, 1973); H. Mommsen, *From Weimar to Auschwitz* (Cambridge, Polity, 1991).
11. M. Broszat, *The Hitler State* (London, Longman, 1981).
12. M. Broszat, 'Soziale Motivation und Führerbindung des Nationalsozialismus', *Vierteljahrshefte für Zeitgeschichte* 18 (1970), 393–403, translated in N. Gregor, *Nazism* (Oxford, Oxford University Press, 2000), pp. 81–4.
13. Fest, *Hitler*, pp. 3–13.
14. K.-D. Bracher, 'The Role of Hitler: Perspectives of Interpretation', in W. Laqueur (ed.), *Fascism: A Reader's Guide* (Harmondsworth, Penguin, 1979), pp. 193–212; cited in I. Kershaw, *The Nazi Dictatorship* (London, Edward Arnold, 1993 edn), pp. 60–1.
15. T.W. Mason, *Nazism, Fascism and the Working Class* (Cambridge, Cambridge University Press, 1995); T.W. Mason, *Social Policy in the Third Reich: The Working Class and the 'National Community'* (Oxford, Berg, 1993).
16. Mason, *Social Policy*, p. xxv.
17. Ibid., p. 282.
18. A. Callinicos, 'Hope against the Holocaust', *International Socialism Journal* (1955), 97–108; also witness the comments on Mason in Toby Abse's review of D. Gluckstein, *The Nazis, Capitalism and the Working Class* (London, Bookmarks, 1999), in *Revolutionary History* 7/3 (2000), 232–41, esp. p. 324; and the series of memories in *History Workshop Journal* 30 (1990), 129–84.
19. Kershaw, *Hitler: Hubris*, p. xxix.
20. Ibid., p. xxviii.
21. Ibid., pp. 511–21, esp. pp. 511, 520. There is also a very detailed account of

German public responses to the events of June 1934 in I. Kershaw, *The 'Hitler Myth': Image and Reality in the Third Reich* (Oxford, Oxford University Press, 1987), pp. 84–95.

22. Kershaw, *Hitler: Hubris*, p. viii.
23. F. Neumann, *Behemoth: The Structure and Practice of National Socialism* (New York, Octagon, 1942).
24. Cited in Kershaw, *Hitler: Hubris*, p. xxvi.
25. In fairness, Kershaw has elsewhere considered the comparison with Russia, both in his own *Nazi Dictatorship*, pp. 17–39, and as the co-editor of a collection of essays making the comparison explicit, namely M. Lewin and I. Kershaw, *Stalinism and Nazism* (Cambridge, Cambridge University Press, 1997).
26. Kershaw, *Hitler, Nemesis*, p. 481.
27. Ibid., p. 487.
28. The classic statement of the great man approach to the past is to be found in T. Carlyle, *Past and Present* (London, Chapman and Hall, 1896, edn), passim.

5. *British Fascism Reconsidered*

A version of this chapter first appeared in *Race and Class* 41/3 (2000), while several of the sources here are also cited in D. Renton, *Fascism, Anti-fascism, and Britain in the 1940s* (London, Macmillan, 2000), pp. 42–70.

1. Z. Sternhell, *Maurice Barrès et le Nationalisme Français* (Paris, Armand Colin, 1972); Z. Sternhell, 'Fascist Ideology', in W. Laqueur (ed.), *Fascism: A Readers Guide* (Harmondsworth, Penguin, 1976), pp. 315–78; Z. Sternhell, *La Droite Revolutionnaire 1885–1914, Les Origines Françaises du Fascisme* (Paris, Editions du Seuil, 1978); Z. Sternhell, *Neither Right Nor Left* (Berkeley, University of California Press, 1986); Z. Sternhell, 'The Anti-Materialist Revision of Marxism as an Aspect of the Rise of Fascist Ideology', *Journal of Contemporary History* 22/3 (1987), 379–400; Z. Sternhell, *The Birth of Fascist Ideology* (New Jersey, Princeton University Press, 1994).
2. Sternhell, *Birth of Fascist Ideology*, p. 3; Sternhell, *La Droite Revolutionnaire*, p. 200; Sternhell, *Maurice Barrès*, pp. 224–32. Hence the title of Sternhell's *Neither Right Nor Left*.
3. R. Griffin (ed.), *International Fascism: Theories, Causes and the New Consensus* (London, Arnold, 1998), p. 238.
4. R.C. Thurlow, 'The Guardian of the "Sacred Flame": The Failed Political Resurrection of Sir Oswald Mosley After 1945', *Journal of Contemporary History*, 33/2 (1998), 241–54, esp. pp. 244, 254.
5. P.M. Coupland, 'The Blackshirted Utopians', *Journal of Contemporary History* 33/2 (1998), 255–72.
6. W. Morris, *News from Nowhere and Other Writings* (London, Penguin, 1993 edn), p. 43.
7. B. and S. Webb, *Soviet Communism: A New Civilisation* (London, Gollancz, 1937).
8. Coupland, 'The Blackshirted Utopians', p. 255.
9. M. Horkheimer, 'Die Juden und Europa', translated as 'The Jews and Europe', in S.E. Bonner and D. Kellner, *Critical Theory and Society* (London and New York, Routledge, 1989), pp. 77–94; G. Orwell, 'Introduction to Love of

Life and Other Stories by Jack London', in S. Orwell and I. Angus (eds), *The Collected Essays, Journalism and Letters of George Orwell, Volume IV, In Front of Your Nose 1945–1950* (London, Penguin, 1968), p. 42.

10. D. Renton, *Fascism: Theory and Practice* (London, Pluto, 1999).
11. Thurlow, 'The Guardian', pp. 243–5.
12. R. Falber, Untitled Report on Fascist Activities, 15 August 1948, among Communist Party papers (CP), in the National Museum of Labour History in Manchester, CP/CENT/ORG/12/7. Incidentally, Thurlow suggests that branches of W.H. Smith would not sell fascist newspapers, when actually we know that Smith's took 1,560 copies of each issue of the *Mosley Newsletter*; see 'Mosley Publications Ltd. vs. Morrison and Others', Transcript of Trial, March 1947, held in the archives of the National Council of Civil Liberties (DCL), in Brynmor Jones Library in the University of Hull, DCL/70/2.
13. C. Watts, 'It Has Happened Here: The Experiences of a Political Prisoner in British Prisons and Concentration Camps during the Fifth Column Panic of 1940–1', unpublished manuscript in Sheffield University library, p. 62; Special Branch, '18B Social and Dance', 21 December 1945, among the Home Office papers (HO) in the Public Records Office in Kew, HO 45/24467/183.
14. *British League Review* (November 1947), Alexander Raven Thomson *Mosley, What They Say, What They Said, What He Is* (London, Raven Press, 1947); 'Why Should Anyone Still Follow Mosley?', *Picture Post* (1 May 1948); T. Grundy, 'My Childhood', *Independent* (28 November 1996), pp. 9–11.
15. Thurlow, 'The Guardian', p. 245.
16. 'Fascists Damage bookshop', *Daily Worker* (15 January 1946). Special Branch, 'Ku Klux Klan', 21 May 1947, in HO 45/24469/361. 'Jewish Factory Set on Fire', *Daily Worker* (5 July 1947). Hackney Metropolitan Police, 'Complaints Against Fascism', 27 September 1947, HO 45/25399.
17. 'A Line of Batons Between', *Daily Herald* (1 September 1947); M. Noble, 'the Battle of Ridley Road', *Challenge* (13 September 1947); *On Guard* (October 1947); 'Ridley Road: 3 Get Prison for Assaulting Jews', *Daily Express* (12 October 1947); *On Guard* (January–February, March, and May–June 1948).
18. Coupland, 'The Blackshirted Utopians', p. 270; Thurlow, 'The Guardian', pp. 245, 247, 250.
19. *Patriot* (4 January 1945, 30 May 1946); *London Tidings* (26 August 1948); *British League Review* (May 1946); *Parliament Christian* (September–October 1944); *At Random* (August 1947).
20. *Mosley Newsletter* (February–March 1946); *Patriot* (15 March 1945); *Unity* (17 January 1947); C.H. Douglas, *The Brief for the Prosecution* (Liverpool, Social Credit, 1945), p. 79.
21. Thurlow, 'The Guardian', p. 266.
22. R. West, 'A Reporter At Large: Heil Hamm!-1', *New Yorker* (7 August 1948), pp. 24–45, esp. p. 42; 'Magistrate Urges Police To Stop Anti-Semitism', *Daily Worker* (24 June 1947); Special Branch, 'Meeting', 30 December 1946, HO 45/24468/317; Special Branch, 'British League of Ex-

Servicemen and Women', 13 April 1947, HO 45/24468/367.

23. For Mr Weitzman MP's speech in the House of Commons in December 1949, see *Hansard*, 470 H.C. Deb. 5s. (7 December 1949), pp. 2042–52, esp. pp. 2043–4.
24. O. Mosley, *The Alternative* (Ramsbury, Crowood House, 1946); R. Skidelsky, *Mosley* (London, Macmillan, 1975), p. 485.
25. *British League Review* (September 1947); *Patriot* (3 April 1945); 'Mosley Men to Seek to Impose a Colour Bar', *South London Press* (4 September 1952); *Gothic Ripples* (21 March 1946).
26. *Independent Nationalist* (22 September 1949); *Social Creditor* (20 August 1949); *London Tidings* (6 September 1947); *Union* (5 March 1949); *Patriot* (15 March 1945, 16 May 1946), A.K. Chesterton and J. Leftwich, *The Tragedy of Anti-Semitism* (London, Robert Anscombe, 1948), pp. 75–7.
27. *Gothic Ripples* (25 February 1948); *Gothic Ripples* (17 March 1946); *Gothic Ripples* (15 August 1946); *New Pioneer* (January 1940); NWM, '25 Points of Policy', unpublished document, 1948, in HO 45/2968/116; *London Tidings* (20 March 1948).
28. Coupland, 'The Blackshirted Utopians', pp. 259, 261; Thurlow, 'The Guardian', p. 246.
29. *Patriot* (14 March 1946); Mosley, *The Alternative*, pp. 63, 150; Duke of Bedford *Why Blunder On?* (Glasgow, Strickland, 1942), p. 9; A. Ratcliffe, *The Truth about Democracy* (Glasgow, Protestant League, 1944), p. 11; *Gothic Ripples* (26 August 1946).
30. Birmingham members of the Union Movement, 'Personalities in the Fascist and Anti-Semitic Movement', DCL/42/5; *On Guard* (March, April and July 1948); HO 45/24468/294; Grundy, 'My Childhood', p. 10; *British League Review* (November–December 1946); Special Branch, 'Gothic Ripples', 15 March 1948, HO 45/24968/15; J. Wynn, 'Memoirs', unpublished manuscript, 2, in British Union Collection, Sheffield University Library; 'Minutes', among the Metropolitan Police papers (MEPO) in the Public Records Office in Kew, MEPO 3/3093; 'A. Norris', in the Jewish Defence Committee's 'Rogue's Gallery', in the archives of the Board of Deputies, BOD/C6/9/3/2; R. Saunders, 'A Tiller of Several Soils', unpublished manuscript, in Saunders Collection, in Sheffield University Library.
31. Peter Pugh of Sheffield University is currently working on a major biography of Raven Thomson.
32. R. Samuel, *East End Underworld: Chapters in the Life of Arthur Harding* (London, Routledge, 1981), p. 275.
33. 'After The Meeting', *Evening Standard* (8 February 1948); *On Guard* (April 1948); 'Minutes', MEPO 3/3093. 'Jew Baiter In Prison', *Daily Worker* (14 September 1949); 'Two Men Fined', *Evening Standard* (31 July 1950).
34. *London Tidings* (25 January 1997); Duke of Bedford, *After the War: Work for All?* (Glasgow, Strickland, 1944), p. 2; *London Tidings* (26 August 1948); *British League Review* (September–October 1946).
35. Special Branch, 'British League of Ex-Servicemen and Women', 15 February 1946, HO 45/24467/209.
36. T. Pocock, 'How Powerful are these People?', *Leader Magazine* (23 August 1947).

6. *Is Fascism Still a Threat?*

1. A version of this paper first appeared as a review article for the journal *Contemporary Politics* 5/4 (1999).
2. C. Mudde, 'Dangerous in the Extreme', *Guardian* (18 October 2000).
3. P. Fysh and J. Wolfreys, *The Politics of Racism in France* (London, Macmillan, 1998), p. 2.
4. Fysh and Wolfreys, *Politics of Racism in France*, p. 1.
5. D. Renton, *Fascism: Theory and Practice* (London, Pluto, 1999), pp. 6–17, 100–16.
6. G. Birenbaum, *Le Front National en Politique* (Paris, Ballard, 1992), pp. 323–4.
7. J.-Y. Camus and R. Monzat, *Les Droites Nationales et Radicales en Frances: Répertoire Critique* (Lyons, Presses Universitaires de Lyons, 1992), p. 107; Birenbaum, *Le Front National*, p. 296; M. Soudais, *Le Front National en Face* (Paris, Flammarion, 1996), pp. 141–55; R. Golsan, 'Introduction', in R. Golsan (ed.), *Fascism's Return: Scandal, Revision and Ideology since 1980* (Lincoln and London, University of Nebraska Press, 1998), pp. 1–18.
8. M. Winock, *Histoire de L'Extrême Droite en France* (Paris, Seuil, 1990); P. Perrineau, 'La Dynamique du Vote Le Pen, le Poids du "Gaucho-Lepénisme"', in P. Pascal and C. Ysmal (eds), *Le Vote de Crise: L'Election Présidentielle de 1995* (Paris, Presses de la Fondation Nationales de Sciences Politiques). There is a similar perspective in J. Marcus, *The National Front and French Politics: The Resistible Rise of Jean-Marie Le Pen* (Basingstoke, Macmillan, 1995).
9. R. Griffin (ed.) *International Fascism: Theories, Causes and the New Consensus* (London, Arnold, 1998).
10. P. Davies, *The National Front in France* (London, Routledge, 1999), p. 2.
11. Davies, *National Front in France*, pp. 3, 5, 6.
12. Davies, *National Front in France*, pp. 78, 224.
13. Fysh and Wolfreys, *Politics of Racism in France*, pp. 131–5.
14. Davies, *National Front in France*, p. 12.
15. Fysh and Wolfreys, *Politics of Racism in France*, pp. 216–17.
16. This article is based on a piece written for the web magazine, *Voice of the Turtle*, http://voiceoftheturtle.org/; also D. Renton and R. Rammeiser, 'Austria Erupts', *Jewish Socialist* 42 (2000), 10–11.
17. *Guardian* (4 October 1999) *Le Monde* (4 October 1999).
18. *Searchlight* (September 1999).
19. At the time of writing, *The Turner Diaries* stands at a more believable but still troubling no. 5,319 in the charts of American Amazon, and is 6,623 in the lists in Britain. By contrast, the second volume of Ian Kershaw's biography of Hitler stands at no. 63.
20. S. King, 'William Pierce', *Searchlight* (July 2000).
21. K. Taylor and N. Lowles, 'Killer Ideas', *Searchlight* (July 2000).
22. Cited in I. Kershaw, *Hitler: 1936–1945: Nemesis* (London, Allen Lane, 2000), p. 151.
23. King, 'William Pierce'.

7. *The Meaning of the Holocaust, Fifty Years On*

1. W. Kansteiner, 'Between Politics and Memory: The *Historikerstreit* and West German Historical Culture of the 1980s', in R.J. Goslan (ed.) *Fascism's Return: Scandal, Revision, and Ideology since 1980* (Lincoln and London, University of Nebraska Press, 1998), pp. 86–129.
2. D. Goldhagen, *Hitler's Willing Executioners: Ordinary Germans and the Holocaust* (New York, Little, Brown and Co., 1996).
3. N.G. Finkelstein and R. Bettina Birn, *A Nation on Trial: The Goldhagen Thesis and Historical Truth* (New York, Metropolitan Books, 1998).
4. N.G. Finkelstein, *The Holocaust Industry: Reflections on the Exploitation of German Suffering* (London, Verso, 2000), p. 3.
5. 'Our anti-Jewish bias', *Guardian* (13 July 2000); also J. Freedland, 'An enemy of the people', *Guardian* (14 July 2000); 'The Holocaust's divided legacy', *Guardian* (17 July 2000); and 'Finkelstein: the row rumbles on', *Guardian* (19 July 2000).
6. J. Rayner, 'Finkelstein's List', *Observer* (16 July 2000).
7. K. Taylor, 'Using the Holocaust', *Searchlight* (August 2000), 10–11; also A. Callinicos, *Socialist Worker* (15 July 2000); M. Simons, 'A Distortion of Judgement', *Socialist Review* (September 2000).
8. Finkelstein, *The Holocaust Industry*, p. 69.
9. For the popular response to the governing coalition, D. Renton and R. Rammeiser, 'Austria Erupts', *Jewish Socialist*, 42 (2000), 10–11.
10. Finkelstein, *The Holocaust Industry*, p. 71.
11. Ibid., p. 81.
12. Ibid., pp. 73–5. For a discussion of the New York City Museum of Jewish Heritage, see S.E. Some, 'Holocaust Museums are Worth the Fight', *New Jersey Jewish News* (March 2000).
13. Finkelstein, *The Holocaust Industry*, p. 72.
14. Ibid., p. 102.
15. Ibid., p. 72.
16. P. Novick, *The Holocaust in American Life* (Boston, Mariner, 1999), p. 103.
17. Novick, *The Holocaust*, p. 147; Finkelstein, *The Holocaust Industry*, p. 22.
18. Indeed, Finkelstein's book began its life as a review of Novick, see N. Finkelstein, 'Uses of the Holocaust', *London Review of Books* (6 January 2000).
19. Finkelstein, *The Holocaust Industry*, p. 5.
20. Ibid., pp. 20–1.
21. See in particular N. Finkelstein, *Image and Reality of the Israel–Palestine Conflict* (New York and London, Verso, 1995).
22. Novick, *The Holocaust*, pp. 3–6; Finkelstein, *The Holocaust Industry*, p. 5.
23. See chapter eleven below; also D. Renton, 'Cable Street Revisited' *Changing English* 5/2 (1998), 189–94.
24. The most recent, indeed 'definitive', edition of the diary was published by Doubleday in 1994.
25. C. Ozick, 'Who owns Anne Frank?' *New Yorker* 73 (6 October 1997), 87; also H. Flanbaum, 'The Americanization of the Holocaust',

Journal of Genocide Research 1/1 (1999), 91–104.

26. Novick, *The Holocaust*, pp. 118–20.
27. This point is made B. Bettelheim, *The Informed Heart* (New York, Free Press, 1960).
28. For more on the adolescent and the Holocaust, see J. Reiter, 'The Holocaust as Seen through the Eyes of Children', in A. Leak and G. Paizis, *The Holocaust and the Text: Speaking the Unspeakable* (London, Macmillan, 2000), pp. 83–96.
29. D. Renton, 'What Future for the past in today's South Africa?', *Soundings* 14 (2000), 31–8.
30. Including P. Levi, *Moments of Reprieve* (London, Abacus, 1985); P. Levi, *If Not Now, When?* (London, Abacus, 1986); and P. Levi, *If This is a Man*, and *The Truce* (London, Abacus, 1987 edn).
31. M. Rogin, '*Spielberg's* List', *New Left Review* 230 (1998), 153–60.
32. A.H. Friedlander, *Out of the Whirlwind: A Reader of Holocaust Literature* (New York, Schocken Books, 1976), p. 11.
33. Novick, *The Holocaust*, p. 214.
34. I have not mentioned the Jewish resistance to the Holocaust. The two key texts here are Bettelheim, *The Informed Heart*; and A. Donat, *Jewish Resistance* (New York, Waldon Press, 1964). Bettelheim maintains that resistance in the camps was minimal; Donat takes the opposite view.
35. L.L. Langer, 'Ghetto Chronicles: Life at the Brink', in L. Langer, *Admitting the Holocaust* (Oxford and New York, Oxford University Press, 1995), pp. 31–40, esp. p. 38.
36. Friedlander, *Out of the Whirlwind*, p. 15.
37. W. Wheeler, *A New Modernity: Changes in Science, Literature and Politics* (London, Lawrence and Wishart, 2000), pp. 106–8.
38. Novick, *The Holocaust*, p. 261.

PART TWO

8. *Degenerate Art and Music*

Some of the ideas for this chapter first appeared in *Socialist Review* (March 1997).

1. Labanyi, 'Images of Fascism: Visualization and Aestheticization in the Third Reich', in M. Laffan (ed.) *The Burden of German History 1919–1945* (London, Methuen, 1989), pp. 151–77, esp. p. 157.
2. For a list of books burned, see J. Noakes and G. Pridham (eds), *Nazism 1919–1945: Volume 2: State, Economy and Society 1933–1939* (Exeter, University of Exeter Press, 1984), p. 402.
3. Labanyi, 'Images of Fascism', p. 158.
4. The text of Hitler's speech is given in Noakes and Pridham, *Nazism: Volume 2*, pp. 399–400; also in D. Welch, *The Third Reich: Politics and Propaganda* (London and New York, Routledge, 1993), p. 27.
5. A Steinweis, *Art, Ideology and Economics in Nazi Germany: The Reich Chambers of Music Theatre and the Visial Arts* (Chapel Hill and London, University of North Carolina Press, 1993), pp. 144–6.

6. A. de Jonge, *The Weimar Chronicle: Prelude to Hitler* (New York, Paddington Press, 1978), pp. 160–1.
7. 'Munchausen', *Entartete Musik: Berlin Cabaret Songs* (CD, London, Decca, 1997).
8. See 'The Concept of Passive Revolution', in A. Gramsci, *Selections from Prison Notebooks* (London, Lawrence and Wishart, 1971), pp. 106–14.
9. One of the most powerful histories of 1923 is written by Adam Fergusson, an economic monetarist: A. Fergusson, *When Money Dies: The Nightmare of the Weimar Collapse* (London, William Kimber, 1975).
10. Gramsci, *Selections*, p. 106.
11. G. Grosz, *Ecce Homo* (Secaucus, NJ, Castle Books, 1965 edn), watercolour ix.
12. De Jonge, *Weimar Chronicle*, p. 156.
13. B. Brecht, 'Theatre for Pleasure or Theatre for Instruction', in J. Willett (ed.), *Brecht on Theatre: The Development of an Aesthetic* (London, Methuen, 1974 edn), pp. 69–78, esp. pp. 70–1.
14. 'Letter to the New York Workers' Company "Theatre Union" about the play *The Mother*', in B. Brecht, *Bad Time for Poetry: Was it? Is it?* (London, Methuen, 1995), pp. 69–73.
15. 'Letter to the New York Workers' Company', p. 73; Brecht also reproduced his criticism as prose for the magazine, *The Masses*, see B. Brecht, 'Criticism of the New York production of *Die Mutter*', in Willett, *Brecht on Theatre*, pp. 81–4.
16. 'But for the Jews advising against it', in Brecht, *Bad Time for Poetry*, pp. 68–9.
17. C. Isherwood, *Christopher and His Kind* (London, Magnum, 1977), p. 72.
18. E. Fischer, *The Necessity of Art* (Harmondsworth, Penguin, 1963), p. 204.
19. Cited in C. Harman, *The Lost Revolution: Germany 1918 to 1923* (London, Bookmarks, 1982), p. 292.
20. De Jonge, *Weimar Chronicle*, pp. 22–3.
21. For Grosz's 1920s Communism, see W.L. Guttsman, *Art for the Workers: Ideology and the Visual Arts in Weimar Germany* (Manchester, Manchester University Press, 1997), pp. 88–93.
22. De Jonge, *Weimar Chronicle*, p. 162.
23. Ibid., p. 47.
24. V. Serge, *Witness to the German Revolution: Writings from Germany 1923*, trans. I. Birchall (London, Redwords, 2000), pp. 205, 210–11.
25. K. Tucholsky, *Deutschland, Deutschland über alles* (Berlin, 1929); also P. Pachnicke and K. Honnef (eds), *John Heartfield* (New York, Harry N. Abrams Publishers, 1992) pp. 148–56.
26. For *Fascist memorials*, see Pachnicke and Honnef, *John Heartfield*, p. 171; for *As in the Middle Ages . . .*', see the illustrations between pages 140 and 141 of this book; for *Millions stand behind me*, see De Jonge, *Weimar Chronicle*, p. 226.
27. Steinweis, *Art, Ideology and Economics*, p. 146.
28. N.G. Finkelstein, 'Daniel Jonah Goldhagen's "Crazy" Thesis: a Critique of *Hitler's Willing Executioners*', *New Left Review* 224 (1997), 39–88, esp. p. 56.
29. T. Mann, *Doctor Faustus* (London, Penguin, 1968 edn), p. 484.
30. G. Lukács, *The Destruction of Reason* (London, Merlin, 1980)
31. Labanyi, 'Images of Fascism', p. 169.
32. 'Theses on the Philosophy of History', in W. Benjamin, *Illuminations* (London, Fontana, 1992 edn), pp. 211–45.

9. *The Anti-fascist Politics of Albert Einstein*

An early version of this chapter appeared as D. Renton 'E = MC²', *Searchlight* (June 2000). A more recent version is due to be published in vol. 7, issue 2 of the journal *Rethinking Marxism.*

1. Einstein expressed his opposition to some of the claims of quantum mechanics. In particular, he was opposed to the claim that at the most basic level, physics is governed by chance rather than rules. Even in his own time, experiments demonstrated that Einstein's opposition to the uncertainty principle was wrong. There is a useful discussion of this incident in N.A. Porter, *Physicists in Conflict* (Bristol and Philadelphia, Institute of Physics, 1998) pp. 106–24.
2. J. Bernstein, *Einstein* (London, Fontana, 1973), p. 91.
3. A Fölsing, *Albert Einstein: A Biography* (London, Viking, 1997), pp. 644–5; S.W. Hawking, *A Brief History of Time* (London, Bantam, 1988), pp. 187–8; also M.J. Klein, 'Albert Einstein', in C. Gillespie (ed.), *Dictionary of Scientific Biography* (New York, Charles Scribner's Sons, 1971), pp. 312–9.
4. Bernstein, *Einstein*, pp. 105–6.
5. For a fuller discussion of this theme, see D. Blackie, 'Revolution in Science', *International Socialism Journal* 42 (1989), 115–36.
6. K. Marx, *Grundrisse* (London, Penguin and New Left Books, 1973), pp. 100–1.
7. J. Medawar and D. Pyke, *Hitler's Gifts: Scientists Who Fled Nazi Germany* (London, Richard Cohen, 2000), pp. 35–6.
8. The classic text describing this process is *Lenin's Imperialism: The Highest Stage of Capitalism*, published as V.I. Lenin, *Collected Works: Volume 22* (London, Lawrence and Wishart, 1985 edn), pp. 185–304.
9. J. Schwartz and M. McGuinness, *Introducing Einstein* (London, Icon Books, 1999), p. 3.
10. A. Einstein, 'Autobiographical Notes', in Schilpp, *Albert Einstein: Philosopher Scientist* (La Salle, Illinois, Open Court, 1970 edn), pp. 1–95; also Bernstein, *Einstein*, pp. 22–3; and M. Jammer, *Einstein and Religion* (Princeton, Princeton University Press, 1999).
11. A. Einstein, *Ideas and Opinions* (New York, Modern Library, 1944 edn), p. 225.
12. The classic history of the Ghetto is M. Edelman, *The Ghetto Fights* (London, Bookmarks, 1990).
13. M. Brodersen, *Walter Benjamin: A Biography* (London, Verso, 1996), pp. 44–5.
14. H.E. Kagan, *Six Who Changed the World* (New York, Thomas Yoseloff, 1963), p. 272; Einstein, *Ideas and Opinions*, p. 197.
15. H. Day, *Einstein et son Pacifisme Relatif* (Paris, Editions Pensée, 1956).
16. Einstein, *Ideas and Opinions*, p. 10.
17. Ibid., p. 82.
18. Ibid., p. 121.
19. Adler's trial is discussed in the memoirs of another Austrian socialist, Julius Braunthal, see J. Braunthal, *In Search of the Millennium* (London, Gollancz, 1945), p. 197.
20. Fölsing, *Albert Einstein*, pp. 402–3, 422.
21. Einstein, *Ideas and Opinions*, pp. 165–73; also 'Albert Einstein's Socialist Principles', *Socialist Worker* (3 July 1999).

22. V.I. Lenin, *Collected Works: Volume 14* (London, Lawrence and Wishart, 1972).
23. 'On the Significance of Militant Materialism', in V.I. Lenin, *Collected Works: Volume 33* (London, Lawrence and Wishart, 1966), pp. 277–36. Trotsky's piece in *Pod Znamenem Marksizma*, no. 1 (1922) does not seem to have been translated into English, but there are references to it in Lenin's piece and in Deutscher's biography, I. Deutscher, *The Prophet Unarmed, Trotsky: 1921–1929* (London and Oxford, Oxford University Press, 1970), p. 180.
24. T.A. Jackson, *Dialectics: The Logic of Marxism and its Critics: An Essay in Exploration* (London, Lawrence and Wishart, 1936), pp. 271–3.
25. Quoted in P. McGarr, 'Engels and Natural Science', *International Socialism Journal* 65 (1994), 143–77.
26. P. McGarr, 'Order out of Chaos', *International Socialism Journal* 48 (1990), 137–59. There are also Marxist accounts of Einstein's work in Blackie, 'Revolution in Science'; R. Havemann, *Dialektik oder Dogma?* (Munich, Wilhelm Goldmann Verlag, 1971); and P. Gasper, 'Bookwatch: Marxism and Science', *International Socialism Journal* 79 (1998), 137–71.
27. Einstein, *Ideas and Opinions*, pp. 165–73; Fölsing, *Albert Einstein*, pp. 644–5.
28. D. Renton, 'Karl Korsch', *What Next?* 16 (2000), 1–10.
29. B. Brecht, *Bad Time for Poetry: 162 Poems and Songs. Was it? Is it?* (London, Methuen, 1995), p. 118.
30. H. Sheehan, *Marxism and the Philosophy of Science: A Critical History; Volume One: The First Hundred Years* (London and New Jersey, Humanities Press, 1985), pp. 416–7.
31. Einstein, *Ideas and Opinions*, p. 225 and passim.

10. *The Battle of Cable Street*

An early version of this chapter was first given alongside Harold Rosen in a round-table discussion at the conference, Marxism 1997. Since then similar pieces have also appeared in the journals *Changing English* 5/2 (1998) and *Jewish Culture and History* 1/2 (1999).

1. The description of events in this section is loosely based on D. Renton, *Fascism, Anti-Fascism and Britain in the 1940s* (London, Macmillan, 2000), pp. 17–20. Further sources appear in the notes below.
2. H. Rosen, 'A Necessary Myth: Cable Street Revisited', *Changing English* 5/1 (1998), 27–34.
3. M. Halbwachs, 'The Social Frameworks of Memory', in L.A. Coser (ed.), *Maurice Halbwachs on Collective Memory* (Chicago, University of Chicago Press, 1992), pp. 37–189, esp. p. 156.
4. P. Piratin, *Our Flag Stays Red* (London, Thames, 1948), p. 25.
5. *Daily Worker* (5 October 1936).
6. Piratin, *Our Flag*, p. 24.
7. Ibid., p. 25.
8. T. Linehan, 'Fascist Perceptions of Cable Street', *Jewish Culture and History* 1/2 (1998), 23–30.
9. *Action* (10 October 1936).
10. *Blackshirt* (10 and 17 October 1936).
11. A. Gibbons, *Street of Tall People* (London, Dolphin, 1996); for the mural, see the illustration on the cover

of Cable Street Group *The Battle of Cable Street* (London, Cable Street Group, 1996).

12. C. Sparks, 'Fighting the Beast: The Lessons of Cable Street', *International Socialism* 94 (1977), 11–14, esp. p. 12.
13. J. Jacobs, *Out of the Ghetto* (London, Janet Simon, 1978), p. 245.
14. Cable Street Group, *The Battle of Cable Street*, p. 19.
15. Ibid., p. 19.
16. D.S. Lewis, *Illusions of Grandeur: Mosley, Fascism and British Society, 1931–1981* (Manchester, Manchester University Press, 1987), p. 127.
17. Interview with Gerry Ross, former member of Labour of Youth, 7 March 1997.
18. Piratin, *Our Flag*, p. 18.
19. M. Beckman, cited in D. Renton, 'Docker and Garment Worker: Railwayman and Cabinet Maker: The Class Memory of Cable Street', *Jewish Culture and History* 1/2 (1999), 95–108, esp. p. 96–7.
20. J. Charlton, *'It Just Went like Tinder': The Mass Movement and New Unionism in Britain 1889* (London, Redwords, 1999), p. 95–8.
21. M. Davis, *Sylvia Pankhurst: A Life in Radical Politics* (London, Pluto, 1999), pp. 36–54.
22 Piratin, *Our Flag*, p. 40.

11. *The British Left and Spain*

1. P. Preston, *A Concise History of the Spanish Civil War* (London, Fontana, 1996).
2. A. Guillamón, *The Friends of Durruti Group* (London, AK, 1996); also C. Ealham, '"Revolutionary Gymnastics" and the Unemployed: The Limits of the Spanish Anarchist Utopia', in K. Flett and D. Renton, *The Twentieth Century: A Century of Wars and Revolutions* (London, Rivers Oram, 2000), pp. 133–55. Guillamón claims that the group was more loyal to the FAI-CNT than Ealham suggests.
3. Hernández's account of the murder was translated by Bob Pitt; see J. Hernández, *How the NKVD Framed the POUM* (London, Pitt Productions, 1995).
4. The context is described in D. Renton, *Fascism: Theory and Practice* (London, Pluto, 1999). p. 78.
5. There is a much more optimistic account of the role played by the PCE and its relationship to the Comintern, in T. Rees, 'The Highpoint of Comintern influence? The Communist Party and the Civil War in Spain', in T. Rees and A. Thorpe, *International Communism and the Communist International* (Manchester, Manchester University Press, 1998), pp. 143–67.
6. N. Branson, *History of the Communist Party of Great Britain 1927–1941* (London, Lawrence and Wishart, 1985), pp. 220–39; G. Matthews, *All for the Cause: The Communist Party 1920–1980* (London, Communist Party, 1980), pp. 10–11.
7. D. Renton, *Red Shirts and Black: Fascists, Anti-fascists and Oxford in the 1930s* (Oxford, Ruskin College Library, 1996), p. 43.
8. See the account by Dave Auty, 'Fighting Fascism', in D. Renton (ed.), *Socialism in Liverpool* (Liverpool, Hegemon Press, 2000), pp. 19–21; also D. Auty, *The Trophy is Democracy: Merseyside Anti-fascism and the Spanish Civil War* (Liverpool, Hegemon Press, 2000).

9. M. Kolzov, 'The Trotskyist Criminals in Spain', *International Press Correspondence* (31 January 1937).
10. *Daily Worker* (11 and 17 May 1937); J. Pettifer (ed.), *Cockburn in Spain: Despatches from the Spanish Civil War* (London, Lawrence and Wishart, 1986), p. 184; D. Caute, *The Fellow Travellers: A Postscript to the Enlightenment* (London, Weidenfeld & Nicolson, 1973), p. 171.
11. The best source for Cockburn's life is his own autobiography, *I Claud* (London, Penguin, 1967).
12. Cited in P. Cockburn, *The Years of the Week* (London, Comedia, 1968), p. 9.
13. *The Week* (25 March 1936, 17 November 1937).
14. The most recent history of the Astors is James Fox, *The Langhorne Sisters* (London, Granta, 1999).
15. Pettifer, *Cockburn in Spain*, pp. 21, 23, 27, 30, 35, 36–7.
16. Ibid., p. 183.
17. J. Coombes, 'British Intellectuals and the Popular Front', in Gloversmith, *Class, Culture and Social Change*, (London, Harvester, 1978), pp. 70–101, esp. p. 72; S. Samuels, 'The Left Book Club', *Journal of Contemporary History* 1/2 (1966), 65–86; P. Foot, *Words as Weapons: Selected Writings 1980–1990* (London, Verso, 1990), pp. 116–18; J. Lewis, *The Left Book Club: A Historical Record* (London, Lawrence and Wishart, 1970), pp. 63, 114.
18. Dewar, *Communist Politics in Britain*, pp. 120–2; Branson, *History of the Communist Party*, pp. 188, 191, 218; Caute, *The Fellow Travellers*, p. 3.
19. V. Cunningham, 'Neutral? 1930s Writers and Taking Sides', in Gloversmith, *Class Culture and Social Change*, pp. 45–69.
20. R. Davenport-Hines, *Auden* (London, Minerva, 1995), pp. 157–62; S. Spender, *Forward From Liberalism* (London, Gollancz, 1937), p. 27; Coombes, 'British Intellectuals', pp. 79–80; B. Crick, *Essays on Politics and Literature* (Edinburgh, Edinburgh University Press, 1989), pp. 48–62.
21. There is an excellent political biography of MacDiarmid in J. Ross, 'Hugh MacDiarmid', in C. Bambery (ed.), *Scotland: Class and Nation* (London, Bookmarks, 1999), pp. 177–99.
22. For the Spanish Trotskyists, see A. Guillamón, *Documentación histórica del trosqismo español* (Madrid, Ediciones de la Torre, 1996); also *Revolutionary History*, special issue on the Spanish Civil War, 4/1–2 (1992).
23. 'The Question of the People's Front', in L. Trotsky, *On France* (London, Pathfinder, 1979), pp. 183–5.
24. The best history of the BOC is A. Durgan, *BOC 1930–1936: El Bloque Obrero y Campesino* (Barcelona, Editorial Laertes, 1996).
25. J. Newsinger, *Orwell's Politics* (London, Macmillan, 1999), pp. 31–41, esp. p. 40.
26. G. Orwell, *Homage to Catalonia* (London, Penguin, 1962 edn), p. 111; there is a useful discussion in A. Zwerdling, *Orwell and the Left* (New Haven and London, Yale University Press, 1974) pp. 76–80.
27. Newsinger, *Orwell's Politics*, pp. 42–61, esp. p. 51.
28. This section is based on Don Bateman's obituary for Cottman, in *Revolutionary History* 7/3 (2000), 286–9.
29. There is a superb series of interviews with twenty-two surviving British

members of the brigades, published as 'They shall not pass', *Guardian* (10 November 2000).

30. A. Durgan, 'Freedom Fighters or Comintern Army? The International Brigades in Spain', *International Socialism Journal* 84 (1999), 109–32, esp. p. 109.
31. Newsinger, *Orwell's Politics*, p. 52.
32. Ibid., pp. 52–3.
33. Branson, *History of the Communist Party*, p. 229; there is a photograph of the Tom Mann Centuria between pages 140 and 141 of this book.
34. Durgan, 'Freedom Fighters', pp. 118–20.
35. Mrs J. McWhirter to H. Pollitt, undated, also H. Pollitt to Mrs J. McWhirter, 30 March 1937, CP/IND/POLL/2/5 in the National Museum of Labour History, Manchester.
36. M. Teasdale to H. Pollitt, 19 April 1937, also H. Pollitt to M. Teasdale, 20 April 1937, CP/IND/POLL/2/5 in the National Museum of Labour History, Manchester.
37. *TGWU Record* 2 (1996); Wilebaldo Solano responded to Carrillo in *El Pais* (14–15 April 1995); his comments are translated by Ian Birchall in *Revolutionary History* 6/2–3 (1996), 275–7.

12. *Interviewing Anti-fascists: 1945–51*

1. M. Beckman, *The 43 Group* (London, Centreprise, 1992).
2. A.W.B. Simpson, *In the Highest Degree Odious: Detention Without Trial in Wartime Britain* (Oxford, Clarendon Press, 1992); T. Linehan, *East London for Mosley: The British Union of Fascists in East London and South-west Essex 1933–1940* (London, Frank Cass, 1996).
3. S.M. Cullen. 'Four Women for Mosley: Women in the British Union of Fascists 1932–1940', *Oral History* 24/1(1996), 49–59.
4. See the article on Cullen's research in *Comrade* 1 (March 1986); also Cullen's obituary for Richard Bellamy, in *Comrade* 18 (April–May 1989).
5. S.M. Cullen, 'Political Violence: The Case of the British Union of Fascists,' *Journal of Contemporary History* 28/2 (1993), 245–68.
6. For the book clubs outside London, see 'Report on Fascist Activities in Lancashire and Cheshire', 3 May 1948, in Communist Party archive, National Museum of Labour History, Manchester, CP/CENT/ORG/12/7.
7. J. Hamm, *Action Replay* (London, Howard Barker, 1983), pp. 150–1.
8. N. Mosley, *Beyond the Pale* (London, Pimlico, 1983), p. 298.
9. *Labour Party Annual Report 1946* (London, Labour Party, 1946), p. 112; *Labour Party Annual Report 1948* (London, Labour Party, 1948) pp. 79–83; *Labour Party Annual Report 1949* (London, Labour Party, 1949), pp. 114–15.
10. For more on the Communist Party in this period, see D. Renton, 'Past its Peak: the Communist Party of Great Britain 1945–1951', *International Socialism Journal* 2/77 (1997), 127–39.
11. The evidence of this lies in the NCCL files, held in the archives of the NCL (DCL) in Brynmor Jones

Library in the University of Hull, at DCL/42/1.
12. For details on specific groups, see DCL/19/1, DCL/41/4a, DCL/41/5, DCL/41/7, DCL/41/8, DCL/42/1, DCL/42/2a, DCL/42/5, DCL/42/6, and DCL/46/4.
13. 'Enthusiasm For New Paper', *On Guard* 1 (July 1947).
14. Hartog, *Born to Sing*, p. 75.
15. Beckman, *43 Group*, p. 55.
16. Interviews with Martin Savitt, 14 January 1997; Royden Harrison, 17 December 1996; Len Sherman, 29 October 1996.
17. Letter from Bill Moore to the author, 4 December 1995.
18. Interview with Morris Beckman, 15 October 1996.
19. Interview with Chanie Rosenberg, 7 October 1996.
20. Interview with Len Sherman, 29 October 1996.
21. Interviews with Martin Block, 1 November 1996; Martin Savitt, 14 January 1997.
22. Interviews with Monty Goldman, 26 February 1997; Royden Harrison, 17 December 1996.
23. Interview with Chanie Rosenberg, 7 October 1996.
24. Interview with Len Rolnick, 9 December 1997. For more on relations between police and anti-fascists, see D. Renton, 'The British State and British Fascism 1945–1951', *Lobster* 35 (1998), 12–19.
25. Interview with Stanley Marks, 28 October 1996.
26. Interviews with Martin Block, 1 November 1996; Martin Savitt, 14 January 1997; Monty Goldman, 26 February 1997; Stanley Marks, 28 October 1996.
27. Interviews with Len Sherman, 29 October 1996; Martin Block, 1 November 1996; Martin Savitt, 14 January 1997; Morris Beckman, 5 October 1996.
28. Interview with Stanley Marks, 28 October 1996.
29. Interview with Stanley Marks, 28 October 1996.
30. Interview with Len Rolnick, 9 December 1997.
31. H. Scott, *Scotland Yard* (London, Andre Deutsch 1970), p. 143.
32. Interview with Morris Beckman, 15 October 1996.
33. Interivew with Len Rolnick, 9 December 1997.
34. Interview with Martin Savitt, 14 January 1997.
35. Interview with Len Rolnick, 9 December 1997.
36. Interview with Martin Block, 1 November 1996.
37. Interview with Malcolm Garland, 8 March 1996.
38. Interview with Royden Harrison, 17 December 1996.
39. Interviews with John Saville, 4 June 1996; Frank Henderson, 10 July 1996.
40. Interview with Chimen Abramsky, 18 February 1997.
41. Interview with Monty Goldman, 26 February 1997.
42. Interview with Duncan Hallas, 16 September 1996.
43. Interview with Chanie Rosenberg, 7 October 1996.
44. Interviews with Martin Block, 1 November 1996; Stanley Marks, 28 October 1996; Morris Beckman, 15 October 1996.
45. Interview with Len Sherman, 29 October 1996.

13. *Sounds of Resistance: the Anti-Nazi League, 1977–82*

1. D. Widgery, *Beating Time* (London, Chatto and Windus, 1986); J. Savage, *England's Dreaming: Sex Pistols and Punk Rock* (London, Faber & Faber, 1991); P. Alexander, *Racism, Resistance and Revolution* (London, Bookmarks, 1978); P. Gilroy, *There Ain't No Black in the Union Jack: The Cultural Politics of Race and Nation* (London, Routledge, 1987), pp. 114–62, esp. pp. 117–18; N. Copsey, *A History of Anti-fascism in Twentieth Century Britain* (London, Macmillan, 2000); R. Messina, *Race and Party Competition in Britain* (Oxford, Clarendon Press, 1989), pp. 102–25; Revolutionary Communist Group, *The Anti-Nazi League and the Struggle Against Racism* (London, Revolutionary Communist Group, 1978).
2. *Temporary Hoarding* 1 (summer 1977); Widgery, *Beating Time*, pp. 40–53, esp. pp. 40, 43.
3. Interview with Ruth Gregory and Syd Shelton, 6 January 1999.
4. C. Coon, 'Rebels against the System', *Melody Maker* (7 August 1976).
5. G. Marshall, *Spirit of '69: A Skinhead Bible* (Dunoon, S.T. Publishing, 1994 edn), p. 68; J. Burchill and T. Parsons, *'The Boy Looked At Johnny': The Obituary of Rock and Roll* (London, Pluto, 1978).
6. Savage, *England's Dreaming*, p. 398; *New Musical Express* (18 February 1978).
7. Marshall, *Spirit of '69*, pp. 73–9; interview with Ruth Gregory and Syd Shelton, 6 January 1999.
8. Marshall, *Spirit of '69*, p. 73.
9. J. Hoyland and M. Flood Page, 'You Can Lead a Horse to Water', *Socialist Review* (June 1978).
10. J. Rose, 'Rocking Against Racism', *Socialist Review* (June 1978); A. Xerox (D. Widgery), 'Long Time See Them a Come', *Temporary Hoarding* 9 (undated, probably spring 1979).
11. D. Goldstone, *Elvis Costello: A Man Out of Time* (London, Sidgwick & Jackson, 1989), p. 19; Savage, *England's Dreaming*, pp. 487–8.
12. 'A Wave of my Own', *New Musical Express* (21 January 1978).
13. Savage, *England's Dreaming*, p. 482.
14. Letter from Keith Flett to the author, 26 December 1998.
15. *New Musical Express* (25 February, 11 March and 8 April 1978).
16. R. Huddle, 'Hard Rain', *Socialist Review* (July–August 1978); D. Widgery, R. Gregory, S. Shelton and R. Huddle, 'Look Get it Straight', *Socialist Review* (July–August 1978); 'Mr. Calico Nickers' was the *Review*'s then editor, Alex Callinicos.
17. *Socialist Worker* (7 October 1978).
18. The article is quoted in full in the (Socialist Workers Party's) *International Discussion Bulletin* 5 (November 1977).
19. Savage, *England's Dreaming* pp. 482–3; interview with Caroline Harper, 10 April 1998.
20. Cited in Savage, *England's Dreaming*, p. 393.
21. *Daily Mail* (15 August 1977); T. Picton, 'What the Papers Said', *Camerawork, Lewisham: What Are You Taking Pictures For?* (London, Half Moon Photography Workshop, 1977), p. 7.
22. Interview with Richard Buckwell, 31 July 1998.
23. K. Leech, *Struggle in Babylon* (London, Sheldon Press, 1988), p. 89.

24. Letter from Ronnie Williams to the author, 4 November 2000.
25. Leech, *Struggle in Babylon*, p. 88.
26. Campaign Against Racism/Southall Rights, *Southall: The Birth of a Black Community* (London, Institute of Race Relations and Southall Rights, 1981); D. North, 'Blair Peach', *Socialist Worker* (28 April 1978); Anti-Nazi League, *Who Killed Blair Peach?* (London, Anti-Nazi League, 1979): Campaign Against Racism and Fascism/Southall Rights, *Southall: The Birth of a Black Community*, pp. 1–3, 56–7; RAR, *Southall Kids Are Innocent* (London, RAR, 1979); the RAR leaflet was based on A. Xerox (D. Widgery), 'Long time See Them a Come', *Temporary Hoarding* 9 (undated, probably spring 1979).
27. Messina, *Race and Party Competition*, p. 118; C. Rosenberg, 'Labour and the Fight Against Fascism', *International Socialism Journal* 39 (1988), 55–92, esp. p. 81, D. Field, 'Flushing out the Front', *Socialist Review* (May 1978); E. Roberts, *Strike Back* (Orpington, Ernie Roberts, 1994), p. 252.
28. C. Sparks, 'Fascism and the Working Class, Part Two: the National Front Today', *International Socialism Journal* 3 (1978), 17–38.
29. D. Potter, *Brimstone and Treacle* (London, Eyre Methuen, 1976), p. 33.
30. Letter from Ian Birchall to the author, 18 August 1998.
31. Interview with Mike Beaken, 22 November 1999.
32. Huddle, 'Hard Rain'.
33. Hoyland and Flood Page, 'You Can Lead'.
34. Widgery, *Beating Time*, p. 112.

Conclusion

1. R. Griffin (ed.), *International Fascism: Theories, Causes and the New Consensus* (London, Arnold, 1998), p. 238.
2. R.G. Collingwood, *The Idea of History* (Oxford, Clarendon, 1946).

Further Reading

As full notes are given for each chapter, the list of secondary sources below is intended as a guide to further reading. These books and pamphlets have been chosen in so far as they contribute to the general argument of this book:

Alexander, P., *Race, Resistance and Revolution* (London, Bookmarks, 1987).

Auty, D., *The Trophy is Democracy* (London, Hegemon Press, 2000).

Barker, M., *The New Racism: Conservatives and the Ideology of the Tribe* (London, Junction Books, 1981).

Benjamin, W., *Illuminations* (New York, Schocken Books, 1970).

Big Flame, *Sexuality and Fascism* (London, Big Flame, 1979).

Billig, M., *Banal Nationalism* (London, Sage, 1995).

Blackbourn, D. and Eley, G., *The Peculiarities of German History: Bourgeois Society and Politics in Nineteenth-Century Germany* (Oxford, Oxford University Press, 1984).

Borkenau, F., *The Totalitarian Enemy* (London, Faber & Faber, 1939).

Bullock, A., *Hitler: A Study in Tyranny* (London, Odhams, 1952).

Byres, T.J., *Capitalism from Above and Capitalism from Below: An Essay in Comparative Political Economy* (London, Macmillan, 1996).

Callinicos, A., *Against Postmodernism: A Marxist Critique* (Cambridge, Polity, 1989).

——, *Theories and Narratives, Reflections on the Philosophy of History* (Cambridge, Polity, 1995).

Copsey, N., *A History of Anti-fascism in Twentieth-Century Britain* (London, Macmillan, 2000).

Deutscher, I., *Marxism, Wars and Revolutions* (London, Verso, 1984).

——, *The Non-Jewish Jew and Other Essays* (Oxford, Oxford University Press, 1968).

Einstein, A., *Ideas and Opinions* (New York, Modern Library, 1944 edn).

Fest, J.C., *Hitler* (Harmondsworth, Penguin, 1974).

Finkelstein, N.G., and Bettina Birn, R., *A Nation on Trial: the Goldhagen Thesis and Historical Truth* (New York, Owl Books, 1998).

Fori, G., *Antonio Gramsci: Life of a Revolutionary* (London, New Left Books, 1970).

Fromm, E., *Fear of Freedom* (London, Kegan Paul and Co., 1942).

Guérin, D., *Fascism and Big Business* (New York and London, Pathfinder, 1974).

——, *The Brown Plague: Travels in Late Weimar and Early Nazi Germany* (Durham and London, Duke University Press, 1994).

Hallas, D., *The Comintern* (London, Bookmarks, 1985).

Heartfield, J., *Photomontages of the Nazi Period* (London, Universe Books,1977).

Hoare, C., *Spain 1936: Workers in the Saddle* (London, Bookmarks, 1996).
Jacobs, J., *Out of the Ghetto* (London, Janet Simon, 1978).
Jay, M., *The Dialectical Imagination, A History of the Frankfurt School and the Institute of Social Research 1923–1950* (London and Boston, Little, Brown and Co., 1973).
Kershaw, I., *Hitler* (London, Longman, 1991).
——, *Hitler: 1889–1936: Hubris* (London, Allen Lane, 1998).
——, *Hitler: 1936–1945: Nemesis* (London, Allen Lane, 2000)
——, *Popular Opinion and Political Dissent in the Third Reich: Bavaria 1933–1945* (Oxford, Oxford University Press, 1983).
——, *The Nazi Dictatorship* (London, Edward Arnold, 1985).
Kitchen, M., *Fascism* (London, Macmillan, 1976).
Korsch, K., *Marxism and Philosophy* (London, New Left Books, 1970).
Leon, A., *The Jewish Question* (New York and London, Pathfinder, 1970).
Lewis, D.S., *Illusions of Grandeur* (Manchester, Manchester University Press, 1987).
London, J., *The Iron Heel* (London, Macmillan, 1974).
Mason, T.W., *Social Policy in the Third Reich: The Working Class and the 'National Community'* (London, Berg, 1993).
——, *Nazism, Fascism and the Working Class* (Cambridge, Cambridge University Press, 1995).
Mayer, A., *Why Did the Heavens Not Darken? The 'Final Solution' in History* (New York, Pantheon, 1990).
Merson, A., *Communist Resistance in Nazi Germany* (London, Lawrence and Wishart, 1985).
Moore Jr., B., *Social Origins of Dictatorship and Democracy* (Harmondsworth, Penguin, 1966).
Neocleous, M., *Fascism* (Buckinghamshire, Open University Press, 1997).
Neumann, F., *Behemoth, the Structure and Politics of National Socialism 1933–44* (New York, Octagon Books, 1944).
Pachnicke, P., and Honnef, K., (eds), *John Heartfield* (New York, H.N. Abrams, 1994).
Piratin, P., *Our Flag Stays Red* (London, Lawrence and Wishart, 1946).
Reich, W., *The Mass Psychology of Fascism* (New York, Farrar, Straus and Giroux, 1946).
Renton, D., *Red Shirts and Black: Fascists, Anti-Fascists and Oxford in the 1930s* (Oxford, Ruskin College, 1996).
——, *Fascism: Theory and Practice* (London, Pluto, 1999).
——, *Fascism, Anti-fascism and Britain in the 1940s* (London, Macmillan, 2000).
——, and Flett, K., *The Twentieth Century: A Century of Wars and Revolutions* (London, Rivers Oram, 2000).
Rossi, A. (Tasca, A.), *The Rise of Italian Fascism* (London, Methuen, 1938).
Sorel, G., *Reflections on Violence* (Glencoe, Illinois, Free Press, 1950).
Sparks, C., *Never Again! The Hows and Whys of Stopping Fascism* (London, Bookmarks, 1980).
Widgery, D., *Beating Time* (London, Chatto and Windus, 1986).

Index